Second edition

OCR
ICT for A2

Glen Millbery and Sonia Stuart

The Publishers would like to thank the following for permission to reproduce copyright material:
Photo credits p. 9 © Winston Davidian/istockphoto.com; p. 10 ©Photodisc/Getty Images; p. 12 © Graça Victoria - Fotolia.com; p. 44, 45 © Steve Connolly; p. 59 The Opte Project, http://www.opte.org; p. 68 SpbPhoto - Fotollia; p. 69 Andrzej Tokarski - Fotolia; p. 75 © Steve Connolly; p. 76 Steve Cole/Photodisc/Getty Images; p. 79 www.domialifestyle.com p. 86, Hodder Education; p. 89 Liaurinko - Fotolia; p. 91 Getty Images/Gallo Images; p. 93 Jae C. Hong/AP Photo/PA Photos; p. 95 SPOT LLC; p. 96 NASA image by Jeff Schmaltz, MODIS Rapid Response Team, Goddard Space Flight Center; p. 97 t © titime 135 - Fotalia, b Kumbabali - Fotolia; p. 99 © Aurora Photos / Alamy; p. 106 © PhotoAlto / Alamy; p. 107 © Blend Images / Alamy; p. 108 © Bill Bachman Plus 91 Technologies Private Limited Alamy; p. 111 © www.maximimages.com / Alamy; p. 112 © Carolyn Jenkins / Alamy; p. 114 © Hugh Threlfall / Alamy; p. 124 r © DWImages / Alamy; p. 124 l © Samantha Craddock / Alamy; p. 131 and 132 © Plus 91 Technologies Private Limited p. 135 © Adam Gault / Alamy; p. 137 t Antonio Gravante - Fotolia, b Tom Gandolfini/AFP/Getty Images; p. 138 © Mark Chapman / Alamy; p. 139 © David Crausby / Alamy; p. 140 © Losevsky Pavel / Alamy; p. 144 Monkey Business - Fotolia; p. 145 © Martin Barraud / Alamy; p. 146 © Will Stanton / Alamy; p. 166 Alexander Shevchenko - Fotolia; p. 167 © Michael Kemp / Alamy; p. 170 goodluz - Fotolia; p. 174 © Digital Vision / Getty Images; p. 181 © PhotoEdit / Alamy; p. 182 jcdaddi - Fotolia; p. 184 Gamma-Rapho via Getty Images; p. 185 David Paul Morris/Bloomberg via Getty Images

Every effort has been made to trace all copyright holders, but if any have been inadvertently overlooked the Publishers will be pleased to make the necessary arrangements at the first opportunity.

Although every effort has been made to ensure that website addresses are correct at time of going to press, Hodder Education cannot be held responsible for the content of any website mentioned in this book. It is sometimes possible to find a relocated web page by typing in the address of the home page for a website in the URL window of your browser.

Hachette UK's policy is to use papers that are natural, renewable and recyclable products and made from wood grown in sustainable forests. The logging and manufacturing processes are expected to conform to the environmental regulations of the country of origin.

Orders: please contact Bookpoint Ltd, 130 Milton Park, Abingdon, Oxon OX14 4SB. Telephone: (44) 01235 827720. Fax: (44) 01235 400454. Lines are open 9.00 – 5.00, Monday to Saturday, with a 24-hour message answering service. Visit our website at www.hoddereducation.co.uk

© Glen Millbery, Sonia Stuart 2013
First published in 2013 by
Hodder Education,
An Hachette UK company
338 Euston Road
London NW1 3BH

Impression number   5 4 3 2 1
Year   2017 2016 2015 2014 2013

Cover photo © Yarche - Fotolia
Illustrations by Integra Software Services Pvt. Ltd., Pondicherry, India
Typeset in ITC Usherwood Std Book 11/15 by Integra Software Services Pvt. Ltd., Pondicherry, India

Printed in Italy

A catalogue record for this title is available from the British Library

ISBN: 978 1444 168624

Contents

Unit 1 Systems, applications and implications

Chapter 1   The systems cycle 1

Chapter 2   Designing computer-based information systems 35

Chapter 3   Networks and communications 55

Chapter 4   Applications of ICT 106

Chapter 5   Implementing computer-based information systems 150

Chapter 6   Implications of ICT 165

Unit 2 Project

Chapter 7   Introduction to the project 191

Chapter 8   Definition, investigation and analysis 198

Chapter 9   Design 211

Chapter 10   Software development, testing and installation 224

Chapter 11   Documentation 237

Chapter 12   Evaluation 244

Chapter 13   Presentation of the report 249

Index 251

Introduction

This book has two sections: G063 – the Exam and G064 – the Project. G063 is worth 60%, G064 is worth 40%. You should also refer to the Exam Technique section from the AS textbook as the same skills apply to G063.

The Theory chapters follow the specification, going through it bullet by bullet. The Project chapter goes through the marking criteria looking at what you need to produce for each component to gain the marks.

There are three main aspects to a good examination: knowledge, application and exam technique. Unless all three are present you will not gain high marks. The aim of this text book is to assist you in getting the grade that you deserve.

The knowledge is a basic understanding of the facts and the specification – it is rote learning and regurgitation. This will assist you in gaining marks in the *identify and describe* questions.

The application is how the knowledge that you have is applied to the context. It is taking the rote learning and tailoring it to fit the specific context of the question. The exam technique is how the keyword in the question tells you what the examiner is looking for in the response and how it will be marked.

When all three elements come together you will achieve a good mark. If one of them is missing then the marks will fall dramatically. This book does not give you all the answers. It gives you the knowledge and allows you to practice that knowledge in a given context. It helps you along the road but it does not replace your own learning. The exam will be in a context and you need to make sure you understand the theory so you can apply it.

G064 has a set mark scheme – it is in the specification that you can download from the OCR website. Look over it and make sure you know what needs to be produced to achieve the marks in each section. The coursework is not about producing complex work but about meeting the need of the client and producing a consistent piece of work – each section flowing logically into the next.

Lastly, good luck, enjoy the course and we hope you achieve the grade you need.

1 The systems cycle

Introduction

This chapter covers the stages that should be followed when developing a system. The tools and techniques that could be used during these stages, many of which will be of use when you are completing the coursework element of the A2 course, are also covered in this chapter. You should also be able to apply your knowledge to a specified scenario.

This chapter covers:

- the systems cycle
- project management
- process modelling.

Describe the following stages of the systems life cycle (definition of the problem, investigation and analysis, design, implementation, testing, installation, documentation, evaluation and maintenance) and how the stages relate to ICT systems

All projects, resulting in a solution to a problem, go through a number of stages before they are complete: the systems life cycle. As the term cycle suggests, there is no clear start or finish point but it may be useful to think that the start is when a new software system is being considered. It may be that an existing system is unable to cope with the demands of the end users or the volume of work has increased leading to a reduction in the efficiency of the current system.

The systems life cycle is a continuous loop with each stage leading into the next.

Each stage within the life cycle has a dependency on the stages that occur immediately before and after it. For example, if you look at Figure 1.1 you can see that the installation stage will depend on the testing stage (the stage before) and the documentation stage will depend on the installation stage.

Problem definition stage

During this stage the feasibility of the proposed system is considered. This stage is also known as the feasibility stage. It is the initial look at the existing system to see how it can be improved or if it is possible to meet the needs of the end users. The result of this stage is a feasibility report.

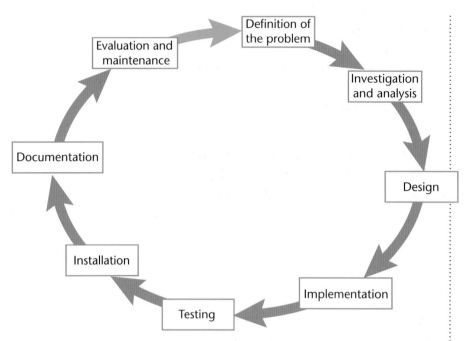

Figure 1.1 The systems life cycle

This stage answers some very important questions:
- Can the need for a new system be justified?
- Is it technically feasible and economically desirable to the end users?

During this stage a number of important questions may be asked. These include:
- Can the solution be designed and implemented within the given constraints of timescale allocated and budget?
- Will the solution have a positive impact on the end users and will the new system bring benefits?
- Will the solution fulfil all the needs and requirements of the end users?

For the project to continue the answer to all these questions must be 'yes': there is the time, money and resources, and the impact of the proposed solution will be positive.

The stage begins with an initial, brief investigation that involves the systems analyst obtaining some general information:
- The system currently being used, its benefits and limitations (i.e. why the existing system is not meeting its user's needs).
- The additional end-user requirements of the new software system (i.e. the purpose of a new system).

The analyst needs to identify why the current system is not meeting the needs of the organisation, why a new software system is needed and what the purpose of the software system is.

There are many reasons why a new system may be required:
- An organisation wants to computerise a part of its operations that is currently done manually.

- The capacity of the existing software system is too small to carry out the work now demanded of it.
- The existing system is now outdated and no longer suits the needs of the organisation.
- The existing system has come to the end of its life and needs to be replaced.

The analyst must be able to clearly identify the general reasons why a new software system is required and the specific needs given by the end users. The client will define process constraints to the analyst. The main process constraints are:

- time
- budget
- hardware choice
- software choice.

The feasibility report is written by an analyst for the management of the organisation needing the new software system. It is very important, therefore, that it is written, as far as possible, in non-technical language so that the contents of the report can be clearly understood. The feasibility report should describe the system from an end-user perspective.

Investigation and analysis stage

This stage follows the definition of the problem and must be fully completed before moving to the design stage. This stage uses the feasibility report (the output from the previous stage) as its main input.

The full nature of the problem to be solved is investigated during this stage. The result of this investigation forms the basis for the analysis.

Different methods can be used for investigating the current system. These include:

- questionnaires
- interviews
- meetings
- document analysis
- observations.

(These investigation methods are discussed later in this chapter.)

The results of the investigation have to be analysed fully to gain a full understanding of the current system. If the investigation has been incomplete, then the new system may not cover all the inadequacies of the current system and will not bring any benefits to the organisation.

Towards the end of this stage the user requirements have to be defined. The user requirements are agreed with the client and will form the basis for the rest of the systems life cycle. The agreed needs are the output of this stage: the requirements specification.

Once the user requirements have been agreed by the client and the analyst then, during the rest of the life cycle, it is important that these user requirements are constantly referred to. By doing this the analyst can be assured that the new system, once implemented, will meet all the user requirements.

If the requirements are not referred back to, then the system may not fully, if at all, meet the needs of the end users. If this situation occurs, then the new system will not be useful to the organisation, thereby resulting in a waste of money.

It may be that some of the functions of the current system have to be incorporated into the new system although these functions may need to be updated. It is more likely, however, that new functions will need to be added to the new system to solve the previously identified problems with the current system.

Design stage

The design stage comes after the investigation and analysis stage has been completed. This stage must be completed before the implementation stage is started.

The design stage follows the set of objectives (the requirements specification) that have been defined in the investigation and analysis stage. It begins to develop the design of the system. The methods of data capture have to be considered to ensure that the format of the data capture and the methods of data capture to be used are compatible with the design of the processing to be used in the system.

Leading on from this, the preparation, input and storage of the data must also be considered. This covers such activities as the design of the user interface and screen layout.

The structure of the data must be defined together with the processing and the validation routines that will be used.

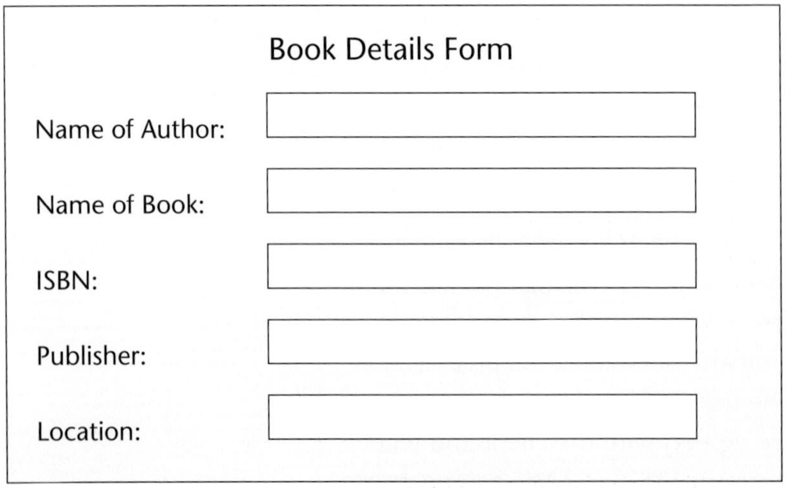

Book Details Form

Name of Author: [   ]

Name of Book: [   ]

ISBN: [   ]

Publisher: [   ]

Location: [   ]

Figure 1.2 Example of a screen form design

The development of any user feedback requirements (e.g. the creation of helpful error messages) should be linked with this.

The validation routines, structure of the data and the processing are likely to form the basis of test plans that are developed as part of this stage.

The design of queries and reports that have been identified as requirements during the investigation stage will need to be considered. The reports may include documents and/or screen reports. The reports should follow, as far as possible, the existing house style of the organisation. The reports will be part of the design of the output that is required from the system. The output requirements should have been defined in the previous stages of the systems life cycle.

The design stage may also involve the development of a project plan. This must be developed in conjunction with the client who may have specified a deadline for the installation of the system.

The main output from this stage is the design specification.

Implementation stage

This stage is also known as the development stage. The implementation stage comes after the design stage has been completed and it must be completed before the testing stage is started. It uses the design specification (the output from the design stage) and is about taking the design forward and putting it into practice.

During this stage the programmers will create the code required for the software solution, including the development of the user interfaces and output. These will have been designed in the design stage, so the programmers will need to ensure that the code matches this. The programmers will also need to develop any macros, processing and queries that are required by the client. The backup and storage of the data should be considered during the creation of the code.

A decision will need to be taken about the strategy to be taken. This is dependent on the system requirements. It may be that off-the-shelf software is purchased and either installed as it is or customised to meet fully the defined needs of the client. Software that is currently available will be much cheaper in terms of time and money than creating custom-written software. The budget constraint defined by the client should be considered when making the decision about which strategy to take.

The output from this stage will be working software code that is ready to be tested.

Testing stage

The testing stage comes after the implementation stage has been completed. The stage must be completed before the installation stage is started. It tests the output from the implementation stage (the software code).

There are two main functions of this stage. They are to find out:

- if there are any bugs or errors in the code
- if the system correctly meets the defined user requirements.

If a high quality and reliable solution is to be installed, then the testing must follow a well-defined and comprehensive test plan. It is acknowledged that the reliability of a software solution increases with the amount of testing completed. However, testing is generally time-consuming and expensive, so, in consideration of the budget set by the client, some compromise may need to be reached. Some software systems need to be more reliable than others and so the purpose of the software will also need to be a major factor when considering how much testing should be completed.

If all the previous stages of the systems life cycle have been fully completed, then the software under test will be well-designed and so should be easier to test.

There are many types of testing that can be carried out at this stage. The type of testing must be appropriate to the purpose of the software.

The test plan to be followed should have been developed in previous stages of the life cycle. This test plan should be followed with the results being recorded. Finding faults with the software, however, may result in the software having to be returned to the previous stage. This demonstrates the iterative nature of the systems life cycle.

Installation stage

The installation stage comes after the testing stage has been completed. It usually runs in conjunction with the documentation stage. This stage uses the output from the implementation and testing stages: the completed and tested software code.

The strategy of installation needs to be decided. There are four main strategies that can be taken when installing a new system. These are:

- parallel
- phased
- pilot
- direct.

These strategies are discussed in Chapter 5.

When making a decision about which strategy to use, the timescale for implementing the new system must be considered. Another consideration is the sensitivity of the data and the effect that any data loss will have on the organisation.

The training of the employees will need to be completed during this stage in the systems life cycle.

Documentation stage

When the system has been implemented and the staff trained it is essential that documentation is given to the end users. Not all of this documentation will be used on a day-to-day basis, but it should be kept in a safe place in case it needs to be referred to at a later date. The documentation that is passed to the end user serves a number of purposes.

The documentation that may be passed to the end user includes:

- detailed program specifications
- recovery procedures
- operating procedures
- user manuals
- test plans, data and logs
- security details
- version details
- technical manuals for the associated hardware.

Detailed program specifications are given to the end user so that if any maintenance is needed at a later date, the programmer completing this maintenance will be able to see clearly how the system was constructed. It is unlikely, but not impossible, that the same team who developed the system will perform any required maintenance.

Security details should be handed over to ensure that the access rights initially set are maintained – staff changes will inevitably occur during the life of a system, so these details will ensure that the security of an organisation is not compromised.

Version details should be passed to the organisation to ensure that the organisation is holding and using the most up-to-date set of documents. As with any iterative activity, different versions of documentation are produced as changes are implemented. Version controls will ensure that changes made to the system can be tracked and that any maintenance performed uses the most recent set of documents.

Additionally, documentation can provide reference material for staff training. Each task and procedure covered by the system should be clearly detailed. This will also enable users to solve any minor issues or problems with the system once they are using it on a day-to-day basis.

The documentation should also provide a detailed explanation of how the system works. This will enable the people working with the system (e.g. technicians) to diagnose and solve day-to-day issues that may arise. The documentation should also contain detail that will help if any maintenance is to be carried out on the system at a later date.

Activities

Investigate and identify why the following pieces of user documentation should be passed to the end user. Explain how each piece of documentation may be used during the life of the system:

- recovery procedures
- operating procedures
- user manuals.

Evaluation and maintenance stage

The final stage of the life cycle is the evaluation and maintenance stage. It may form the basis on which the decision is taken to begin the life cycle again. The linkage between this stage and the definition of the problem demonstrates the iterative nature of the life cycle.

The solution should be evaluated once it has been implemented. If the timescale of the life cycle has been long then it may be that some of the user requirements have changed. This can be identified during the evaluation and can be rectified through maintenance. Maintenance is the process of ensuring that a system continues to meet the needs of its users. Further details about maintenance can be found in Chapter 5.

The inputs and outputs of stages of the systems life cycle are shown in the following table.

Stage	Input	Output
Problem definition		Feasibility study
Investigation and analysis	Feasibility study	Requirements specification
Design	Requirements specification	Designs
Implementation	Designs	Completed system
Testing	Completed system / test plans	Working system / test logs
Installation	Working system	Installed system

Question

Describe the following stages of the systems life cycle:

a) design

b) implementation.

Describe the advantages and disadvantages of different approaches an analyst might use when investigating a system: questionnaires, interviews, meetings, document analysis, observation

There are different methods that can be used to gather the information during the investigation and analysis stage of the systems life cycle. They include:

- questionnaires
- interviews
- meetings
- document analysis
- observations.

The analyst will select the most appropriate method of investigation for the task. The choice will depend on:

- the people involved
- the type of information being gathered
- the place where the investigation is to be carried out.

Each method of investigation has benefits and limitations. Based on these, and the factors given above, the analyst may use more than one method during the investigation stage.

Questionnaires

Questionnaires are an excellent way of gathering information. However the questionnaire must be structured correctly, the return of the questionnaires must be strictly controlled and the questionnaire must be sent to relevant end users.

The questionnaire should be structured clearly and provide opportunities for short answers based on facts and figures and descriptive answers. The balance of type of questions will ensure that all the information required by the analyst will be gathered.

The return of a questionnaire may cause a problem to the analyst. One idea maybe to put a time constraint on the return of the questionnaire (e.g. 'Please return within five working days'). Another idea may be to distribute the questionnaire at a meeting and collect them in at the end of the meeting – this is not always feasible and the use of this approach should be carefully considered beforehand.

When designing a questionnaire it is important to consider who the questionnaire is aimed at. End users of a system can interpret questions differently depending on their job role within the organisation.

Figure 1.3 Example questionnaire

Interviews/meetings

The analyst can clarify that the information already gathered is correct by interviewing, or holding meetings with, users. If the questions are well-planned, interviews can reveal new information and give the analyst the opportunity to understand the system from the end-user's perspective. However, interviewing end users can be problematic if the organisation has a number of geographically distributed branches or offices.

The analyst should always carefully plan an interview. The questions to be asked must be unambiguous to ensure the information required is gathered.

One of the main benefits of interviewing is that the planned questions can be modified as the interview progresses. An answer might be given that raises some relevant and/or additional information that the analyst has not considered. If this occurs it may be beneficial for a checklist of points to be drawn up to ensure that all the points that need to be considered are covered.

Sometimes meetings and interviews do not go as planned. This may be because:

- people are unable or unwilling to answer the questions (e.g. the procedures defined by the management of the organisation are not being followed and staff do not wish to draw attention to it)

Figure 1.4 Interviewing an end user

- irrelevant or unnecessary information may given in response to a question (e.g. it may be that the question is ambiguous and may need to be restructured, or a topic under discussion may lose its focus leading to irrelevant dialogue taking place)
- insufficient information may be given in response to a question
- inaccurate information may be given in response to a question. The interviewer may not be aware of any inaccuracy until the responses from other investigations are collated.

If the system to be designed is to meet the needs of the organisation, then it is important that the analyst has all the relevant information. This situation may mean that the interviewer has to ask more questions in order to gather the required information.

It is very important that the analyst talks to all different types of end user, from management to staff of all levels, and that the interviewee feels comfortable and at ease with the questioning. A good interview will enable a rapport to be developed between the interviewer and interviewee. This rapport may prove to be important if further interviews are needed or further information has to be gathered.

There are four factors that the analyst should consider when arranging interviews or meetings:

- Who to interview or invite to the meeting.
- Where and when to conduct the interview or meeting.
- What questions to ask.
- How to record the answers to the questions.

If all these points are carefully considered, then the interview or meeting will go well and all the information required by the analyst should be gathered.

Document analysis

The analysis of documentation used in the current system is a good way of identifying the format of the input, processing and outputs that occur in that system.

The drawback is that this method of investigation can only be used when the information flow is document-based. This method can be used to clarify the information given by the end user and can also trace the source and recipients of a particular piece of information used by the current system. The analyst should collect copies of all documents used by the current system.

The most common documents analysed include invoices, purchase orders, goods received notes, receipts, stock records and customer records.

Figure 1.5 Example of documents used in a system

Observation

If several activities are taking place in the system being investigated, then observation (or shadowing) may be the best method for collecting the information.

Observing someone doing their job is better than asking someone to describe it. Over a period of time, the possibility of anything being forgotten or missed is reduced. Observation is suitable on a factory production line, for example, where there will not be much documentation for analysis and, because of the nature of the activity, interviewing or questionnaires are inappropriate.

The analyst observing a system will be able to identify all the processes that occur, how long the user takes to perform a specific task and what hardware, software (if any) and people are involved.

One thing the analyst must be aware of is that people are involved in a system. The analyst must always ask the permission of the people involved before beginning their observation or shadow. To ensure that the observation or shadow gathers the information required the following factors should be carefully considered:

- How the findings will be recorded.
- Where and when the observation/shadow will take place.
- What part of the current system will be observed.

Questions

1 Explain why an analyst might use the technique of observation.

2 Identify **two** situations when observation would be appropriate.

Method	Benefits	Limitations
Questionnaires	• Large numbers of people can be asked the same questions, therefore comparisons are easy to make (e.g. 72% of people said they were unhappy with the current system). • Cheaper than interviews for large numbers of people. • Anonymity may provide more honest answers. • Factual information required can be easily gathered.	• Must be designed very carefully. Questions need to be unambiguous. • Cannot guarantee 100% return. • It is difficult to gain a realistic view of the use of a system.
Interviews	• A rapport can be developed with the people who will use the system. • Questions can be adjusted as the interviews proceed – additional questions can be added to gather more information.	• Can be time-consuming and costly. • Poor interviewing can lead to misleading or insufficient information being gathered. • It might be impossible to interview every relevant person in a large organisation.
Meetings	• A group of people, possibly from a specific department, can attend a meeting. • Discussions can take place with different views being expressed. • Can be used to gather or give information. • Body language can be seen.	• The discussions can lose focus resulting in the questions not being fully answered. • Some staff may not attend as jobs and tasks still need to be completed while the meetings are being held.
Document/ record analysis and inspection	• Good for obtaining factual information (e.g. volume of sales over a period of time, inputs and outputs of the system).	• Cannot be used when input/output information is not document-based.
Observation	• The effects of office layouts and conditions on the system can be assessed. • Work loads, methods of working, delays and 'bottlenecks' can be identified. • Potential to experience all aspects of job role.	• Can be time-consuming and costly. • Problems may not occur during observation. • Users may put on a 'performance' when being observed.

Questions

1 Describe how interviews could be used as an investigative method.

2 What are the advantages of using meetings as an investigative method?

3 What are the disadvantages of using observation as an investigative method?

Describe the following software development methodologies: prototyping and rapid application development (RAD)

A major problem with the traditional structured life cycle model is the duration of the activities that have to take place. There is usually a long time delay between the definition of the problem and the implementation of the solution. In some cases this may mean that the delivered system does not fully meet the current requirements of the organisation it has been designed for.

This problem could be solved by using a different software development methodology.

Prototyping

Prototypes are a first attempt at a design, which is then extended and enhanced through the use of iterations. The prototyping methodology stresses the early delivery to the end users of an incomplete, but working, system that can then be changed following feedback from the client. Typically, a prototype simulates only a few aspects of the software system and may be completely different from the final solution that is implemented.

The main purpose of a prototype is to allow the end users of the software to evaluate the proposals for the design of the software by actually trying them out, rather than having to interpret and evaluate the design based on descriptions.

Prototyping can take place at different stages of the development life cycle, but the use of this methodology must be planned to ensure maximum feedback is obtained from the end users of the system.

This methodology is popular because it can be used to verify that what the designer has conceptualised is what the end user requires, thereby fully meeting the need. End users can often find it difficult to define their exact requirements. This may be because they do not exactly know or find it difficult to imagine how, for example, the user interface will need to look when the solution has been completed.

Prototyping can also be used by end users to describe requirements that the designer may not have considered, so controlling the prototype can be a key factor in the relationship between the designer and the end users.

By creating a prototype, concepts can be demonstrated, design options can be tried out and problems with possible solutions can be investigated. For example, a prototype of a screen design for a user interface could be developed to test the appropriateness of the layout. It would not be necessary, in this case, to develop the data files that are queried or written to using the screens. However, when the screen design has been agreed, then the data files can be developed as a prototype to ensure that the end users are happy with the way they interact.

There are two main ways of prototyping:

- evolutionary
- throw-away.

Evolutionary prototyping is when an initial prototype of the system is developed and evaluated by the end users. Using the feedback from this a second prototype is developed and then evaluated. This process continues with each prototype and evaluation making the system closer to what the end users require. Finally, on the last evaluation, the system meets all the requirements.

Throw-away prototyping is when a working model of various parts of the system is developed after a short investigation. The prototype is developed and evaluated by the end user, but this prototype is not used in the final solution: it is thrown away! This enables the end users to give, and receive, quick feedback. This means that any refinements can be done early in the development. Making changes early in the development life cycle is cost effective because there is nothing to redo. If a project is changed after considerable work has been done, then small changes could require large efforts to implement since software systems have many dependencies.

Question

Describe the evolutionary and throw-away prototyping methodologies.

Benefits of prototyping methodology

Reduced time and costs

Prototyping can improve the quality of requirements and specifications provided to developers. Changes cost exponentially more to implement because they are detected later in development, so early clarification of what the user really wants can result in faster development and smaller development costs.

Improved and increased user involvement

Prototyping requires the involvement of users. This enables them to see and interact with a prototype providing better and more complete feedback and specifications. Misunderstandings that can occur when each side believes the other understands what they said are fewer. The end users know the problem better than the designer, so increased user involvement can result in a better and more appropriate final product that is likely to satisfy the end users' needs in terms of look, feel and performance.

The designer can obtain feedback from the end users early in the project. This will, hopefully, ensure that the software made matches the software specification. This can also check that the deadlines proposed can be successfully met.

Disadvantages of prototyping methodology

Confusion between the prototype and the finished system

End users can think that a prototype, intended to be thrown away, is actually a final system that merely needs to be finished. This can lead them to expect the prototype to match accurately the final system. Users can also become attached to features that were included in a prototype for user evaluation and then removed from the final system.

Excessive development time of the prototype

The main aim of prototyping is that it is supposed to be done quickly. It is very tempting to develop a prototype that is too complex, leading to the development time being extended. This would also lead to an increase in the cost of the resources needed.

It would not be appropriate to use this methodology where user requirements are well established or the system is a standard one used by the organisation.

Rapid application development (RAD)

Another approach to shortening the project duration is rapid application development (RAD). The RAD methodology is based on a life cycle that is both iterative and evolutionary.

One of the main aims of RAD is to produce a software solution within a relatively short duration. The typical duration of a RAD system is less than six months. This duration is generally considered to be the longest period over which user requirements will stay static.

The short duration, along with increased opportunities for user involvement, are the two main benefits of RAD. These will, hopefully, ensure that no changes to the end-user requirements will appear towards the end of the development process. During the RAD process, there are a number of tools that can be used by the developers to build the graphical user interface (GUI) that can be seen and evaluated by the end user. The use of these tools will assist end users to visualise the GUI and to provide helpful feedback to the development team before the system is implemented.

RAD has two main features. The first is the use of joint application development (JAD) workshops. These are requirement gathering workshops that aim to develop a set of requirements that, hopefully, will not change before the system is implemented.

The second feature of RAD is timeboxing. This means that the requirements of the system are defined in small 'chunks', each of which is considered using a JAD. Each 'chunk' is allocated a specified timescale which must not be exceeded. At the start of each timebox the objectives are defined and, at the end of the timebox, these are evaluated. If requirements are not successfully completed, then they may be added to another timebox or dropped. The requirements that are not implemented are those of lowest concern because they have been prioritised.

If the requirements of several consecutive timeboxes cannot be completed, then the overall system may need to be reviewed.

Activities

Investigate software systems that could be developed using the prototyping methodology.

This should ensure that the incomplete requirements do not pile up and cause excessive delays to the overall product.

RAD attempts to maintain overall control over the development process, but also provides continual feedback on the progress of a project. This means that if there is any slippage in the defined time schedule, then plans can be adjusted.

RAD is also helpful to the end users of the system being developed. They are party to the evaluations, which means they are continually involved. This involvement should ensure that the system, once developed and implemented, fully meets their defined requirements.

Benefits of RAD

- The end user is involved at all stages and the system is implemented within six months. This should ensure that the final system fully meets the defined requirements.
- End users do not have to define all the requirements of the system at the beginning of the process.

Disadvantages of RAD

- The solution developed may, on the surface, meet the end-user requirements but the functionality may not be acceptable. For example, if the system is tested using a small number of users then it may not fully function when many end users try to use the system concurrently.
- The project manager, who is overseeing the development of the system, will need to keep very tight control over the whole development process and the team. The timescales defined must be adhered to otherwise the solution will not be developed within the six-month deadline required by RAD.

Question

Describe the RAD methodology.

Describe the purpose of test data and explain the importance of testing and test plans

When a system has been created (implemented) then it must be tested to ensure that, as far as possible, it is free from errors. Testing checks that a system works as intended.

There are set procedures that should be followed to ensure that a system works. These procedures are grouped together to form a test plan. Testing is important and should:

- make sure that the system (software) meets the design specification
- make sure that the system returns the correct results and actually works

- give confidence to the end users: they will have more faith and confidence in a new system if it has successfully completed and passed all the tests.

It is important to understand the difference between an error and a fault. An error is a human action that produces an incorrect result. A fault is a manifestation of an error in the system – these are also known as bugs or defects. A fault may cause a software failure; it is a deviation of the software from what is expected.

Reliability is also a key factor in testing. Reliability is the probability that the software will not cause the failure of the system for a specified time under specified conditions. Testing is about ensuring the software is reliable.

Errors occur with software because people are not perfect. While they are working under constraints, such as deadlines, they can, due to the stress and pressure, make mistakes.

The amount of testing that is carried out on a system depends on the risks that are involved. A safety critical system, which would cause more risk if it failed, would need more rigorous testing than, for example, a stock database.

Testing is about trying to identify faults and rectifying them, thereby increasing the reliability and quality of a system.

When carrying out tests, it is important to consider other factors that may have an impact on the system. These may include contractual (part of the handover of the system) or legal (industry standards) requirements.

It is sometimes difficult to determine how much testing should be carried out. However, it is unlikely that all the faults will be found during the testing process. Large software vendors release patches to solve any bugs or errors found after the software has been released.

Test data

The data that is selected for testing is important and should cover:
- Normal data: The data that is used every day. It is data that is correct and should not generate any errors on data entry.
- Extreme data: The data that is also correct, but is at the upper and lower boundaries of tolerance. It should not generate any errors when entered because it is normal data.
- Erroneous data: The data that is incorrect. It may be outside the boundaries of tolerance or be of the wrong data type.

Test plans

A test plan has to be developed before testing is carried out. This is a formal document that lists the tests that will be carried out on the system.

The test plan should ensure that the tests cover:

- the requirements
- pathways
- validation routines
- a comparison of the actual performance against the design specification.

The test plan structure, as explained further in Chapter 9, is shown below.

Test number	Description of test	Type of test	Data used	Expected result

- Test number: a unique identifier for each test.
- Description of test: an everyday language description of what is being tested.
- Type of test: normal, extreme, erroneous (incorrect).
- Data used: the data that will be entered to run the test. It must be specific and, if relevant, indicate where it will be entered. All data used must be given.
- Expected result: what you expect to happen when you run the test. For normal tests it should be a positive result. Incorrect data should result in an error message.

The format of the test plan is important because the test plan should be in sufficient detail to enable a third party to recreate exactly the tests and the actual results obtained. The test plan may also be included in the documentation that is passed over following the installation of the system.

The test plan aims to document clearly how each test will be carried out. The input data and expected output should be clearly defined. This will enable any discrepancies between the expected output and the actual output to be identified clearly. Any tests where there is a difference between the actual and expected output (results) will need to be re-tested once remedial action has been taken to rectify the fault. These will need to be added to the test plan to ensure that it stays complete.

Questions

1 Describe the importance of a test plan.

2 When should a test plan be changed?

3 Explain the purpose of test data.

Describe the contents of the requirements specification, the design specification and the system specification, distinguishing between them

Requirements specification

The requirements specification is usually developed by the systems analyst. It will be developed following investigations that have been carried out on the system.

The requirements specification should clearly define what the system is to do and how this should be achieved. It should also describe all the interactions the users will have with the software.

The defined functional (what the end user wants the system to do) and non-functional (the end-user-defined limitations relating to response time/hardware/software/programming language) requirements should also be included within the requirements specification.

The contents of a requirements specification will also include:
- the objectives/purpose of the system
- the scope of the system
- the proposed timescale for the project
- end-user-defined constraints including budget, time, hardware and software choices
- a contract.

Design specification

The design specification is usually developed by the systems designer. The specification is usually created following the investigations. The contents of the design specification may have a different focus dependent on the type of system that is being developed. For example, if a website is being developed, then it would be appropriate to include the links between the web pages and how these pages would be organised.

This would not be appropriate if a database system is being developed. However, both the website and the database might include data entry forms. The design for the data entry forms would be included in the design specification.

The design specification usually includes:
- the purpose of the system
- assumptions, limitations or constraints
- the inputs – documents and screens/interface
- the outputs – documents and screens/interface
- error messages
- the colours/fonts/sizes, including the consideration of the corporate image/house style, to be used

- validation rules
- processing requirements/queries
- data structures
- modelling diagrams (e.g. data flow diagrams, entity relationship diagrams and state transition diagrams)
- the hardware
- the software/programming language to be used
- test plan.

System specification

The system specification defines the requirements for the new system. These include, for example, the facilities and outputs that the new system should provide. The requirements are developed and formulated from the results of the investigation of the current system. The system specification should include:

- operation requirements: what operations the system should carry out
- information requirements: what information the system should provide to the end users
- volume requirements: for example, how much volume of processing is to be handled
- general systems requirements: for example, the degree of data accuracy needed, security issues, the need for an audit trail, the flexibility of the system and its ability to adapt to growth and change.

Question
Describe the contents of the design specification.

Describe the roles and responsibilities of the following members of the project team: project manager, systems analyst, systems designer, programmer and tester

Many people are involved in the development of a system, both at specific or all stages of the systems life cycle.

The main members of the project team will be the project manager, systems analyst, systems designer, programmer and tester. Each member of the team has a different role and responsibility. If, however, the project team is small then it is possible that one person may take on more than one of these roles and responsibilities.

Project manager

The main role of the project manager is to plan and control the whole project. The project manager is, if required, responsible for identifying potential problems and issues, and, if they arise, for rectifying them.

After consulting with the end user and other members of the project team, the project manager will set the deadlines for each stage of the project. This task is completed at the beginning of the project to ensure that the system being developed is delivered to the end user on schedule. This enables the project manager to have, at any given point during the development, an overall understanding of how the project is progressing. This may, if the project is falling behind the defined time schedule, involve the rescheduling of any tasks, and of associated resources such as time, staff and money. One of the other associated roles of the project manager is to oversee the project team.

The budget allocated by the end user will need to be agreed at the start of the project. The project manager is responsible for ensuring that the budget is adhered to and that any slippage in costs is notified to the end user (i.e. the project manager should try to ensure that the project costs do not exceed those set by the end user).

The project manager must ensure that all the associated project reports and documentation are correctly completed during the project. This may involve consultation between all members of the project team to ensure that the documentation provides accurate and complete details.

The systems life cycle is an iterative process, so the project manager is responsible for ensuring that each stage (and any associated tasks) of the life cycle is completed before the next stage is started. As each stage or task is completed the project manager should provide progress reports to the end user of the system.

Systems analyst

The main role of the systems analyst is to analyse the existing system. During the analysis the analyst will investigate the current system using appropriate investigative methods.

The results of the analysis will enable the systems analyst to assess the suitability of the current system for upgrading.

After the investigations, the systems analyst must develop a plan for developing the proposed system. As part of this the analyst must specify:

- the procedures involved (computerised and manual)
- how the data is to be captured
- the software required to process the data
- how the data is to be output
- the hardware that is required
- how the staff will be trained to use the new system.

The systems analyst is mainly responsible for the development of the feasibility report (the output from the investigation and analysis stage of the systems life cycle) including the requirements specification.

A major part of the role of the systems analyst is to liaise with the staff in the organisation. Those who work in the organisation will have expert knowledge of how the current system works and how it could be improved.

Systems designer

The systems designer will build on the findings of the systems analyst in order to design the new system. The designer's role is central to the process of designing, developing and implementing the defined requirements of the system. The roles and responsibilities of the systems analyst and designer are very similar and, if roles have to be combined in a project team, these roles can be given to the same person.

The role usually involves planning and designing the system so that hardware, software and communication technologies all integrate and interact. The systems designer will be involved with the development of the new system until it has been implemented. The roles and responsibilities of a systems designer may include:

- completing the requirements analysis
- working with programmers and the end users
- planning and designing the system
- confirming the systems analyst's proposal (i.e. the choice of hardware, software and network requirements for the system)
- developing, documenting and revising system design procedures, test procedures and quality standards
- creating an architectural design with the necessary specifications for the hardware, software, data and staff resources.

Programmer

The programmer will create software that is required for the system being developed. A programmer can be a specialist in one area (e.g. a language) of computer programming or be a generalist who writes code for many kinds of software. Most systems, unless very specialised, such as for air traffic control, will be programmed by an applications programmer.

The programmer will be responsible, within the project team, for developing the applications system or for modifying an existing software solution to meet the defined needs of the end user.

When the system has been developed, then one of the responsibilities of the programmer is to create the technical documentation.

Tester

The main role of the tester is to find any bugs and errors in a system once it has been created, and to rectify them before the system goes live. All aspects of the system should be tested, including the associated manual procedures. The testers may not have been involved in the development of the system. The tester will often deliberately try to 'break' the system.

The tester's responsibilities include developing and using test plans to test the programs and modules that are included in the system. The tester must ensure that the system is free from bugs and errors by using a variety of tests. These may include white box and black box tests. It is the responsibility of the tester to ensure that a range of test data is used, including normal, extreme and erroneous, to cover all aspects of the system.

The test plans will need to be created to enable a third party to carry out the testing without having to refer to the tester who created the plans. The tester will also need to record the results of the tests, usually on a test log. The test plans and logs may form part of the technical documentation which is passed to the end user when the system has been implemented.

Questions

1 Describe the role and responsibilities of a systems designer.

2 Describe the role and responsibilities of a programmer.

Describe, interpret and create critical path analysis (CPA) and Gantt charts and for each explain its suitability for use in a given application

A project manager can use several project planning tools when planning a project. Among these are critical path analysis and Gantt charts.

Critical path analysis

Critical path analysis (CPA) shows the relationship between the different parts of the project. A large project is usually made up of many interrelated smaller ones. CPA can be defined as the process of identifying how the tasks within a project fit together so that all tasks occur in a logical order with minimal delay and resourcing issues. The analysis is based on the assumption that some tasks will be dependent on others and have to be completed prior to moving on.

It is important that enough time is allocated to each project task to enable it to be completed before moving to the next dependent task(s). If enough time has not been allocated to a task or if that task is delayed, and no slack time has been built in, then the delivery of the project may be delayed.

CPA lets the project manager identify the critical path through a project i.e. the order in which the component tasks have to be completed and, usually, the path that takes the maximum time.

CPA assists the project manager to analyse and plan the order in which tasks in a project should take place and to define by when they should be completed. By doing this, resources can be provisionally allocated. The project manager is, essentially, charting the path that must be taken to ensure that the project is successful.

Any task that relies on another being completed first is called a dependent or sequential activity (task). A task that can happen at any time is called a non-dependent or parallel activity (task).

When developing the CPA the project manager should ensure that tasks are not scheduled before the earliest start date or before the completion of prior task(s) on which they might be dependent. Most software-based project planning tools have an automatic function that checks these.

Slack time, lead and lag, also needs to be built in so that any unforeseen issues do not lead to slippage of the completion date.

CPA helps plan all tasks that must be completed as part of a project. It acts as the basis for preparation of a schedule and for resource planning. During the management of a project a CPA diagram can be used to monitor the project goals and can help to identify where remedial action needs to be taken to get a project back on course.

The benefit of using CPA within the planning process is to help develop and test the plan to ensure that it is robust. CPA formally identifies tasks which must be completed on time for the whole project to be completed on time. It also identifies which tasks can be delayed if resource needs to be reallocated to catch up on missed or overrunning tasks.

A further benefit of CPA is that it helps identify the minimum length of time needed to complete a project. If a project needs to be speeded up, then the CPA diagram can help identify which project tasks need to be completed more quickly to complete the project within the available time.

The main disadvantage of CPA diagrams is that they can be difficult to understand.

How to create a CPA diagram

1 List all activities in the plan. Detail, for each activity the earliest start date, estimated length of time it will take, and whether it is parallel or sequential. If tasks are sequential, show which stage they are dependent on.

2 Plot the activities as a circle and arrow diagram. In these, circles show events within the project, such as the start and finish of tasks.

The number shown in the circle allows you to identify each event easily. Circles are sometimes known as nodes. An arrow, sometimes known as an arc, needs to connect the circles. This arrow shows the activity needed to complete that task. A description of the task is written underneath the arrow with the length of the task shown above it. It is usual that all arrows run left to right. Looking at Figure 1.6 it is clear that task 70 cannot be started until tasks 40, 50 and 60 have been completed. Also, tasks 40 and 60 are dependent on task 30 being completed.

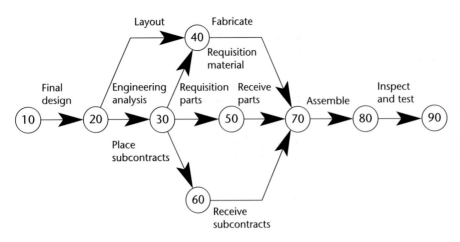

Figure 1.6 Example of a CPA diagram

Gantt chart

A Gantt chart is a diagram that shows each task as a block of time. Each block of time is labelled with the title/description of the task and the amount of time the block represents. A Gantt chart assists the project manager in planning because it will show how long each activity/task is expected to take and the order in which these will occur.

A Gantt chart will also model how long the overall project will take and where 'pressure' points can be expected. These points may occur when a number of tasks need to be completed prior to moving to the next part of the project or when all members of the project team are working at maximum level and all resources are allocated.

A Gantt chart has four main features:

- Milestones: important checkpoints or interim goals for a project.
- Resources: it often helps project teams to have an additional column containing numbers or initials that identify who is responsible for a task.

Activities

To make a cup of tea:

- The kettle must be filled with water (1 min).
- The kettle must be boiled (2 mins) and while this is happening the tea must be put into the teapot (1 min).
- When the kettle has boiled, the water must be poured into the teapot (2 min).
- The tea must brew (2 mins) while the cups are got from the cupboard (1 min).
- The tea is poured from the teapot into the cups (1 min).

Using the tasks shown above develop a CPA diagram for making a cup of tea.

- Status: the progress of a project can be seen by filling in task bars to a length proportional to the amount of work that has been finished and by 'ticking off' tasks that have been completed.
- Dependencies: an essential concept that some activities are dependent on other activities being completed first.

The critical path is shown on a Gantt chart as the longest sequence of dependent tasks.

Figure 1.7 shows a Gantt chart for building a house. The tasks are shown on the left side of the chart with the timescale shown along the top. Each task is shown as a blue rectangle with the dependent tasks being linked by a black arrow. Tasks that are completed at the same time are shown in the same time slot.

Chapter 9 covers more about Gantt charts.

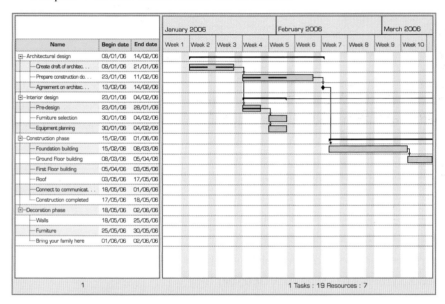

Figure 1.7 Example of a Gantt chart

How to create a Gantt chart

1 List all the tasks that need to be completed. For each task, show the earliest start date, the estimated time it will take to complete the task and if the task is dependent or non-dependent.

2 Set up a chart, with the total timescale across the top.

3 Plot the tasks, one per line, on the chart. Start each task at the earliest start and draw a solid horizontal line to show how long the task is expected to last.

4 Link the dependent tasks.

Questions

1 Describe Gantt charts as a tool used in project planning.

2 How is the critical path defined?

Describe, interpret and create data flow diagrams and flowcharts, and for each explain its suitability for use in a given application

Data models will need to be completed during a system's life. If all the information collected previously exists, then all the information needed to complete the data modelling will be available.

Various techniques can be used during the design stage, all of which will enable a system to be developed that fully meets the needs of the organisation and of the end users.

Among the tools and techniques that can be used are:

- data flow diagrams (DFDs)
- flowcharts.

The choice of tools and techniques used will depend on the type of system being developed. However, it is possible to combine more than one tool or technique when fully designing a new system.

Data flow diagram

Data flow diagrams (DFDs) show how data moves through a system. They focus on the processes that transform incoming data flows (inputs) into outgoing data flows (outputs). The processes that perform this transformation create and use data that is held in data stores.

A DFD will also show what and who the system interacts with in the form of external entities. Examples of external entities include people and other systems.

There are many different sets of symbols that can be used when constructing DFDs. It does not matter which set of symbols is used, but it is important that once the set of symbols has been selected that they are used consistently and are not changed part way through the analysis stage. One set of symbols that could be used is shown in Figure 1.8.

- External entities are used to represent people, organisations or other systems that have a role in the system under development but are not necessarily part of it. They either put data into the system or receive data from it.
- A process represents an activity that takes place within, and is linked to, the system. All activities within a system have a process attached to them. A process models what happens to the data. It transforms incoming data flows into outgoing data flows. Usually a process will have one or more data inputs and produce one or more data outputs.
- A data store shows where data is stored. Examples of data stores include a database file, a paper form or a folder in a filing cabinet. A data store should be given a meaningful descriptive name (e.g. customer file).

Figure 1.8 Examples of DFD symbols

- Data flows indicate the direction or flow of data within the system. Data flows provide a link to other symbols within the DFD. Each flow should be given a simple meaningful descriptive name.

A DFD does not show the hardware or software required to operate the system. The analyst will use the DFD to show:

- the external entities that the system interacts with
- the processes that happen
- the data stores that are used
- the flow of the data and information.

There are certain rules about which DFD symbols can be linked. These are shown in the next table.

Data flow links	Data store	External entity	Process
Data store	✗	✗	✔
External entity	✗	✗	✔
Process	✔	✔	✔

The table shows that it is not possible to link an external entity with another external entity or a data store with an external entity.

Three of the symbols used in a DFD must also be labelled further.

The process box is labelled with a number that should represent when in the system the process is taking place. The process box should also state what the process is. For example, the process shown in Figure 1.9 is the third process and shows the creation of a purchase order.

The data stores are labelled to indicate the type of data store they are. The two main types are:

- D: a computerised data store (e.g. records in a database).
- M: a manual data store (e.g. a filing cabinet or paper form).

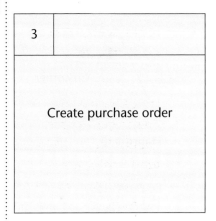

Figure 1.9 The DFD process symbol

M3	Purchase order		D3	Purchase ledger

Figure 1.10 The DFD data store symbol

A data store can be used more than once in a system. This is called a repeating data store. If a data store is repeated, then the same numbering and description is used, but a second vertical line is inserted as shown in Figure 1.11.

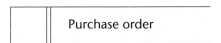

Figure 1.11 The DFD repeating data store symbol

The external entities are labelled with the name of the person, organisation or system they represent. The external entity shown in Figure 1.12 shows the Customer as an external entity.

Figure 1.12 The DFD external entity symbol

It is possible to have repeating external entities. As with the data stores, the original name is kept and a line is used to show that it is repeated (Figure 1.13).

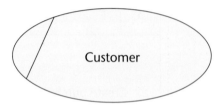

Figure 1.13 The DFD repeating external entity symbol

DFD levels

There are many different levels of DFD. The Level 0 (L0) or context diagram gives a summary of the system. It shows the main external entities and the information that flows into and out of the system.

A Level 0 DFD does not show the processes that occur or the data stores that are used within the system – it simply provides an overview of the system under investigation.

Some systems will have more than one external entity, and the process of constructing the Level 0 DFD will be the same despite the number of external entities and flows involved.

The main aim of the L0 DFD construction is to identify the flows of data that occur between the system and the external entities. The flow of data has a source (where the data comes from) and a recipient (where the data goes to). It is convention that the initial flows in the system are shown as the top flows in the L0 DFD, while the flows that happen last are at the bottom.

A Level 1 (L1) DFD provides an overview of what is happening within the system. The system is represented in the L0 DFD by the central process box. The overview includes types of data being passed within the system, documents and stores of data used (data stores), the activities (processes) and the people or organisations that the system interacts with (external entities).

This information may be put into a data flow table which will give the analyst a clearer understanding of the flows of information. It may also be easier for the client to check that all the flows are present. This table can also be used to construct the L0 DFD.

Ten-step plan for constructing a L1 DFD

There is a wide range of methods that can be used to construct a L1 DFD. One method is given here.

1 Read through the information collected during the investigation and analysis stages.
2 Sort the information into clear sections identifying the people or organisations external to the system under investigation but who interact with it, the documents used in the system under investigation, and the activities that take place within the system under investigation.
3 Produce a data flow table.
4 Convert external users to external entities.
5 Convert documentation to data stores.
6 Convert activities to processes identifying when in the system the activity takes place, who is involved, and any data stores used.
7 Look at the inputs and outputs for each process with the data stores that are used and use data flows to 'link' these.
8 Link each data store and external entity with the associated process.
9 Link the processes (remembering the rules about labelling processes).
10 Check for consistency (e.g. check the initial findings to ensure all documentation has been included, check the flows between external entities given on the context diagram are included, and check with the end users of the current system to ensure nothing has been forgotten).

The analyst should perform some final checks before the DFD is shown to the organisation. These are detailed in the list below.

- Does each process receive all the data it needs?
- Does any data store have only data flows out and not in?
- Does any data store appear to hold data that is never used?
- Are all data flows consistent across the L0 and the L1 DFD?
- Are all external entities shown on the L1 DFD also shown in the L0 diagram? Are all flows labelled? Are they documented in the data dictionary?
- Are there any data flows between two external entities, between external entities and data stores or between two data stores?
- Do any data flows cross other data flows on the diagram? If they do, use repeating external entities or data stores.

Flowcharts

Flowcharts are a diagrammatical representation of the operations or processes involved in a system. They are good at showing a general outline of the processing that is involved in the system under investigation but, generally, they do not relate very well to the actual software system which is eventually developed. Different shaped symbols are used to represent different actions.

There are many different sets of symbols that can be used. As with DFDs, it is important that once a set of symbols has been selected it is used consistently throughout the flowchart. One set of symbols is shown in Figure 1.14.

Flowcharts can be used to model all kinds of systems, not just computer systems. They can be used to break a process into small steps or to give an overview of a complete system.

People who are not involved in the IT industry can easily understand them. However, flowcharts do not translate easily into code and they can sometimes become so complex they can be hard to follow.

For these reasons flowcharts are used by the analyst to give a generalised overview of a system or of the functions that make up a specific process.

There are some rules that must be followed when developing a flowchart:

● Every flowchart must begin with 'Start' and finish with 'End'.
● A decision must have two flows coming from it: 'Yes' and 'No'.

Before a flowchart is developed, it is important that the analyst gains a clear understanding of a system by clearly defining any input, output, decisions and processes that occur. Once this information has been clearly defined then the flowchart can be developed.

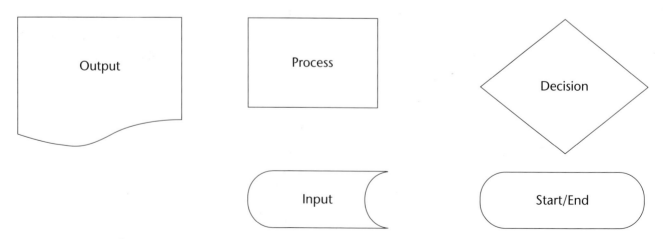

Figure 1.14 Some flowchart symbols

Example

A van hire company needs to take decisions about whether a van needs to be serviced, valeted or repaired after each hire period before it is hired out again. The information needed is taken from the van history log.

- A van needs to be serviced if it is more than six months or the mileage is more than 8000 since the last service.
- A van needs to be valeted if it has been hired out five times since the last valeting.
- A van needs to be repaired if there are any dents or scratches on it.

The process of taking a decision of what action is required (if any) has to be identified by asking the following questions:

- Is it six or more months since the van was last serviced?
- Has the van done 8000 or more miles since the last service?
- Has the van been hired out five times since the last valeting?
- Are there any scratches or dents on the van?

Based on the answers to these questions, a decision on a range of actions can be taken. It is possible that the answer to more than one of the questions is 'yes' and, therefore a number of actions may need to be completed on one van.

The actions that may be taken are:

- Service the van.
- Valet the van.
- Repair any dents or scratches.
- Do nothing.

The information needed to make the decisions and take the appropriate actions is found in the van history log.

Chapter summary

Stages of the systems life cycle

Definition of the problem
Investigation and analysis
Design
Implementation
Testing
Documentation
Evaluation and maintenance

Different approaches to investigating a system

Questionnaires
Interviews
Meetings
Document analysis
Observation

Activities

Using the example, draw a flowchart to represent the process that occurs when deciding on what actions need to be taken with a van on its return to the company.

Software development methodologies
Prototyping
Rapid application development (RAD)

Testing
Purpose of test data
The importance of testing and test plans

Requirements specification

Design specification

System specification

Roles and responsibilities
Project manager
Systems analyst
Systems designer
Programmer
Tester

Project planning tools
Critical path analysis (CPA)
Gantt chart

Modelling tools
Data flow diagram (DFD)
Flowcharts

Chapter tests

Test 1

1 Describe the contents of:

- the requirements specification

- the system specification. [8]

2 Describe the testing and installation stages of the systems life cycle. [6]

3 Describe the purpose of test data. [4]

Test 2

1 Describe the role and responsibility of the project manager. [6]

2 Describe the rapid application development (RAD) software development methodology. [6]

3 Describe flow diagrams and explain how they can be used in the systems life cycle. [8]

2 | Designing computer-based information systems

Introduction

This chapter covers the different computer-based processing and operating systems that are available. An understanding of these will help you to understand the principles of design. You should also be able to apply your knowledge to a specified scenario.

You will learn about:
- processing systems
- designing the user interface.

Compare batch, interactive and real-time processing systems in terms of processing methods, response time and user interface requirements

Processing systems process data. There are many different types of processing systems but the most commonly used are batch, interactive and real-time. These are known as modes of operation (operational modes).

The decisions about which mode(s) should be used in a system are taken during the design phase of the life cycle. The operating system will then manage the functioning of the operational mode that is being used.

Batch

Batch processing systems process batches of data at regular intervals. The amount of data that is processed by a batch system is usually large with the data being of identical type. Batch processing could be used to produce utility bills, bank statements or payroll data.

The data in a batch system is collected together into batches, sent for processing, stored and processed at an appropriate time. No user interaction is needed in a batch processing system. The time when batch processing is carried out tends to be when there is least demand on the processor, such as at a weekend or at night. This means that there is less disruption to daily work so peripherals remain accessible.

A major disadvantage of batch processing is the delay, hours or days, between collecting the data and receiving the output. The user interface requirements of a batch processing system tend to be code-based.

Payroll processing is one of the most common uses of a batch processing system. Each pay date, weekly or monthly, the payroll details for each employee are collected. The details that are collected could include hours worked, monthly salary, overtime completed and sick days to be deducted from payment. These details are then processed with reference to a master file that holds the details of employees' hourly pay rates, tax and national insurance details, and other regular deductions to be made such as pension contributions. The output from the system is the payslips for all employees.

Interactive

An interactive processing system is also known as a transactional processing system. This type of system handles transactions one at a time. Each transaction must be fully processed, the response given to the user and any associated files updated before the next transaction is processed.

The amount of data input for each transaction is generally small and is usually entered, interactively, by the user using a form on a screen. The input method is usually by means of a keyboard.

The user inputs responses to pre-defined questions on an input form that is displayed on a GUI. A database is then searched based on the responses. The results of the search are shown on the screen. The questions and responses are in a very structured, fixed format. The user effectively has a dialogue with the system, but without being able to deviate from responding to the questions asked on the input form or from the preferred options presented.

A typical use of an interactive or transactional processing system is for booking tickets. This type of system could be used to book any type of ticket without the risk of double-booking because each transaction is dealt with in turn.

For example, consider a customer who wants to buy a flight ticket. The details of the departure and destination airports along with the preferred dates of travel are input. When these details are submitted, the system checks the database for the seat availability. The flights that are available, based on the requirements given on the form, are shown on the screen. The flight is selected and a confirm action takes place. At this point the seat is confirmed as being booked – this means that no other customer can book that seat on the flight.

Real-time

A real-time processing system processes data at the time the data is input. The data must be handled within a specified maximum time limit. The time limit will depend on the user requirements and the processing the system has to carry out.

It is usually accepted that the data will be processed as soon as it is received, thereby affecting the database records immediately.

This means that as soon as the user enters some data and the appropriate action is taken to confirm the data, then the processing will take place. The time taken to provide a response to the user must also be very quick. The response time of a real-time system is critical, but, depending on the user requirements, it should be less than four seconds.

A real-time system is generally accepted as being one that reacts fast enough to influence behaviour in the outside world. An example of a real-time system is an air-traffic control system. Real-time systems can also be found in embedded applications (systems within another system) such as mobile phones.

Summary

	Batch	**Interactive**	**Real-time**
Processing methods	Processed when the system is not busy and off-line.	Each transaction is completed before moving onto the next.	Data is processed as soon as it is received by the processor.
Response time	Delayed: there is a delay between the data being input and the results. This can be overnight or days.	Dependent on action from end-user.	Very quick, based on user requirements, but usually less than four seconds.
User interface requirements	Usually code-based.	Graphical User Interface (GUI).	Usually based on the user's requirements.

Question

Describe a batch processing system.

Describe the difference between types of operating systems (single-user, multi-user, multi-tasking, interactive, real-time, batch processing and distributed processing systems) by identifying their major characteristics

An operating system (OS) is a program (or suite of programs) that controls the entire operation of the computer system. The operating system will also manage the functioning of the operational mode(s) being used.

An operating system is software that is responsible for allocating various system resources, such as memory, processor time and peripheral devices (e.g. printers and monitor). All application programs will use the operating system to gain access to the system resources.

There are many different types of operating systems, including:

- single-user
- multi-user
- multi-tasking
- interactive
- real-time
- batch processing
- distributed processing.

Single-user

A single-user OS provides access for one user at a time to use the computer. The OS can support more than one user account but only one account can be used at any one time. This means that someone using the computer must log off their account before someone else can log on.

When a single-user OS is used the processor is dedicated to the user, so multi-tasking can be performed.

Multi-user

A multi-user OS lets more than one user access the system at the same time. The access to a multi-user OS is usually provided by a network. A common setup is a network with a single-user OS connected by the network to a server that has a multi-user OS.

The multi-user system manages and runs all the user requests ensuring that they do not interfere with each other. Peripherals that can only be used by one user at a time, such as printers, must be shared among all users requesting them.

Multi-tasking

A multi-tasking OS involves the processor carrying out more than one task at a time, for example an author might use a word processor while using the internet. Most multi-tasking operating systems are not controlling two things at once; to do this would require multiple processors. The processor is completing part of one task, then changing to do part of another task, and then returning to the first task. This process continues until the two tasks are completed. Switching between tasks is very fast so it appears to the user that the computer is doing both tasks at the same time (concurrently).

The latest processors can run multi-tasks, or threads, at the same time providing that the OS can manage the activities.

Interactive

An interactive OS is one in which there is direct user interaction while a program is running.

Real-time

A real-time OS is one that has been developed for real-time applications. Real-time operating systems are typically used for embedded applications, that is, for systems within another application. An example of this is the engine management system of a car.

Batch processing

A batch OS is given a set of tasks to run without any user intervention: the programs are collected, stored and run at an appropriate time, which might be at night or at the weekend when there is least demand on the processor. Another time when a batch OS may complete jobs is just before the results are required, for example, payroll calculations just before the end of the month.

Distributed processing

A distributed processing system comprises a number of computers connected together. Each computer completes part of the processing. When all the processing has been completed the results are combined to meet the requirements of the user.

Questions

1 What is the difference between a single-user and a multi-user OS?

2 How does a batch processing system differ from an interactive OS?

Explain the use of colour, layout, quantity of information on screen, size of font, complexity of language and type of controls when designing a human–computer interface

A designer must consider the needs of the user at all times when designing a human–computer interface (HCI).

A designer must consider:

- use of colour
- layout
- quantity of the information on the screen
- font size
- complexity of language
- type of controls.

Colour

During the design process a designer should always consider the colours being used. This will include consideration of the existing corporate (house) style of the business. The colours used on the HCI should, as far as possible, follow the corporate colours. However, the suitability of these colours within the HCI should also be taken into account.

The colours selected for use in the HCI should not clash (e.g. bright pink and orange), and they should be easily read by the user. Care should be taken to ensure that a user with a sight impediment, such as colour blindness, can also use the HCI.

Colour can also be used to trigger a user's memory. For example, areas where mandatory information should be input could be in a different colour to optional information.

The number of colours used should be limited to four per screen and seven for the whole sequence of screens.

Colours can be used to code information (e.g. overdue accounts in red, non-overdue accounts in green). If this strategy is used, then the designer must make sure the user understands the code and that the colours used match the user's expectations (e.g. to a mapmaker blue means water, but to a scientist blue means cold).

Certain colours can be used to draw the user's attention. The most effective colours for this are white, yellow and red.

If displayed information needs to be separated, then colours from different parts of the spectrum (red/green, blue/yellow, any colour/white) should be used. If similar information is shown, then colours which are close neighbours in the spectrum (orange/yellow, blue/violet) should be used.

It is important to remember that around 9% of the population is colour-blind, with red/green blindness being most common. Colour-blind people can discriminate colours using black and white shades, but designers should check that the use of colour is not going to affect the performance of those users.

Activities

Investigate the colours that should be used if a user has:
- colour blindness
- dyslexia.

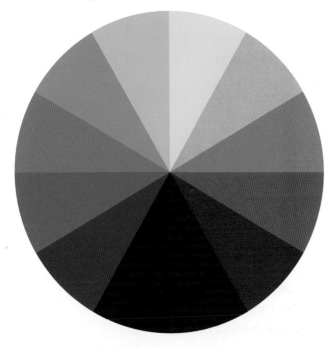

Figure 2.1 A colour wheel

Layout

A designer must ensure that a consistent layout is used on all the screens of the HCI. The layout should follow the house style or corporate image of the business. The layout should follow, as far as possible, the layout of the original source documents used.

The layout of the information on the HCI should flow in a logical order. This should be applied to the information given to a user as well as to the information that has to be input by the user.

In addition, any buttons that are used (e.g. Back or Next) should also be in the same place on each screen of the HCI.

Clearly marked exits should be included in simple and helpful language and they should be in a consistent place on all screens.

The layout should include some white space. This is the amount of empty space (no text or images) on the HCI. Too little white space will mean that the HCI is difficult to read and use, too much white space will make the HCI look bare.

The layout of the HCI should, as far as possible, be consistent with the other applications that are used by the user. Labels and buttons should correspond with the user's idea of what will happen and their previous experience.

Information that needs attending to immediately should always be displayed in a prominent place to catch the user's eye (e.g. warning messages and alarms).

Information that is not needed very often (e.g. help facilities) should not be displayed, but should be available when requested. For example, a Help icon or menu option should appear on every screen.

Less urgent information should be placed in less prominent positions on the screen in a specific area where the user will know to look when this information is required.

Again, the consistency of the layout will enable users to become familiar with the layout quickly, so increasing confidence and learning.

Quantity of the information on the screen

The quantity of the information on the screen of the HCI is linked to the amount of white space that is used.

The amount of information available on the screens of the HCI should enable users to use the screen effectively and to complete their tasks. However, a designer must be aware that too much information on the screen can slow down the user because they have to read more information.

Too much information on the HCI can confuse a user when trying to locate the required information. If this happens then the user can begin to lose confidence, the rate of learning will decrease and so the rate at which tasks are completed will diminish.

Font size and style

The text used on the HCI must be in a font style that is clear and in a font size that is easy to read.

Font styles such as Verdana, Arial and Times New Roman are clearly legible. Other fonts are very difficult to read (e.g. Brush Script MT or Edwardian Script IT).

The size of the font used on the HCI is also important and needs to be appropriate to the HCI, to the text in question and to the users. It would be very difficult to use the HCI if the entire font were size 8.

The font style and size of instructions must be clear and consistently used on the HCI and associated screens. Any error messages should also use the same font size and style.

Complexity of language

The complexity of the language should be kept as low as possible. Any error messages and instructions used should be given in simple language.

If a user is faced with the error message 'Runtime error at line 89670', then they will probably not know what it means and so they will not know what they should do to rectify the error.

The language used should be helpful and simple, but should not be perceived as condescending by the user. The designer should also be aware of the readability of the language used. Technical language should be kept to a minimum, but should be fit for purpose.

Types of control

Controls can be included in the design of the HCI to ensure ease of use.

There are many different types of control that can be used. The designer should select the controls to be included in the HCI to ensure that the user can complete their tasks with ease.

Among the controls that could be used are buttons, forms and menus.

Buttons

Buttons can be used to take the user to a specified page or to run a selected action/command. A macro can be run by the user clicking a button. For example a command button can be added to a database user interface to run a search, or to sort or edit data. A button can also display pictures or text.

In HCI terms, a macro is a set of stored commands that can be replayed by pressing a combination of keys or by clicking a button. A macro enables the user to automate tasks that are performed on a regular basis. This is done by recording a series of commands to be run whenever that task needs to be performed. The complexity of the macro is only limited by the task requirements and the ability of the user.

Activities

Investigate other font styles and sizes that are available on the word-processing software available at your centre.
Ask a sample of ten or more people to rank the font styles and sizes in order of usability for an HCI.

Activities

Investigate the different readability tests that are available.

Once the macro has been recorded, then it can be run by pressing the keys assigned to it when it was recorded. A macro can also be activated by clicking an assigned button placed on the GUI. A macro will only run when the application program with which it is associated is being used. A macro will not run on its own or with a different application program.

Among the advantages of using a macro are:

- a repetitive task can be performed by using a simple action (e.g. pressing a key, clicking a button)
- errors may be reduced because the instructions included in the macro are run automatically and are the same every time
- inexperienced users can perform complex tasks by using a pre-recorded macro.

Among the disadvantages of using a macro are:

- error messages may occur if the conditions when the macro is run are different from those when it was recorded
- users must know and remember the key combination to run the macro (if one is required)
- a macro is pre-programmed so it may not do what the user wants
- if the macro is run from a different starting point than intended, then it may execute incorrectly
- a user can correct errors only if they have some knowledge of how the macro was recorded.

Forms

Forms can be used to assist data entry. A form can give the user help and guidance on what data should be input. Instructions to the user and error messages can be included on forms. It is also possible to include some validation when forms are being used in a system interface. A form may include drop-down boxes for data selection, option boxes and fill-in boxes, which can automatically help a user. Form controls can be used to increase the interactivity with the user and improve usability.

A common example of the use of an automatic fill-in box is when a postcode is entered and the street name and town automatically appear. The user has only to type in the house number.

Menus

Menus enable a user to select actions. There are several types of menu that can be used, including full-screen, pop-up and drop-down. Each type of menu gives the user available choices of actions.

In addition to the considerations mentioned above a designer must ensure that the HCI is easy to learn and use. This will minimise the training required and the number of instructions that will need to be learned and remembered by the user.

Activities

Investigate different form controls that are available and describe how they could be used on a HCI.

Explain the concept and implication of good methods of human–device communications, particularly human–computer interfaces (HCI) using command line interfaces, menus/sub-menus, graphical user interfaces (GUIs), natural language (including speech input–output) and forms dialogue

Many devices use an embedded human–computer interface (HCI) to enable the user to complete tasks, for example mobile phones, satellite navigation systems and washing machines.

A group of devices will have a common purpose, for example the main purpose of a mobile phone is to make phone calls. Some mobile phones enable users to complete other tasks in addition to the primary purpose of making phone calls and so they will have different HCIs (e.g. compare a BlackBerry and an iPhone) to communicate with the user. The mobile phones have embedded systems that enable the user to perform selected tasks.

A BlackBerry (Figure 2.2) lets the user select the task they need to complete using menus and sub-menus. These are not customisable by the user. The menus that are given are those that are embedded in the HCI.

In addition to making phone calls, a BlackBerry lets the user email, use an organiser, browse the internet and access instant messaging. All these options are available by selecting appropriate menus and sub-menus.

An Apple iPhone (Figure 2.3) uses a GUI as the main means of HCI. Users can customise the GUI. They can rearrange the icons they see and also add or delete their own icons to the GUI. The iPhone does use some menus. If a menu is being used, then the back button (to move up the menu structure) is always displayed at the top left of the screen.

Some satellite navigation (satnav) devices (Figure 2.4) use a natural-language HCI which lets a user input the address or postcode that they need to travel to by speaking them.

The satnav uses speech, as an output, to direct the driver to their destination.

If the required destination is input through the use of a form, then the satnav will offer the user destinations based on each element of the postcode input. The user is able, based on a part input, to select the destination they need.

Figure 2.2 A BlackBerry phone

Figure 2.3 An Apple iPhone

As technology advances, more devices will begin to use different HCI methods. The designers of these devices must ensure that the HCI is appropriate to the tasks that the users need to complete and that the advances in technology do not render the devices incapable of delivering their primary function.

Question

Explain how a natural language input could assist users of a satnav system.

Figure 2.4 The TomTom GO 530

Explain how a potential user's perception, attention, memory and learning can be taken into account when designing an interface

When designing a user interface, a designer will have to consider many issues that are related to the potential user. Among these are the user's perception, attention, memory and learning. The use of the interface must be made as intuitive as possible. This means that a designer will have to draw on their knowledge of the user's perception, attention and memory. Designers should ensure that a new interface matches, as far as possible, the current system being used.

Perception

A user will perceive input from the sights and sounds taken from the user interface. Most users will have preconceived ideas that they will draw on when using the interface. For example, most users when faced with a graphic or text in red will have the perceived idea that this will mean 'stop'. Conversely text or graphics in green will, based on the perception of the user, indicate 'go'.

These common perceptions should be considered by the designer. If a user feels comfortable with the interface then, theoretically, their confidence with the interface will increase.

In addition to a user's perception of the colours used in the user interface, the use of sounds is also important. Users can perceive sounds as being happy or sad. This could relate to a sound that indicates a positive response (happy) or a negative response (sad).

If a user hears a sad (negative) sound, then their perception will be that they have done something incorrectly or even that they cannot correctly use the system. Conversely, when a user hears a happy (positive) sound, then their perception will be that they have done something right and that they are using the system correctly.

Activities

Investigate sounds that might be perceived as being happy or sad.

Attention

The designer needs to consider the attention span of a user. Most users have a limited attention span, which is also linked to the amount of time they can look at a screen. One way that a designer can maximise the use of a user's limited attention span is to make the screens uncluttered with the layout in a logical order. (See also the later section on Memory.)

The most important information on the screen needs to be obvious with the screens clearly labelled. Any area where data/information has to be inserted by the user also needs to be clearly labelled. The use of pop-up messages could also help keep a user's attention.

A designer could also use flashing graphics, sounds or pop-up messages to draw a user's attention to an action on the screen. These features should, however, be used sparingly as too many features can detract from the use of the screen. A user's attention span can become shorter if there are many features on a screen. Similarly, if the screen is permanently filled with, for example, flashing graphics, a user could become confused and feel uncomfortable with the screen.

Most screens will include some menus and sub-menus to help the user complete tasks. These menus should remain, as far as possible, consistent. The menus should be in the same place on the screen, and the words used should mean the same on each screen. In addition, if sub-menus are used, then these should relate to the same words on each screen and again be consistent. If graphics are used to denote a task, for example a pair of scissors to denote the action 'cut', then the graphic for this action must always be the same.

The screens will also need to have a consistent layout i.e. buttons or groups of buttons should be in the same place on all screens. If the user has to search for information on each screen, then their attention span will decrease.

Screens should also be designed with a consistent colour scheme which might link to the corporate style of the organisation for which the interface is being designed.

Figure 2.5 shows how a company can ensure that screens are laid out consistently with good use of the corporate style. The figure also shows how the menus and sub-menus are consistent on all screens.

Memory

Users will often use the same screen on a day-to-day basis, and as they do so they will memorise the actions required to use the interface. However, there will always be parts of a user interface that will be used infrequently and for which memory cannot be relied on. A designer must ensure that these screens are also easily used.

Figure 2.5 Screen consistency

A designer must try to ensure that the actions required to use the interface are held in a user's short-term memory. This can be achieved through the use of a consistent and uncluttered page layout.

As far as possible a designer should consider the pre-existing knowledge of the user. It may be that user is already familiar with the interface and is simply using screens that they do not often use. If this is the case, then a designer must ensure that the user's existing knowledge will enable them to use the less familiar screens.

As the user moves through the interface from page to page they will be making use of their short-term memory. If the designer has considered, and used, consistency between screens, then this will help the recall of the skills and knowledge required to use the interface effectively. This in turn, will increase the speed at which the user learns to use the interface.

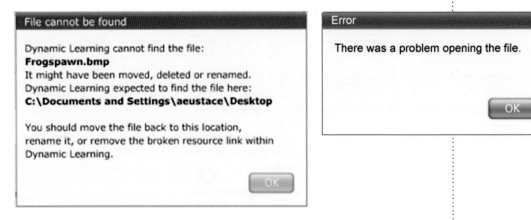

Figure 2.6 Error messages: helpful (left) and unhelpful (right)

Learning

All users need to learn to use an interface. One of the considerations that a designer must take into account is how easy the interface is to learn. As far as possible the interface must draw on the previous experience of the user. Again, this is achieved by using consistent, but not distracting, screen layouts, colour and menus.

On-screen help, in the form of pop-up messages or an easy-to-use help feature, will help a user learn about the interface more quickly. These messages will need to help a user easily correct their errors or learn how to complete an unfamiliar task.

Figure 2.6 shows a helpful error message and an unhelpful one. The helpful message will help a user to correct the error they have made, so increasing the speed with which they learn to use the interface. If a user was given the unhelpful message, it would not help them continue with their task (although it might help the programmer who created the system).

Describe mental models and how they can be applied to the design of a user interface

Users of computer systems can be divided into two groups: those who have some understanding of the operation of a computer and those who have little or no understanding.

Users in the first group are generally able to carry out tasks more quickly and more effectively than those in the second group.

Users who have little understanding of the operation of a computer will generally read and follow a set of instructions with no clear comprehension of how the tasks are being processed by the computer. This may lead to an uncertainty, and possibly some panic, about how to deal with any messages that appear on the screen and which are not defined in the instructions being followed by the user.

When a 'new' user saves a file, it is often the case that they will be unable to locate the file again at a later date. This is because the user has a limited understanding of how the filing system of a computer works.

If a user has a mental model of the computer and has some knowledge of how it works, then they should be able to use the computer more effectively. The mental model a user has when working with a computer is based on the way people process tasks. The processing that is carried out will be based on various types of input. These inputs will based on, for example, sound and images, as well as experience.

The mental model of the user will not only cover such operational functions as the use of RAM, menus, sub-menus and file management, but should also cover the generic features of the software package being used. For example, if a user is creating a word-processed document, then the generic concepts of automatic word-wrapping at the end of a line of text and of text formatting, will enable the user to produce an effective and appropriate document.

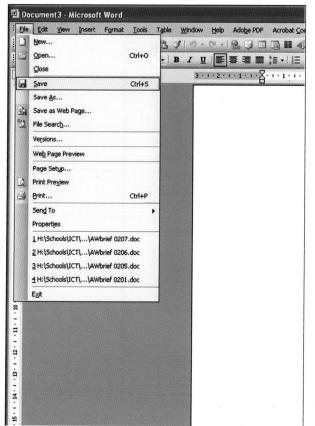 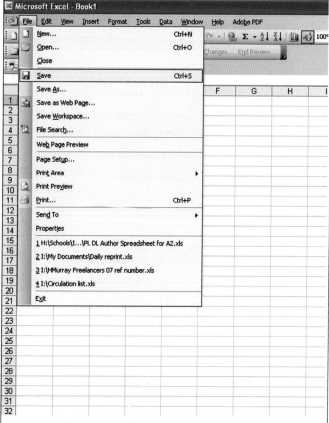

Figure 2.7 Menus

A user's mental model should let them envisage the results of an action. They will then use this experience in the future to predict the actions that may be needed in another situation. This means that the mental model forms the basis of any further interactions with the computer and should enable the user to predict the performance of the computer based on past experiences. The action of the computer will then, hopefully, match the action that they intend to take or have taken. Figure 2.7 shows the file menus from a word-processing and a spreadsheet package. A user's mental model lets them base their actions to save a file in the spreadsheet package on those experienced in the word-processing package.

The development of an effective user interface will have to take account of the fact that different users will have different mental models. In general, this is related to the user's experience of using the interface. The designer must design the interface to ensure that the intention of the user is translated by the interface into the appropriate activity or action. Conversely, the action of the computer should match that anticipated by the user.

The actions of the computer can then be matched by using audio-visual indicators. For example, Figure 2.8 shows the print dialogue box from a word-processing package. The options that can be selected and set by the user can be highlighted (a visual indication) by stepping through the box areas by pressing the tab key.

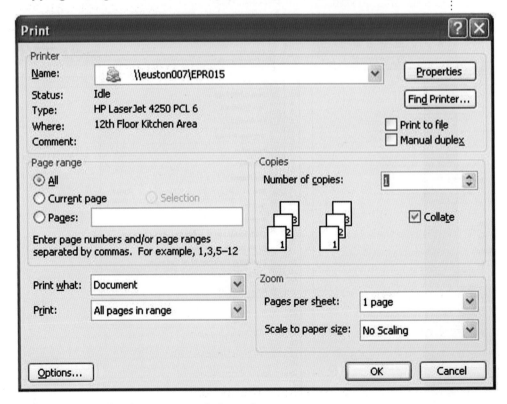

Figure 2.8 Visual indication on a dialogue box

The design of a user interface must take into account the perception of the majority of users. This means that a designer of the interface will have to maintain a natural method of completing an action by the user. When this action has been completed the interface display must reflect the current, and accurate, state of the system. This accuracy will then enable a user to carry out further actions.

Explain the importance of designing a system model that matches closely the user's mental model

A designer must consider the mental model when designing a system model. This ensures that the final product matches the mental model as closely as possible. One of the most important reasons for this match is to ensure that the user does not 'get lost' while using the system. The system must, as far as possible, build on the experience of the user to ensure that previous experience can be used when the user is faced with any problems that might occur. This might mean the use of the same audio cue when an error occurs, or the display of a useful error message.

Users will bring their own preconceptions to any system. These will be based on their own mental model of a system. The designer must try to provide a convergence between the user mental model and the system model being created. For example, a user will expect the command 'open' to open a document or file. By ensuring that these expectations are met when the system is designed then the confidence of the users will increase as they use the system model.

Another reason for the system matching the mental model is that the speed with which the user will learn to use the system confidently will be increased.

Describe the user interface design tool known as the Model Human Processor, developed by Card, Moran and Newell, and its application

The Model Human Processor (MHP) attempts to portray the user of a computer system as a computer with memory areas and processors.

The MHP was developed by Card, Moran and Newell in their book titled *The Psychology of Human–Computer Interaction*, published in 1983. Figure 2.10 shows a very simplified version of the model.

Information is received through the eyes and ears: this is the input. The information is then passed to the Working Memory by the Perceptual Processor. The Working Memory comprises two separate storage sections: one for visual images and one for auditory images. The Working Memory also includes those sections of the Long-term Memory that are currently of interest to the users and those sections that are required so the current task can be completed. This process can be related to the process of loading data from a disk into RAM.

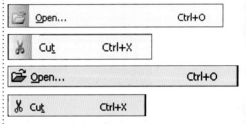

Figure 2.9 Use of a graphic consistently in different applications (Excel at the top and Word at the bottom)

Activities

Investigate the similarities within different applications produced by the same vendor.

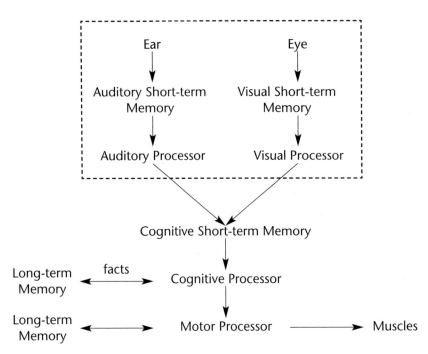

Figure 2.10 The MHP model

The Recognise–act Cycle of the Cognitive Processor can be related to the fetch–execute cycle. On each cycle the current contents of the Working Memory are used to trigger actions to be carried out by the Motor Processor.

The MHP draws on the appropriate information held in the Long-term Memory to enable a task or action to be completed. For example, the Working Memory could hold the information that 'a left click of the mouse is needed' but the information required to complete this process will be held in the Long-term Memory.

The Working Memory demonstrates the importance of the user's short-term memory for the successful completion of tasks. If the memory becomes full of information before a task or action can be completed then the user will have to pause or re-read supporting documentation. As a result of this the user may start to make mistakes. To avoid these mistakes the user will often break a task down into manageable sections. The software interface that is being used must enable this to happen. For example, menus should be hierarchically divided to ensure the user can select exactly what they are looking for.

In summary, the MHP draws an analogy between the processing and storage of a computer with the perceptual, cognitive, motor and memory activities of the computer user.

This is done by a visual or audible stimulus being captured by the user with the physical attributes of the stimulus being decoded. For example, a user's attention is drawn to a box on the screen. The response that is needed will then be interpreted by the user.

A motor response is then initiated to satisfy the response needed, for example, the click of a mouse button.

The application of the MHP

The model can be applied to many situations related to the use of computers. However, the application the model was developed for is that of the design of a user interface.

Examples of how the model can be applied to the design of a user interface include:

- logically ordering inputs, possibly those required from the user
- using an on-screen flashing cursor to show where data is to be input
- using an audible stimulus (e.g. a beep sound) to indicate when an error has been made by the user.

Question

Describe the user interface design tool known as the Model Human Processor.

Chapter summary

Processing systems
Batch
Interactive
Real-time
   – in terms of processing, response time and user
    interface requirements.

Types of operating system
Single-user
Multi-user
Multi-tasking
Interactive
Real-time
Batch processing
Distributed processing

Designing and using a human–computer interface
Colour
Layout
Quantity of on-screen information
Size of font
Complexity of language
Type of controls

Methods of human–device communications, particularly HCI

Command line interfaces

Menus/sub-menus

Graphical User Interfaces (GUIs)

Natural language (including speech input–output)

Forms dialogue

Designing an interface

A potential user's:

  – perception

  – attention

  – memory

  – learning

should be taken into account

Mental models

How they can be applied to the design of a user interface. The importance of designing a system model that matches closely the user's mental model.

The user interface design tool known as the Model Human Processor, developed by Card, Moran and Newell, and its application.

Chapter tests

Test 1

A business is developing an online ordering system. A user interface will need to be designed.

  1 The ordering system will be a real-time system. Describe the processing method and response time of a real-time system. [6]

  2 Explain how the user's perception and attention should be considered when designing the interface for the online ordering system. [6]

  3 Identify and explain **two** examples of how the Model Human Processor could be applied when designing the interface. [4]

Test 2

A publishing company is updating the invoicing system that is currently in use.

  1 Explain how a user's memory should be considered when the invoicing system interface is being designed. [3]

  2 Explain how the layout and quantity of information on the screen should be considered when designing the HCI. [4]

  3 The new system will use a batch processing operating system. Describe a batch processing operating system. [4]

3 | Networks and communications

Introduction

This chapter is about communications. It is particularly about computer-to-computer and human-to-computer communication – the former requiring at least two computers linked in some manner as a network. A large part of the chapter concerns networks.

You will need to know the features, characteristics, advantages and disadvantages of different types of networks, network components and the use of the networks.

You will learn about:

- types of network
- hardware and software required for a network
- different methods of communication
- implications of networking.

Compare the characteristics of a local area network (LAN), a wide area network (WAN) and a virtual network

A network is a series of nodes that are connected together by communications media (e.g. wireless, cable, satellite). A node can be a peripheral, a computer or a networking device such as a switch or hub.

Networks can be divided into two main types: the local area network (LAN) and the wide area network (WAN).

Local area network

A LAN (Figure 3.1) is a network that covers a relatively small area such as a room or building, for example within a school, library, doctor's surgery or small business.

Some of the characteristics that make up a LAN are:

- nodes are in close proximity to each other – within a locally defined area
- nodes have direct connections between them
- nodes are connected only by cables that are owned by the company
- ability to share local peripherals.

Activities

Using the flash network simulator at http://www. teach-ict.com/gcse_new/ networks/hardware/ resources/NWB_SIM.swf, add devices and computers to create your own LAN, similar to that you might find in a doctor's surgery or in a person's home.

Basic LAN Topology

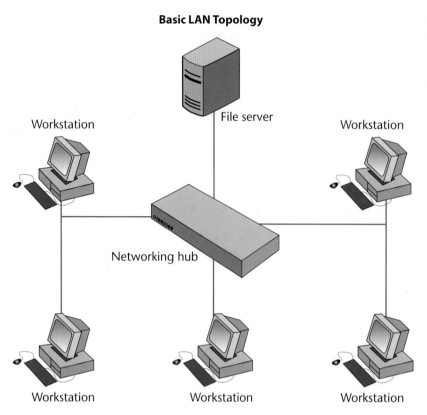

Figure 3.1 A LAN

Wide area network

A WAN (Figure 3.2) has machines that are geographically remote – they are not limited to a geographical area. It utilises a variety of telecommunication media. The components of a WAN are owned by different people.

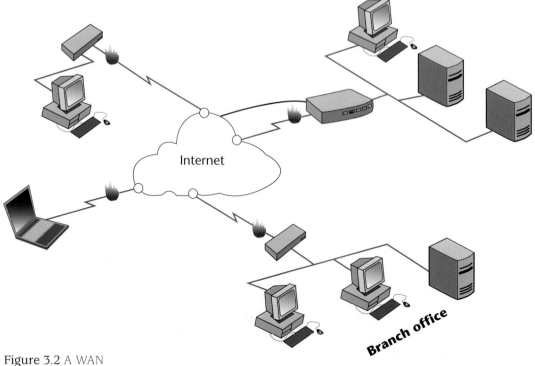

Figure 3.2 A WAN

Some of the characteristics that make up a WAN are:

- nodes are geographically remote – there can be large distances between them
- nodes are connected by telecommunications lines, satellites and other equipment that are owned by third parties.

Virtual network

There are two types of virtual networks:

VPN (Virtual Private Network)

VLAN (Virtual Local Area Network)

The VPN allows computers to communicate with each other as if they were within a single LAN, but without knowing that they may be part of a bigger network.

A virtual network could exist within a single LAN so that a set of computers could communicate only with each other, even though there are other physical connections. In Figure 3.3, the computers in the dotted border are part of a virtual network. They do not know that any of the grey computers exist on the network because the switching device that connects them all together is 'hiding' the other computers.

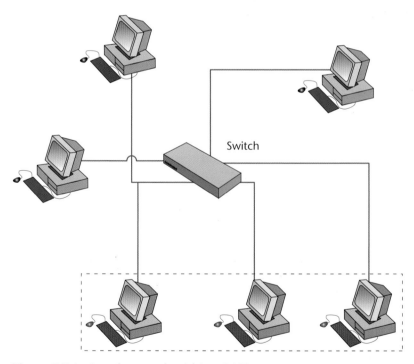

Switch

Figure 3.3 A virtual network within a LAN

A virtual network could also exist across more than one LAN through a WAN or the internet. In Figure 3.4, the green computers are part of a virtual network. They operate as if they were part of a single LAN. Other computers and devices cannot communicate directly with the green computers on the virtual network. Data for a virtual network travelling through cables on a LAN does not affect data from the LAN or other virtual networks.

Activities

Describe how your home network is configured to another student. Get them to draw the network configuration based on what you have told them.

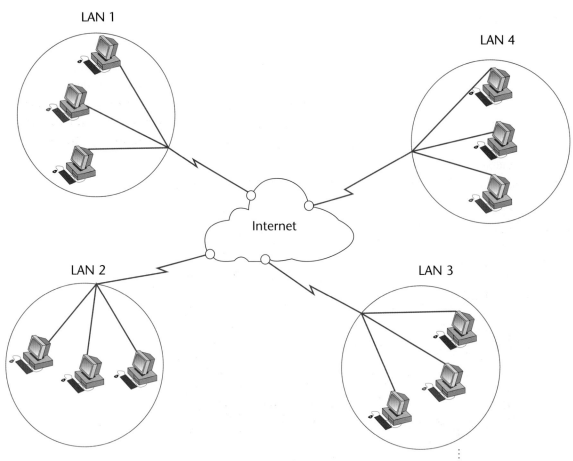

Figure 3.4 A virtual network within a WAN

In a virtual network, users will have access to the same services they would on a single LAN, such as print sharing, file sharing and application sharing.

A VLAN is a way of separating the traffic on a LAN so that different broadcast domains are created. It allows devices that are common to be grouped together, such as printers, IP phones, IP cameras and wifi devices. Maximum bandwidth can be allocated to the VLAN so that it does not use up all the bandwidth and leaves some spare. It increases security, simplifies network administration and creates the backbone for a scalable system.

Questions

1 Describe **two** characteristics of a LAN.

2 Describe **two** characteristics of a WAN.

3 Describe **two** characteristics of a VLAN.

Describe the characteristics and purpose of intranets, the internet and extranets

Internet

The internet is a vast collection of interconnected computers for the main purpose of sharing data. It uses the Transmission Control Protocol/Internet Protocol (TCP/IP) program to allow the exchange of data between devices.

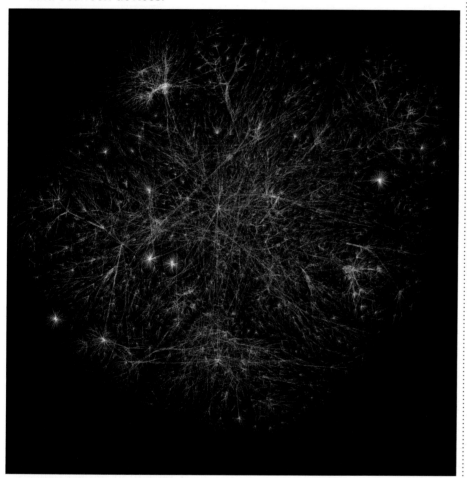

Figure 3.5 Paths through a portion of the internet as visualised by the Opte Project

One of the biggest benefits and problems of the internet is that it is outside of any government's control. (Governments can attempt to filter or restrict access but they cannot control the content – attempts to do so have resulted in the content being relocated to countries with laws that allow that content) The fact that it cannot be turned on or off or controlled is a large advantage.

The data that is transmitted across the internet can be used for many different purposes. Websites are one of the biggest areas of the internet:

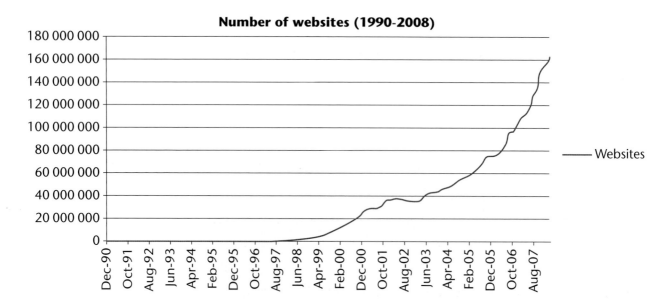

Number of websites (1990-2008)

As can be seen, the growth is quite amazing and continues to be so. Other uses of the internet include email, in particular webmail (the email client is a web page rather than an application on the computer. Skype (video conferencing) and FTP (accessing files on a remote server) are also uses of the internet.

Intranet

An intranet is the internet on a small scale. It is used within an organisation and is configured so that the users must be authorised before they can make use of its facilities. This usually means that they need to provide some credentials, such as a username and password. If an organisation has a LAN (Local Area Network) then the Intranet will be accessible to all users in the LAN.

The intranet provides the same facilities as the internet. It allows users to communicate with each other, whether by email or messenger. Users can work together on shared documents which are stored in a central location and web pages can be set up to disseminate information.

Extranet

An extranet is a private network that is built on top of, and uses, the internet. It is commonly used to access an organisation's intranet – it is easiest if thought of as the intranet accessed from any authorised computer on the internet. It uses VPN technology to maintain security. All the features of an intranet are available via an extranet, but with the added characteristic of remote access.

The purpose of an extranet is to allow authorised access to all the resources and facilities of an intranet for anywhere in the world that has an internet connection.

Activities

You are the network manager for a small photographic studio that has ten employees. You have a LAN. Identify the facilities that the staff would require from an intranet and for each facility, give examples of how they would use it. Draw up a table to show the examples.

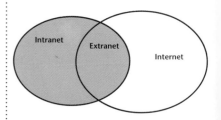

Figure 3.6 Venn diagram showing the internet, intranet and extranet

Describe client–server and peer-to-peer networks giving advantages and disadvantages of each

Networks can be configured as client–server networks or peer-to-peer networks.

Client–server

This is a computer network (Figure 3.7) with a single centralised computer (the server) that is connected to less powerful computers (the clients). The clients run programs and access data that are stored on the server.

The server can perform different roles including:

- file server
- applications server
- backup server
- print server
- mail server
- proxy server

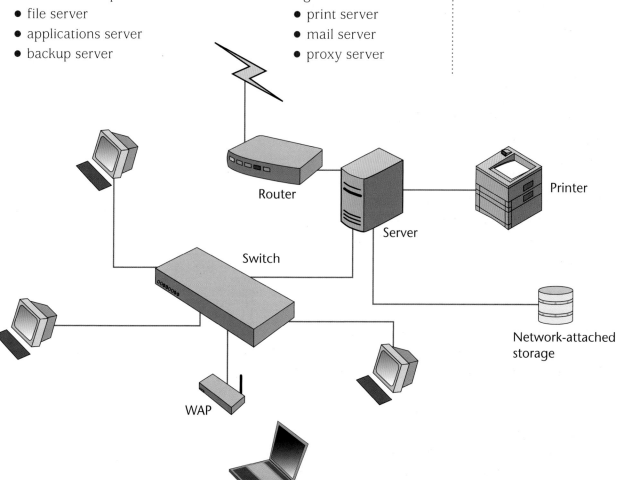

Figure 3.7 Client–server network

A client–server network is commonly found in medium- to large-sized businesses and will involve a degree of network management to keep them running at their best. There is usually security on the server that prevents open access by the clients.

One of the key advantages of a client–server network is centralisation. Responsibility for backups, software installation and antivirus updates is transferred from the individual computers (clients) to the server. This makes sure that all the clients' software is up to date, free of viruses and their data is backed up whether the individual user remembers to or not.

The disadvantages focus on the management and reliance on a single device. If the server fails, access to the resources is removed. Management of a network becomes more complicated the larger it becomes.

The advantages and disadvantages are summarised below as a comparison with a peer-to-peer network.

Client–server	
Advantages	**Disadvantages**
• Backup, security and antivirus software are centralised, thereby removing responsibility from the individual.	• The server costs money, as does the network operating system because additional equipment is required.
• The user does not do any of the management of the computers. There is usually a network manager to do this.	• A network manager is required and this costs money because the network is complicated and cannot usually be run by an everyday user.
• Network processing is done centrally, not at individual computers, freeing the individual clients to do what the user wants without interruption.	• There is a reliance on the central server. If it fails, no work can be done.
• The facilities of the server (e.g. the data and programs) are available from any client, allowing hot-desking.	• Large data files (such as video files) and programs run from the server can slow the network down.

Peer-to-peer

This is a network of computers in which each computer acts as both client and server. Each computer can access any of the others, although access can be restricted to those files that a computer's user chooses to make available. There is no one powerful computer; each peer is equal.

A peer-to-peer network is commonly found in a small business or in a home.

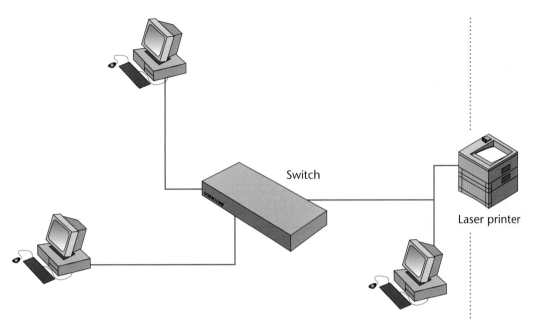

Figure 3.8 Peer-to-peer network

The advantages of a peer-to-peer network are based around the resilience of the individual machine: there is minimal dependence on other machines so it can operate independently. The cost is less, a server is not needed and the management can be conducted by an everyday computer user.

The disadvantages are based around the responsibility of the individual to maintain it: updating the antivirus utility, running backups and installing software patches.

Generally, the advantages of a peer-to-peer network are the disadvantages of a client–server network, and the disadvantages of a peer-to-peer network are the advantages of a client–server network.

Peer-to-peer	
Advantages	**Disadvantages**
● Only normal computers are required. There is no need to purchase an expensive server, which saves money. ● Each user manages their own computer. This means that a network manager is not required. ● The set up for peer-to-peer (e.g. file sharing/printer sharing) is done via wizards within the software. Only limited technical knowledge is required. ● There is no reliance on a central computer. Each peer can act independently regardless of the state of the other computers.	● Each computer is fulfilling more than one role (e.g. it might be printing or file sharing). This increases the load and slows the computer for the individual user. ● The data can be stored on any computer. There is no organisation to data storage: a file that a user was using on a different machine might have been moved/deleted by the owner of that machine. ● Responsibility for security, antivirus and backup software is down to the individual user and if they forget, it can have consequences for all machines.

Questions

1 Define what is meant by a client–server network.

2 Define what is meant by a peer-to-peer network.

3 Describe **two** advantages of a peer-to-peer network in a home.

4 Describe **two** disadvantages of a peer-to-peer network for a large company.

5 Describe **two** advantages of a client–server network for a large company.

6 Describe **two** disadvantages of a client–server network in a home.

Explain the importance of bandwidth when transmitting data

Bandwidth is how much data can be transferred along a communications channel in a given amount of time.

$$\text{bandwidth} = \frac{\text{volume of data}}{\text{time}}$$

Bandwidth is often given in bits per second (bps). This is the number of bits that can be transferred each second. This is not to be confused with Bps, which is bytes per second (one byte is eight bits, the equivalent of one character).

Think of bandwidth as a water pipe. Different diameters of pipe carry different amounts of water. The water through the pipe is flowing at the same speed but with a wider pipe, more water can be transferred in any given second.

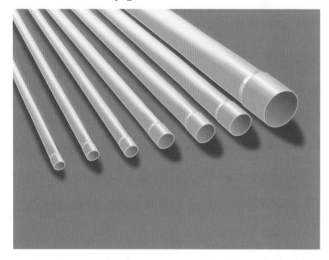

Figure 3.9 A bandwidth analogy

Activities

Look at http://voip.about.com/od/voipband width/a/speedtest.com Select one of the speed test sites and check your internet speed. Discuss why these results might not be accurate and what can affect them.

What is the impact of bandwidth?

The impact of bandwidth depends on what you are doing. There are activities using the internet that will require a lot of bandwidth to work.

Bandwidth affects the time that it takes to download and upload files. If you have bought a film from an online store, such as NetFlix, there are two ways to watch it. You can wait for it to download completely and then start watching it or you can download some and then start watching it (progressive download), hoping that the download will continue just ahead of what you are seeing. This is known as streaming.

Bandwidth affects downloading because of the time it takes. A large bandwidth will reduce the time it takes for the file to download. A low bandwidth will mean that it takes a long time to download. However, the time taken to download the file does not affect the viewing/listening of the file once it is downloaded.

The effect of too low a bandwidth on streaming is that the film might stop while more is downloaded. The sound and picture might get 'out of sync' or the image might pixelate.

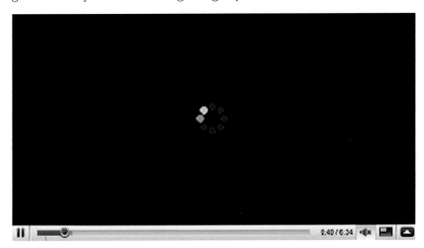

Figure 3.10 Waiting during video streaming

Bandwidth has implications on time-dependent applications, for example video conferencing, which needs high bandwidth to display moving images.

Questions

1 Define what is meant by bandwidth.

2 How long would it take to download a 640 MB (megabyte) movie on an 8 Mbps (megabits per second) internet connection?

3 Why is a large bandwidth important when streaming video?

Activities

Take the bandwidth test at http://library.thinkquest. org/27887/gather/digital_ talk/quizzes/bandwidth.htm Analyse how different types of communication media (cables, wireless, optical) govern the bandwidth available.

There are different means by which a signal can be transmitted. Communication media, such as cable, wireless or optical, deliver data. Each of these is covered below.

There are lots of different factors that affect the bandwidth of the communication media. You could have the same communication medium in different houses, but get a different bandwidth.

Cable

There are different types of cable.

Cable type	Description	Identification	Maximum bandwidth*
Fibre-optic	Fibre-optic cable is a flexible, transparent fibre made of glass or plastic. It is slightly thicker than a human hair.	Figure 3.11 Bundled optical cable	In a laboratory, a bandwidth of 69.1 Tbs (terabits per second) has been achieved.
Co-axial (coax)	This has an inner conductor (a core) surrounded by an insulating layer that itself is surrounded by a conducting shield (copper braid).	Copper braid Signal wire Insulation Outer plastic sheath Figure 3.12 Co-axial cable	Download speeds of 1.5 Gbs have been recorded.
Copper	These come in the form of twisted pairs (commonly UTP and STP).	Figure 3.13 Twisted pair cable	A bandwidth of 100 gigabit Ethernet (100 Gbs) has been achieved.

*The maximum possible bandwidth for each type. The figures are correct at the time of writing, but advances in technology might mean they are incorrect at the time of reading.

Optical

This is the use of either 'unshielded' light or 'shielded' light guided within fibre-optic cable to transmit data. The optical transmission used is:

- infrared
- laser.

With 'unshielded' optical communication, line of sight is required between the transmitter and receiver. Infrared is commonly used in short-range communication between devices, such as remote controls. Infrared communication has achieved speeds of up to 1024 Mbs.

The term 'laser' is an acronym for Light Amplification by Stimulated Emission of Radiation. Speeds of up to 10 Gbps are common between devices.

Wireless

This is the transmission of data between two points without the use of wires. In broad terms, this definition also encompasses the use of optical methods to transmit the data (but the frequencies used are lower). Since optical methods have already been covered, this section will focus on:

- wifi
- satellite
- Bluetooth®.

Wifi is generally accepted to be implemented and administered using radio waves as the transmission media.

Satellite communications work in the microwave portion of the radio spectrum and connect a dish on the ground to a satellite in space. Data can be shared over great distances as long as there is line of sight between the dish aerial and satellite.

Bluetooth® is a technology standard for exchanging data over short distances using short-wavelength radio transmissions.

Activities

Compare the maximum bandwidth available with wifi, satellite and Bluetooth®.

Questions

1 Given two houses, with the same cable, what factors could reduce the bandwidth available in one compared with the other?

2 Describe **two** different types of optical technology used as a communication medium.

3 Describe **two** different types of wireless technology used as a communication medium.

4 Describe **two** different types of cable technology used as a communication medium.

Compare the role of the following network components: switches, hubs, wireless access points, network interface cards, wireless network interface cards, routers, repeaters, gateways, firewalls and servers (file, applications, mail, proxy, print, backup) and justify where their use would be appropriate

A network is made up of different components. Each component has a different role to play.

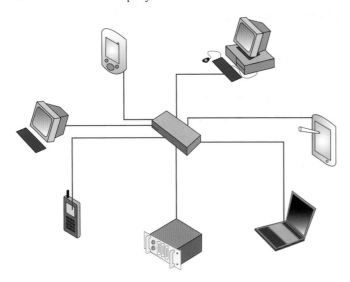

Figure 3.14 A typical network

Network interface card

A network interface card (NIC) is a piece of hardware that connects a computer to a network through a physical connection – a cable. Each NIC has a unique identifier – a MAC (media access control) address.

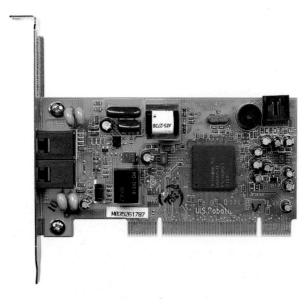

Figure 3.15 A network interface card

Wireless network interface card

A wireless network interface card (WNIC) has the same functionality as an NIC except that the connection from the device to the network is wireless, that is there is no physical connection. A WNIC also has a MAC address.

Wireless access point

A wireless access point (WAP) is a device that allows a WNIC to connect to it, and transfers the data to the rest of the network. A WAP is commonly connected by cable to the network (although you can connect WAPs together) and it allows multiple devices to be wirelessly connected to a network.

It is common to combine a WAP with other functionality, so, for example, in a home network the WAP might be combined with a switch or a router. The WAP broadcasts an identifier – a service set identifier (SSID). This can be password protected to prevent unwanted devices from connecting to it.

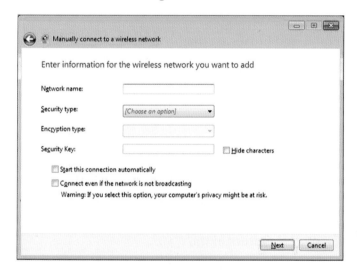

Figure 3.16 SSID/password set-up page

Hub and switch

On the surface, hubs and switches are similar devices. They are concentrators for the network and allow communication between different devices.

When referring to hubs and switches, you will come across the term 'port'. A port is an interface between a computer and other computers or peripheral devices. It is an outlet in the hardware that a plug or cable connects to.

In a hub, a signal comes into one of the ports and this is copied to every port that the hub has, with the exception of the one where the signal originated from. For example, imagine a four-port hub as shown in Figure 3.17.

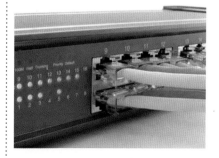

Figure 3.17 Hub

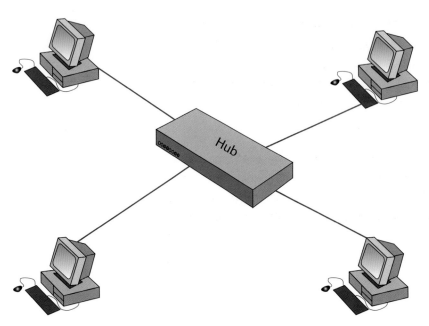

Figure 3.18 Connecting to a hub

A computer on port 1 sends a signal to the computer on port 4. The hub will receive the incoming signal on port 1 and broadcast that signal out on the three other ports so computers 2, 3 and 4 receive the message. The signal is not intended for computers 2 and 3 so they will ignore it.

In a switch, there is a MAC address table. This is a table that contains the MAC address of every connected device and the port number that the device is connected to. When a message is received, it looks to see the destination, looks up to find the port and forwards the message to that port only.

In the example shown in Figure 3.18, using a switch, the switch will receive the incoming signal on port 1, look up the address in the table, and broadcast that signal out on port 4 only.

This means that a switch, when compared with a hub, will reduce the network traffic as less data is being sent. This in turn will decrease packet collisions, which reduces resends. Each computer is not receiving every message (which it has to read to find out if it is meant for it) so its workload is lessened.

Router

A router connects different networks together. It receives data packets and examines them. A data packet contains address information, part of which includes a destination – where the packet is destined for. A router uses the destination information to determine where a packet should be forwarded to. A router will use a routing table and routing policy to move packets onwards to their destinations. It is likely that a data packet will be forwarded between many different routers until it reaches its destination.

Repeater

A signal sent over a distance deteriorates before reaching its destination. This is attenuation. Each type of communication medium (wireless, optical, cable) has distance imitations and a repeater can be used to extend the distance that the signal can travel (Figure 3.19).

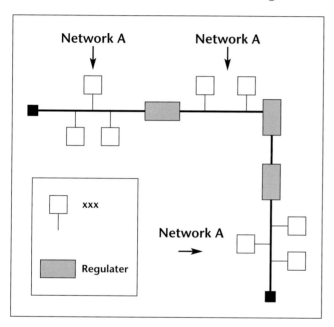

Figure 3.19 Repeaters connecting network segments

A repeater amplifies (i.e. strengthens) and retimes the signal before passing it onwards.

Gateway

Gateways link networks that are not using the same protocols. It converts the data from one protocol to another before passing the data to the new network. The gateway can also control who and what uses the link.

The main benefit of a gateway is that it allows networks to be connected that might not otherwise communicate. This is particularly important with legacy systems.

Firewall

There are two types of firewall: software and hardware. The function of each type is similar: to keep a network secure. A firewall does this by using a set of rules to examine the incoming and outgoing data packets to see whether they should be let through or blocked (Figure 3.20).

Activities

Watch the movie at http://www.warriorsofthe.net/movie.html and make notes on the different hardware devices that make up a network.

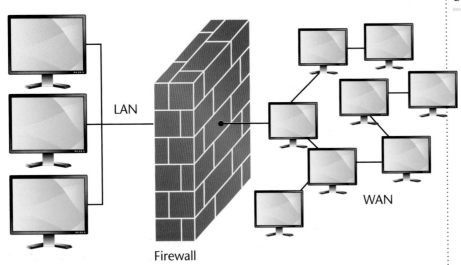

Figure 3.20 A firewall

Servers (file, applications, mail, proxy, print, backup)

A server is a computer on a network that manages resources. These resources determine the type of server. Resources can include:

- applications
- printing
- mail
- proxy
- file (storage)
- backup.

A physical server can perform one or more of the above functions.

- **Applications server** – This distributes programs to computers and monitors their use. For example if you have only ten licences for a particular program, the server will allow only ten individual clients to run that program. An application server can also be used to update programs when the software manufacturer releases updates.

- **Printer server** – Clients connect to the print server and download the drivers of the printers connected to it. It can monitor the printing and record who is printing what and how many copies. Printer servers can also allocate priority to print jobs allowing some users to jump the print queue and go straight to the top.
- **Mail server** – This stores the mailboxes of individual users. It sends and receives mail and distributes messages to the user. It can be combined with filters for obscenity, large attachments and viruses.
- **File server** – This controls the storage. When a user logs onto the network they can access the files that are stored in their user area. If users change clients, they can still access their files. This is because the files are stored centrally on the file server. A file server also controls access rights, so only an authorised person can access particular files. It can also provide a shared area that multiple people can access. This is useful for a team working on shared files.
- **Backup server** – This has responsibility for backing up and restoring files, folders and databases. The backup server will not only restore the file but also the permissions (access rights) associated with the file. The backup can be set on a schedule. The backup server is likely to have storage attached and this storage does not have to be in the same physical location – it could be in a different building or even in the cloud.
- **Proxy server** – This sits between a network and the internet. It allows the machines in a network to be anonymous and it acts as a single point for passing requests to and from the internet. It speeds up web access by having a cache of web pages. A proxy server has a set of rules, for example undesirable sites or words that cannot used, and it can log and report on users' activities (see Figure 3.21).

Activities

Investigate different backup schedules that can take place, for example complete or incremental.

Questions

1 Describe **two** features of a switch that are used to control data.

2 Describe **three** different types of server found in a network.

3 Why do NICs have a MAC address?

4 Compare a hub and a switch.

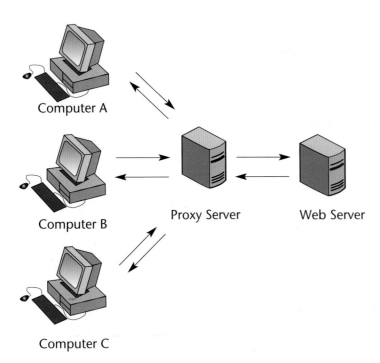

Figure 3.21 A proxy server

Describe optical communication methods (infrared, fibre optic, laser), giving their advantages and disadvantages and typical applications

Optical communication is the use of light to transmit data.

- Infrared is used mainly in remote controls to communicate with a TV, DVD or video player/recorder. It is short range and requires a direct line of sight to work. The power consumption required for infrared is very small, which makes it useful in remote controls.
- Fibre-optic communication is the transmission of light through a transparent cable. It is useful because the fibre-optic cable is capable of very high bandwidth. Fibre-optic cables are flexible, which means they can be installed round corners. They are also small, meaning that a large number of them can be run in a small space. Light is not affected by electrical interference, so fibre-optic communication is useful in places such as power rooms.
- Laser communication works by sending and receiving a laser beam. Direct line of sight is required and the signal can be interrupted by fog and cloud. Lasers are used to connect LANs together, in particular where physical connection is not possible, such as in different parts of a town.

Describe wireless communication methods (Bluetooth®, radio), their advantages, disadvantages and typical applications

Bluetooth® has a range of about 10 m and does not require two devices to be in line of sight of each other. It is commonly used to connect peripherals, such as headphones (Figure 3.22), to mobile phones. The connection can be secured between the two devices with a pass key.

Figure 3.22 Bluetooth® earpiece

Radio is the use of radio frequencies to transfer data. This is commonly referred to as wifi. Wifi allows devices to connect without cables to a network. This gives the user the freedom to move around a room and the ability to connect multiple devices without being limited by the number of ports on a hub.

The signal can be made secure with a pass code and no line of sight is required. However, the further away a device is from the WAP, the weaker the signal and the lower the bandwidth. Devices can also interfere with the signal – microwave ovens for example can affect the bandwidth.

Describe the facilities of the following communication applications: fax, email, bulletin (discussion) boards, tele/video conferencing and instant messaging and compare their use for a given task

There are a number of different applications that two or more individuals can use to communicate. The applications that they can use have different advantages, disadvantages and features.

The facilities of the different applications are merging over time. Different software companies are incorporating features into their programs that blur the boundaries that used to define the different types. For example, the ability to send files through instant messaging is very similar to email.

For a communication to take place, there needs to be a minimum of two people – the sender (author) and the recipient. The author can compose a message using text, sound or images. The recipient can be one or more people.

Fax

A fax is an image of a document or picture that is transmitted as data via a telecommunications link.

There are two main methods of sending and receiving a fax: by computer or by specialist machine (a fax machine – Figure 3.23).

A fax is sent to a fax number, which is a specific telephone number that is set up to receive faxes. It can either be associated with a fax machine or it can be a virtual number.

A fax number that is a real number has a fixed location, that is it is located in an office and has a physical fax machine plugged into it.

If both the sending and receiving equipment can deal with colour, then a fax can be sent and received in colour. The equipment can hold an address book and can dial a single person in the address book or can be set up to dial multiple contacts.

Fax machines can be set up so that a security number is required before the fax is printed out.

A fax can also be sent from a computer (Figure 3.24). There are programs that will act as a fax machine – sending to numbers kept in your address book, and sending images of any attachments.

Figure 3.23 Fax machine

Activities

Investigate two programs for sending faxes. List any features that are common and any that are different.

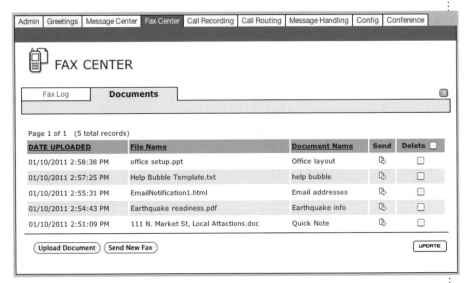

| Admin | Greetings | Message Center | Fax Center | Call Recording | Call Routing | Message Handling | Config | Conference |

FAX CENTER

| Fax Log | **Documents** |

Page 1 of 1 (5 total records)

DATE UPLOADED	File Name	Document Name	Send	Delete ☐
01/10/2011 2:58:38 PM	office setup.ppt	Office layout		☐
01/10/2011 2:57:25 PM	Help Bubble Template.txt	help bubble		☐
01/10/2011 2:55:31 PM	EmailNotification1.html	Email addresses		☐
01/10/2011 2:54:43 PM	Earthquake readiness.pdf	Earthquake info		☐
01/10/2011 2:51:09 PM	111 N. Market St, Local Attactions.doc	Quick Note		☐

(Upload Document) (Send New Fax)   [UPDATE]

Figure 3.24 Fax program interface

A virtual number is a number that exists on the internet. The fax is sent to the virtual number, which receives the transmission, saves it as a picture file and then forwards the picture, as an attachment, via email (Figure 3.25).

Figure 3.25 Virtual fax number working

	Fixed number	Virtual number
Security	Keypad can be set up to protect the information, but anyone with the key can read the fax.	The fax can be sent to a specific email account so only one person has access to the fax.
Location	The number is in a fixed location and you have to be in the physical location to read the fax.	As the fax is sent to an email address, anywhere that has a connection can receive email and so read the fax.
Hardware	A specific fax machine is required and this must have paper in it to print out the fax.	A standard computer with internet access and email can be used. Neither specialist equipment nor paper are required.
Editing	The fax is sent as an image and, in both cases, the fax contents cannot be edited.	

Some common features of fixed number and of virtual number faxes are:

- both send as images
- both send to numbers – there is no need for the machine/program sending to know what device it is sending to
- both can receive a receipt saying that the fax has been sent – they cannot tell if it has been read or by whom.

> **Tip**
>
> When answering a question on faxes, make sure you give as much detail as you can about how the fax is being sent and received because this will affect the advantages, disadvantages and features you discuss.

Email

Email is a method of exchanging digital messages from an author to one or more recipients.

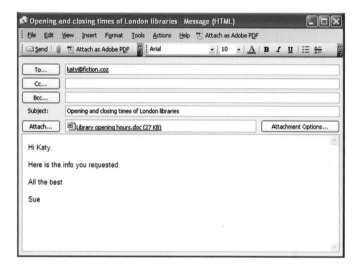

Figure 3.26 Email interface

At its basic level, an email is text, but it can have attachments associated with it. Any digital file can be an attachment, for example:

- an image file
- a sound file
- a movie file
- an application file (e.g. a word document).

Many types of device can send and receive emails. They are not limited to use on a standard computer.

Email allows you to send messages to many people (by using distribution lists) and you can send carbon copies and blind carbon copies. It is possible to add a digital signature to the message and encrypt it to increase security.

The recipient's email software can send a confirmation of delivery and opening, but with some software it is possible to cancel this. A receipt of delivery and opening is not the same as being able to prove that it was read.

Some email software can filter out junk mail and organise messages by preset rules, such as auto-replying with out-of-office messages. Email messages can often be formatted in a variety of different ways.

Email gives a 24/7 service to anywhere in the world. An email address is a single point of contact that can be picked up anywhere in the world, so the location of the recipient is not an issue.

Email programs can either be on the device or web-based. The latter is where the emails are accessed through a web browser.

Bulletin boards

A bulletin board allows online discussion where users can post messages and read messages from other uses.

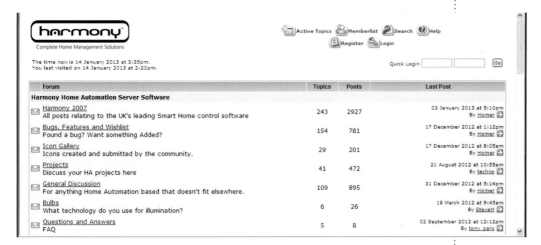

Figure 3.27 Discussion board

A bulletin board accessed through the internet can be used to give information in messages or contain links to downloadable documents, videos etc. Messages can be text or images.

A bulletin board is accessible anywhere in the world and can have many recipients.

A general discussion board is not secure (it is open to the general public), but sometimes parts of the bulletin board and downloadable documents are password protected.

A bulletin board can set up threads of conversations and ensure that all elements are kept together. Users can be notified by email of new postings.

Bulletin boards are usually focused on a single topic or idea, and the posts are related to that topic, for example cycling, a football club, a programming language or an author.

Tele/video conferencing

Conferencing is where more than two people are taking part in the same conversation. 'Tele' means 'at a distance', and teleconferencing is similar to telephoning, that is it is voice only, but with multiple participants. Video conferencing is similar, but allows participants to see one another and to view sound and images when they are separated by some distance.

Both types of conferencing can be done via a direct line or across the internet. If it is done via a direct line, then it is secure, whereas across the internet it is not.

The equipment required can range from a simple (web camera) to a complex setup. Smartphones with cameras now have the capability of video conferencing (Figure 3.28).

Figure 3.28 Apple® iPhone® and running FaceTime®

The individuals involved in the conference need to be present at the same time and there might be a slight delay that makes conversation difficult. The image size is not likely to be large. If the bandwidth is not sufficient, then the sound and the image might become unsynchronised and the image might stutter and pixelate.

In some software, the conference can be recorded for playback at a later time. It might also be possible to include file sharing.

Instant messaging

This is where a message is sent and 'instantly' received. The actual reception time will depend on network traffic, so the message might be delayed. Also, if the recipient does not have the device switched on, it will not be immediately received.

Two types of messages can be sent:

- **Online** – Messages can only be sent if the recipient is connected to the network. The moment either party is not connected the message cannot be sent or received.
- **Off-line** – Messages can be sent to recipients who are not connected – when they do connect, they will receive the message.

Figure 3.29 BlackBerry Messenger

Instant messaging can give delivered and read receipts and in some applications, images and documents can be transferred. It is also possible to combine instant messaging applications so they work across computers, phones and tablet devices and synchronise themselves.

There can be issues (see the next section on social networking for more detail), including the expectation that you are always available, the speed of typing an instant message and sending it without checking/reading it first.

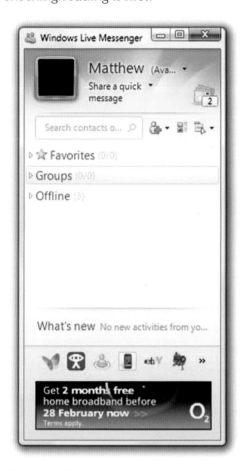

Figure 3.30

Instant messaging makes use of emoticons and abbreviations and these can often be misused or misunderstood. There are limited options for emotion or sarcasm in instant messaging and sometimes messages can be taken the wrong way.

Questions

1 Compare the use of fax and email for communicating between an office in the UK and one in China.

2 Compare instant messaging with video conferencing.

3 Describe **three** facilities of a bulletin board.

4 Describe the security features available on fax, email and bulletin boards.

Discuss the use and implications of social networking

Social networking is the use of technology and devices to link individuals together in a network. Social networking media include Facebook, Twitter and Google+, for example. The features of social networking allow you:

- to follow an individual – this might be reciprocated or it could be one way
- to post images – either individually or in an album
- to create subgroups which can be protected or open
- to add comments
- to send messages directly to other people.

Activities

Describe the common and different features in the three social network media given in the table.

Feature	Facebook	Twitter	Google+

The use of social networking is to engage the individual in an online environment where they can contribute. There are different types of users: some who actively post, some who post occasionally and lurkers. Nonnecke and Preece (2000)[1] indicates that 'lurkers make up over 90 per cent of online groups' and Ridings, Gefen and Arinze (2006)[2] have proposed that a lack of trust represents one of the reasons explaining lurking behaviour.

Social networking has brought the celebrity closer to the fan. Anyone can 'follow' a celebrity and get information on their thoughts, likes and dislikes. This can increase the fan base of the celebrity and, as a consequence, increase the amount the celebrity can charge for advertisements and appearances because more people are likely to turn up to see them or take notice of them.

It can also have the opposite effect (see Figure 3.31).

---

1   Nonnecke, B. and Preece, J. (2000). *Lurker demographics: Counting the silent.* Proceedings of CHI 2000, The Hague, ACM.

2   Ridings, C., Gefen, D. and Arinze, B. (2006). *Psychological barriers: Lurker and poster motivation and behavior in online communities.* Communications of AIS **18** (16).

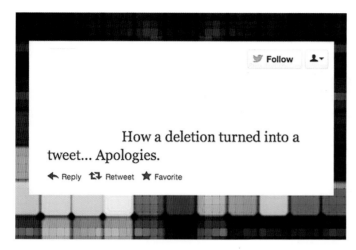

Figure 3.31 Headline showing negative effect of social media

As the celebrity is constantly under observation, the persona they might have developed for the fans might be different to their real one. It might also be that they find it difficult to 'let their hair down' because their every move, look and appearance are photographed, documented and sent to a social networking site. There is a pressure on the celebrity to look their best at all times or suffer the comments that will inevitably follow.

For individuals, it allows them to keep in contact with the day-to-day lives of their friends and relatives, to share photos (especially since the majority of photos are digital and it is becoming easier to upload straight to social networking sites).

Of course, the downside is the banality of some of the posts and comments. There is also the digital footprint that is being left behind. The experiences and actions of people's youth follow them as they mature (Figure 3.32).

Employee loses job before starting due to negative Tweet

Figure 3.32 Headline showing how social media creates a digital footprint

What may have seemed fun and a laugh at the time – the embarrassing photo, the drunken escapade – follows you and can be seen by future universities and employers.

Questions

1 Describe the advantages of using social networking for a family.

2 Describe the disadvantages of using social networking in a company.

3 Compare the use of social networking by a celebrity and an ordinary person.

Compare different types of broadband connection and analyse suitable situations where the use of each would be appropriate: asymmetric digital subscriber line (ADSL), cable, wireless, leased line, satellite

Broadband is a term that describes the type of internet connection.

Asymmetric digital subscriber line

Asymmetric digital subscriber line (ADSL) uses standard copper cable that is used for telephoner, but utilises frequencies on the line not used by voice. This means that the line can be used for data and voice (PSTN) at the same time (Figure 3.33). ADSL utilises the existing phone network so there is minimal disruption in implementing it because additional cabling is not required.

Asymmetric is a key term that applies to all types of broadband connection. When a connection to the internet is made, the traffic flows in two directions:

- **Upstream** – from the computer to the internet (uploading)
- **Downstream** – from the internet to the computer (downloading).

Asymmetric means there is a difference between two things, or to put it another way, the two things are not the same (Figure 3.34). When used to describe upstream and downstream communication, it means that the download bandwidth is greater than the upstream bandwidth. If you consider that ADSL is used primarily in homes, then downloading is more common than uploading. This is why it is quicker to download an email with a picture attachment than to send one. Another term that can be applied to ADSL is duplex. There are two types of duplex:

- **Full duplex** – messages can be sent and received at the same time
- **Half duplex** – messages can be sent or received, but not both together at the same time.

ADSL is full duplex.

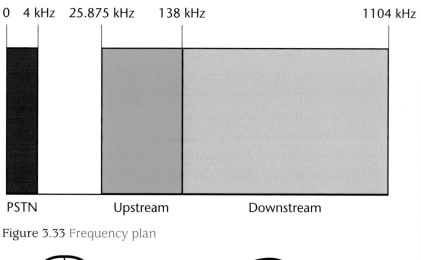

Figure 3.33 Frequency plan

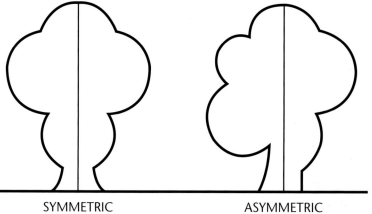

Figure 3.34 Symmetry and asymmetry

Contention ratio is another term that crops up when talking about broadband connections. This is the potential maximum demand on the available bandwidth, that is it is a measure of how many users are trying to use the bandwidth at any one time.

Contention ratios are difficult to calculate. A contention ratio of 50:1 means that 50 properties are sharing the available bandwidth. This is not the same as the number of users – each property might have multiple users. If each property had four users, then you will have 200 users sharing the bandwidth. It is more common to see phrases such as 'guaranteed minimum bandwidth' – this still only applies to the property and not to each individual user in the property.

ADSL is 'always on'. This means that it is permanently connected.

Activities

Investigate the limitations of ADSL and why it is not possible for every home in the UK to have an ADSL connection.

Cable

This is the use of fibre-optic cable to deliver a broadband connection. Cable broadband is usually bundled with telephone and television so you get an all-encompassing service from a single provider, such as BT or Virgin.

The advantages are that the bandwidth is higher, which gives greater download speeds. Cable is also asymmetric and full duplex – the same as ADSL.

The disadvantages are based around the infrastructure. The cables required need to be specifically laid at significant cost.

Wireless

This is the use of the 3G mobile telephone network to exchange data (e.g. connecting a laptop to a mobile phone or tablet for downloading and uploading data).

Figure 3.35 Apple iPad and iPhone

A laptop can also make use of a wireless dongle (a USB device that plugs into the laptop and connects to the internet) or it can use a MiFi device. A MiFi acts as a WAP/router and allows a fixed number of devices to connect to it. It connects to the internet through a 3G connection, giving the devices internet access.

Note

This is not the same as the use of a WNIC and a WAP.

Figure 3.36 MiFi device

Limitations depend on the device, but there are three main ones:
- signal strength/reception
- battery operation
- credit.

The bandwidth is limited. It is improving, but it is still not as good as a physical cable.

The advantages are the flexibility. There is no need to be in a fixed location to connect to the internet.

Leased line

A leased line connects two locations to each other. There is nothing in between and it is not shared between any other locations. This makes the line secure.

This means that there is a contention ratio of 1:1 – all the available bandwidth is available to the two users. A leased line is full duplex and symmetric.

Leased lines are expensive because they are not shared. A dedicated line needs to be installed and this can cost extra money.

Satellite

If you live in a remote area, too far away for ADSL, or in a bad 3G signal area, one option is satellite.

There are two different types of satellite broadband:
- one-way
- two-way.

Note

It is possible to change the upload and download speeds to create an asymmetric line as required.

Activities

Investigate different organisations that could make use of a leased line and how they might use it.

Note

Do not confuse satellite broadband with satellite television or satellite phone.

One-way satellite communication is where the download is done via the satellite, but uploading is completed using a telephone and modem. This is used where there is a fixed telephone line and the user is normally static.

Two-way satellite communication is where data is both uploaded and downloaded via the satellite. This is used in remote areas where the user is more mobile.

Satellite broadband has limited bandwidth and high costs (both set-up and ongoing).

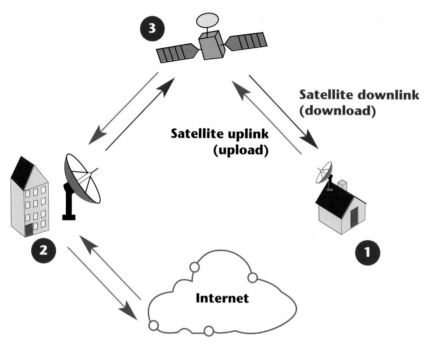

Figure 3.37 Satellite phone set up

Activities

Copy and complete the table.

Type	Bandwidth	Typical use	Advantages	Disadvantages
ADSL				
Cable				
Wireless				
Leased line				
Satellite				

Questions

1 Compare ADSL and leased-line methods of broadband connection for use in a home.

2 Describe **two** different methods that can be used to connect a laptop to a 3G network.

3 Describe contention ratio and why it is not a good indicator of bandwidth.

4 Explain **two** situations where the use of two-way satellite broadband would be the preferred option for broadband connectivity.

Describe how a mobile phone network operates (cellular and satellite) and the advantages and disadvantages of cellular and satellite mobile phone systems and their use

There are two types of mobile phone network: cellular and satellite. We do not distinguish between them, calling them mobile phone networks. In the USA, a mobile phone is called a cell phone, making the distinction.

Cellular phone network

A mobile phone sends and receives communications (voice, data etc.) by radio waves. Outgoing signals are transmitted from the phone to the nearest base station and incoming signals are sent from the base station to the phone at a slightly different frequency.

The base station links the mobile phone to the rest of the mobile and fixed phone network.

Figure 3.38 Base station mast

When a signal reaches the base station, it is then transmitted to the fixed telephone network in one of two ways:
- telephone cables
- radio links between an antenna at the base station and another at a terminal connected to the main telephone network.

The country is split up into cells. A base station provides signal coverage to a cell (Figure 3.39). The base stations are connected to each other by switching centres. These track calls and pass calls from one base station to the next (e.g. if the user is in a vehicle).

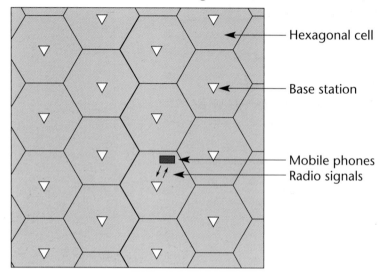

Figure 3.39 Mobile phone cells

A cell is drawn as a hexagon with the base station in the centre and a slight overlap. In reality the country is not split into multiple hexagons. The exact shape depends on three factors:
- **Local terrain** – this includes hills, trees and buildings.
- **Frequency band** – the higher the frequency the smaller the cell.
- **The capacity needed for a given area** – the number of connections in a given area, rural requiring less than a town. Base stations are typically spaced about 0.2–0.5 km apart in towns and 2–5 km apart in the countryside.

The actual process is described using many three-letter acronyms (TLAs), but in general:
1 When the mobile phone is switched on it makes a connection to the base station that gives it the strongest signal.
2 The phone is allocated a frequency (different incoming to outgoing).

3 The base station passes on information about the phone that has just connected to it to a central computer – this is so that any messages, voice mails etc. can be passed to the base station and then on to the phone.

4 The base station is the link to the fixed telephone system.

When the mobile phone connects to make a call a number of things are done by the system:

- It checks that the user account for the phone has enough credit to make the call.
- It checks that the phone is allowed to make the call (e.g. is the SIM blocked or are there certain numbers blocked on the account, such as international calls?).

If these check out correctly, the call can be placed.

The mobile phone today does a lot more than make phone calls. Its many uses make it comparable with a desktop computer.

Satellite phone network

A satellite phone is a type of mobile phone that connects to a satellite. A user can use one in a similar way to a cellular mobile phone as it has many of the same functions, such as the ability:

- to make and receive telephone calls
- to send text messages
- to access the internet (although slow)
- to video conference.

As with cellular phones, satellite phones use different service providers. Access in different locations will depend on the service provider and contract, and not all providers and contracts will give access in all areas.

There are two main types of satellite that the phone system uses:

- geosynchronous satellites
- low Earth orbit satellites.

Geosynchronous satellites

These are satellites that are in geosynchronous (or geostationary) orbit. A geosynchronous orbit is one where the satellite is in a fixed position over the same point on the surface of the Earth at all times. It does not move from that fixed position, so if you look up in the sky and can see a geosynchronous satellite, it will be in the same position every time you look for it.

Figure 3.40 Satellite phone

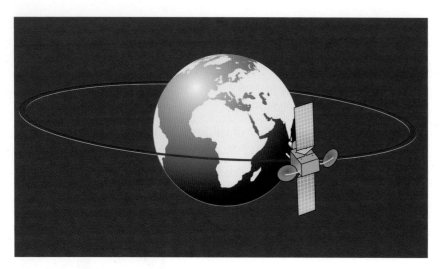

Figure 3.41 Geosynchronous orbit

With any satellite communication there is a delay because of the distance the signal travels – this is called latency. Occasionally on television news broadcasts the voice and the image become unsynchronised or a presenter needs to delay questions to avoid talking over replies.

The two main disadvantages of geostationary satellites are that:

- the best latitude for a satellite to remain in geostationary orbit is up to 70 degrees either side of the equator – this means that areas in the Arctic and Antarctic (place where a satellite phone would be very useful) will not have coverage
- line of sight is required between the phone and the satellite – if you are in a deep valley, in the middle of a city surrounded by tall buildings, or if anything blocks the signal (like trees or thick cloud), then you will have difficulty connecting to the satellite.

Low Earth orbit satellites

These are not in a fixed position over the same point, but circle the Earth. This means that at regular intervals the satellite will be overhead, but will soon move on. It will be over a particular phone user for between 4 and 15 minutes during each orbit. After that time, the phone user will need to wait for either the same satellite to come around again or for another satellite to orbit into range.

As with geosynchronous satellites, line of sight is required, but it is possible to get a connection even if the phone user is in a steep-sided valley because the satellite moves.

Activities

Copy and fill in the table.

Type of mobile	Advantages	Disadvantages	Typical uses
Cellular			
Satellite			

The advantages and disadvantages of a mobile phone are similar whether it is a cellular or a satellite phone.

There are three big limitations:

- credit
- battery
- signal.

Figure 3.42 Mobile phone

There are also disadvantages that are related to the use of the phone, for example: their antisocial use on trains or using it at the dinner table! There is also the expectation that people are always available – it does not matter where you are if the phone rings or a text is sent, there is a feeling that it needs to be responded to rather than left and dealt with later – very few phone calls go unanswered. This is not just true of teenagers, but also of adults and of employers.

However, the advantages are also to do with accessibility and never being out of touch – giving that feeling of security, particularly to parents in that they can contact their children and vice versa if need be. Of course, the additional functions of the phone bring other advantages – games can alleviate boredom, cameras remove the need for a separate device and so on.

Questions

1 Describe how a mobile phone network operates.

2 Describe **three** factors that need to be taken into account when planning the position of a base station.

3 Describe **three** limitations of a mobile phone and how these apply to cellular and satellite phones.

4 Describe how a satellite phone network works.

5 Describe the advantages of having a cellular mobile phone on you at all times.

Describe how satellite communications systems are used and work in global positioning, weather, data transfer systems and television, explaining the advantages and disadvantages of using satellites for these applications

Global positioning systems

Global positioning systems (GPS) use satellites and a device on the ground with radio signals sent and received between them. Each GPS satellite transmits data that includes its location and the exact time at that location.

The signals from the satellites are received by the GPS receiver on the ground at slightly different times. The receiver uses this information to determine its position on the ground. The data from at least four satellites is required to give an accurate position (Figure 3.43).

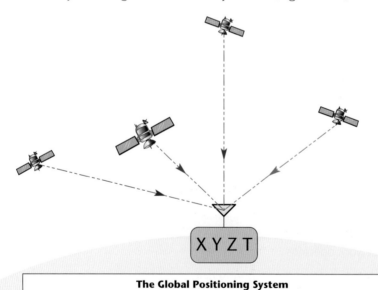

The Global Positioning System
Measurements of code-phase arrival times from at least four satellites are used to estimate four quantities: position in three dimensions (X, Y, Z) and CPS time (T).

Figure 3.43 Satellite triangulation

GPS is used to give directions to vehicles via satnav devices such as that made by TomTom. Satnav devices have up-to-date maps and can be used to plot routes. The GPS location is placed on top of the map and displayed to the driver. Route-finding systems can also give information on speed and estimated time to a destination. They can also use information from other sources to give an indication of traffic on the route.

GPS is also used in aircraft and boats to give the current location. It is useful for walkers in an emergency because it gives a precise location with very little error and makes it easier for the emergency services to find them (Figure 3.44).

Figure 3.44 Spot messenger device

The disadvantage is that the reliance on the device means that people are not learning traditional skills, such as map reading, and if the device goes wrong or malfunctions, they have nothing to fall back on. There is also the distraction of the device to consider, especially when driving. A line of sight to the satellite is required which means it will not work in all weather conditions or locations, such as in storms or if trekking through a jungle.

Weather

Weather satellites are used to measure and monitor the weather and climate of the Earth.

Their main use is in forecasting the weather. By monitoring the clouds, the ocean currents and winds, computer systems can use the data to determine the likely forecast for the coming days.

Weather satellites can see more than clouds, they can also see the lights surrounding cities, the effects of pollution and storms, as well as disasters such as fires, ash clouds and oil spillages. They help monitor climate and environmental aspects, such as ice mapping, ocean currents and boundaries and deforestation.

Activities

Investigate the photos taken by satellites of the same location on Earth at different times. How are these photos used to determine geographical information such as climate change? How else might the photos be used?

Figure 3.45 Satellite image of storm

The satellites can take 'normal' photos and also thermal or infrared images to give different information that can be analysed.

Data transfer

Unless the satellite is passive and does not transmit or receive data, it is involved in some way in data transfer, which might be photos, voice or television systems.

Satellites (Figure 3.46) are also used to transfer data on the internet (e.g. satellite broadband discussed earlier in the chapter).

The advantages and disadvantages are generic and covered at the end of this section.

Television

Satellite television (Figure 3.47) gives access to a wider range of channels than is available otherwise. It also allows access to television in areas that might have difficulty picking up a digital signal.

There are two main types: free-to-air and subscription.

As well as obviously needing the satellite, for satellite television to work, you need a decoder – this may be a separate box or it may be built into the television.

In a subscription service, all homes receiving the satellite signal are receiving all the channels – the decoder then filters the channels you have subscribed to watch.

With satellite television, the communication is only one way. Additional interactivity is provided by the telephone connected to the box.

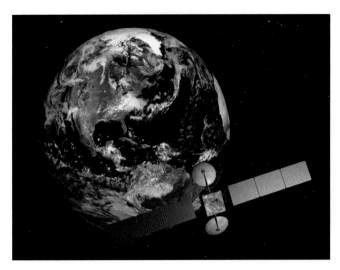

Figure 3.46 Communications satellite

Figure 3.47 Domestic satellite receiving aerial

The main advantages of satellite television are the quality of the signal, accessibility to the number of channels and the availability of the signal from anywhere with a line of sight to the satellite.

The main disadvantages are the requirement for a satellite (which is expensive), a possible requirement for planning permission, and that the receiver aerials can be unsightly. The signal can be lost in severe weather conditions (such as storms) and the dish can become misaligned so a specialist is needed to adjust it.

General advantages and disadvantages

There are some general advantages and disadvantages to satellites. Advantages include the number of people that can access the signal from a single satellite. The type of satellite restricts where the signal can be picked up, but anyone in range, with the correct equipment, can access the signal.

Disadvantages include the cost – of the satellite and the launch to get it into orbit. There is also the difficulty of repair if anything goes wrong. Satellites are also vulnerable to space debris and solar storms.

Questions

1 Describe the disadvantages of using a route-planning GPS system in a car.

2 Describe how GPS works.

3 Describe the advantages of using satellite systems to record climate changes.

4 Describe the advantages of using a satellite to receive television signals.

Describe how mobile technology and networks can enable communication from anywhere in the world

This section brings together the content from the other areas of the chapter – the different hardware devices in a network and the types of mobile network.

Communicating from anywhere in the world depends on the available technology. There are, as you have seen, two main telephone systems (other than traditional land lines) – satellite and cellular. Satellite requires a specialised type of phone, type of contract and type of satellite. Cellular requires the signal strength and a suitable contract with a company.

Then there is the use of the infrastructure in the country where you are. This might be a wifi hotspot, an internet connection through the LAN at a hotel or an internet café.

There are lots of variables and different pieces of equipment that could be required to get a connection.

Figure 3.48 Remote communications

Different methods of connection are:

- connect a fixed computer into a fixed network via an NIC
- connect a mobile computer into a fixed network via an NIC or a WNIC
- connect a mobile computer into a mobile network by tethering to a phone (connected to a 3G network or a satellite network) or by using a MiFi (connected to a 3G network).

Of course, additional hardware (such as hubs, switches, routers etc.) is required once the computer is connected in order to connect to the internet.

Questions

1 Describe the hardware required to enable a sports reporter to file their story electronically from a football stadium.

2 Describe the hardware required to connect to a mobile network in a hotel.

Discuss the implications of being able to communicate from anywhere in the world using mobile technology and networks

Distance is no longer an issue. It used to take months to get information to and from relatives in, for example, Australia. Now, with email, Skype (or similar) and mobile phones, it appears to be instantaneous. This brings with it implications.

It is possible to travel the world and still stay in contact. Months without communication are no longer necessary because modern technology gets messages through, whether they are text messages, emails or video conferencing signals.

The implications are dependent on the type of technology, the cost, the availability of the signal and the type of use.
The main groups affected are:

- parents
- children
- employees
- employers.

Questions

1 Explain the implications for a child of being able to communicate with their parents from anywhere in the world.

2 Explain the implications for a company of being able to communicate with their employees wherever they are in the world.

Explain the importance of standards for communicating between devices and explain how protocols are used to enable this communication

Where you have more than one device it is necessary to have a set of rules that both devices follow so they can communicate (or 'talk to each other').

The method used is a 'standard'. The implementation of that standard is achieved by a protocol.

Additional benefits include the fact that companies and individuals can purchase devices from different locations knowing that if they meet the standard, then they will work with existing equipment.

This leads to the fact that any manufacturer can produce hardware that meets the standard and this brings in competition, and competition is one factor that can keep prices low.

Protocols are the rules used by the standard to enable the communication. They determine how the message is to be sent and received. There are different protocols for different services, such as:

- **SMTP** – governs the sending and receiving of email
- **TCP/IP** – governs communication across the internet
- **FTP** – governs the sending and receiving of files across a TCP network.

1 Explain the advantages to a company of its hardware complying with a recognised standard.

2 Describe the importance of protocols when communicating.

Chapter summary

Characteristics of a LAN
Local area / close proximity
Cables owned by company
Direct connection possible

Characteristics of a WAN
Geographically distant
Third party own cables
Uses external telecommunications equipment

Characteristics of a virtual network
Links computers together to create a virtual LAN
Subset of a WAN or a LAN
Physical location is irrelevant

Purpose of intranet
To share documents internally
To give access to shared files

Purpose of internet
Infrastructure to allow services to run
Allows access to email/ftp/WWW

Purpose of extranet
Uses internet to allow access to intranet
Security required to access resources

Client–server
Single centralised server and connected clients
Allows backup, antivirus and software install/maintenance to be performed centrally
Requires technical knowledge
Reliance on server – if it fails, network fails

Peer-to-peer

No powerful central machine

User takes responsibility for machine

Peer can slow down if others are using its services

Bandwidth

Volume of data over time

Important for time-sensitive downloads

Cables

Co-axial cable

Copper

Fibre optic

Wireless

Wifi

Bluetooth®

Satellite

Optical

Infrared

Laser

Network components

Switch

Hub

Wireless access point

Network interface card

Wireless network interface card

Routers

Repeaters

Gateways

Firewalls

Servers

File

Application

Mail

Proxy

Print

Backup

Communications applications

Fax

Email

Bulletin (discussion) boards

Tele/video conferencing

Instant messaging

Social networking

Facebook, Google+ and Twitter etc.

Connects people together

Post status and thoughts

Broadband connection

ADSL

Cable

Wireless

Leased line

Satellite

Compare by

  – Connection

  – Symmetry

  – Bandwidth

Mobile phone network

Cellular

Satellite

  – Geosynchronous

  – Low Earth Orbit

Limitations

  – Signal

  – Battery

  – Credit

Advantages

  – Location

  – Ability to contact

Satellite communications systems

GPS

Weather

Data transfer

Television

Global connectivity

How to connect from anywhere in the world
  – A fixed computer into a fixed network
  – A mobile computer into a fixed network
  – A mobile computer into a mobile network
Implications of connecting from anywhere
  – Always in contact
  – Work life balance
  – Parental reassurance

Importance of standards

Common language
Protocols (the rules)
Brings competition
Cheaper prices

Chapter tests

Test 1

Harveys is a new employment agency. They have hired an empty office and need to set up the ICT equipment.

1 Describe the advantages of setting up a client–server network. [4]

2 Describe **three** different types of servers they could need. [6]

3 Identify and describe **three** different items of hardware required to set up a wireless network in the office. [6]

4 Explain the importance of standards when purchasing networking equipment for the new office. [6]

5 Describe the advantages of using copper cable to connect the computers together. [4]

6 Compare ADSL or cable broadband connection for Harveys. [4]

7 Explain how *Harveys* could make use of social networking. [6]

Test 2

Ollies is a second-hand classic car business. They have three employees and an office. They have expanded and purchase classic cars from all over the world.

1 *Ollies* makes use of mobile phones. Describe the process when an employee uses their mobile phone to collect an answer phone message that has been left for them. [6]

2 Explain the advantages to *Ollies* of being able to contact their employees anywhere in the world. [6]

3 Describe the advantages to *Ollies* of using social networking sites. [4]

4 *Ollies* has set up an intranet in their office. Describe the characteristics of an intranet. [4]

5 When abroad, the employees make use of an extranet. Describe the characteristics of the extranet they would use. [4]

6 *Ollies* needs to arrange shipping of the cars from abroad to the UK. They can communicate with the shipping agent by fax or email. Compare the use of fax and email to communicate with the shipping agent in China. [4]

7 *Ollies* employees use satnav to find their way to sellers' addresses. Describe how the GPS on a satnav works. [4]

8 Describe **two** disadvantages of using GPS satnav. [4]

4 Applications of ICT

Introduction

This chapter is about the different ways ICT is used in society. This might be at home or in a business setting. ICT can be used in many different ways and can be used to enhance the experience of a user but, as you will learn, ICT also has limitations. You should also be able to apply your knowledge to a specified scenario.

This chapter covers:

- applications and limitations of ICT
- converging communications and information technologies
- distributed databases
- systems.

Describe the advantages and disadvantages of the following software-based training methods: online tutorials, computer-based training, video conferencing

At home and in business, people need to be trained to use computer systems and software. This training can be completed in many different ways, including the use of an actual teacher.

Software-based training can be defined as being any computer program, whether local or delivered through the internet, that can assist the learner in learning something. The training can include tests, checkpoints and revision.

It can be easier and more cost-effective to use software-based training. This includes online tutorials, computer-based training and video conferencing. There are advantages and disadvantages to each of these methods to both the learner and, if used, the teacher/trainer.

Online tutorials

An online tutorial is an interactive method of learning that is computer-based and is usually web-based. This means it is always available and can be used by many people at the same time. It is usually context sensitive and shows the user, through the use of video, sound and text, what to do to complete a task.

Figure 4.1 Using an online tutorial

Advantages	Disadvantages
• Learning can be completed 24/7. • Tutorials can be accessed at anytime from anywhere as long as an internet connection is available. • The content of the tutorials is consistent. • Tutorials can be stopped, paused and started as needed. • The tutorials can be revisited and reused as often as required. • A tutorial is usually written to support a specific task so it can be easy to access a tutorial to meet your needs. • Tutorials contain text/sound/video so they can be stimulating. • Videos/animated graphics can be used to demonstrate skills – easier than trying to explain a practical skill with words.	• Learners need to have high levels of motivation because the learning is usually done individually. • Technical issues might be difficult to deal with in isolation. • High development costs. • Lengthy development time – if the skills being taught are software based then newer versions maybe released before the tutorial is completed. • If a new software skill is required then an appropriate tutorial might not be available.

Computer-based training

The computer-based training (CBT) method has several useful features that enable the learner (who is completing the training) to progress through the training and the teacher/trainer to monitor the progress of each learner.

CBT can record what the learner is doing, the mistakes they are making and tailors the information given out to assist the user to correct any problems. For example, if the learner has difficulties with a particular area of a module, but can do the rest of the module without problems, the CBT component could automatically move them onto the next module. This could stretch the learner on the areas where they were successful, but also continue to revise the areas where they had difficulties.

Most CBT packages enable a learner to access their profile using a user ID and password. The package will then show the learner what modules they have completed, and any scores in tests they have taken. It can show the modules that have still to be completed and identify the point at which the learner left the training.

Feedback might also be provided by the CBT package. This might be at the end of each module or on questions to be answered throughout the module. Based on these results suggestions can be made as to whether a particular topic needs to revisited.

Some CBT packages might be overseen by a teacher/tutor. It will be possible for them to monitor the progress of each learner. This is particularly useful if the learners are in different places. It might also be possible for the teacher/tutor to see how long a module is taking learners to complete, the scores that are being achieved by each learner in each set of questions or test and use these to identify learners who are performing poorly or well in any given module.

Figure 4.2 Using CBT

Advantages	Disadvantages
<ul><li>The learner can work at their own pace.</li><li>Sections can be revisited if the learner is unsure about any concept introduced.</li><li>Different methods of learning are used – video/sound/images.</li><li>Feedback can be given at the end of each completed section or module to highlight areas of weakness or strength.</li><li>The learner can pause/leave a module and return to the same place at a later date.</li><li>Each module can set targets to be shown on the feedback – enables a learner to identify the next module to be completed.</li><li>The teacher/trainer might be able to see the progress being made by each learner.</li></ul>	<ul><li>The learner might develop computer use related health issues.</li><li>Motivation is needed to carry out the training.</li><li>A basic level of ICT skills is needed – the training might not be ICT related.</li><li>Limited access to a teacher/trainer if help and guidance is needed.</li><li>Learner might be tempted to skip through modules and so not develop the skills/knowledge required.</li></ul>

Video conferencing

Video conferencing means that a group of people, usually located in separate locations, can see and hear each other. Each location will need equipment to enable the video conference to take place. The equipment needed will include cameras, speakers, a (large) screen and projectors. The learners at each location are then able to see the teacher/tutor and ask questions.

Practical skills can be demonstrated by the teacher/tutor, which can be easier to show than trying to explain through speech or text.

Video conferencing could be used by learners who are located far distances away from the teacher/tutor, for example consultant surgeons are using video conferencing to demonstrate new surgery techniques to other surgeons located all over the world.

Figure 4.3 Using video conferencing in a learning situation

Advantages	Disadvantages
● Larger groups of learners can take part in the training than if just held on one site. ● Many sites, over a wide geographic area, can be included in the training. ● Travel costs and time can be significantly reduced. ● Accessibility of courses can be increased.	● The equipment can be very sensitive to noise and so demonstrations could be disrupted. ● The equipment needed can be expensive. ● Technical issues might be difficult to deal with if locations are separated. ● Technical issues/problems could lead to the disruption/cancelling of a training session.

Questions

1 Describe **two** advantages of the use of video conferencing to train learners in a practical skill.

2 Describe **two** disadvantages to a learner of the online tutorial training method.

Discuss the limitations of using ICT in society today and how advances in technology might overcome some of these limitations

ICT is used in many areas of society today by people completing a vast number of tasks. However, there are some limitations to using ICT.

The limitations of a piece of technology are what is wrong with it now, that is what it cannot do but that is required by a user. For example, the technology being used to complete a task might not fully meet the user requirements and fail to complete a task satisfactorily.

To overcome the limitations new developments and advances need to be made. The advances and developments come about as a result of the identification of limitations: a catch-22 situation.

Intel's co-founder, Gordon Moore, observed that the number of transistors on a computer chip doubles approximately every two years. Since Moore said this in 1965 this has been the main principle of the ICT industry.

The capabilities of many digital electronic devices are strongly linked to Moore's Law, including processing speed/power, memory capacity, sensors and the number and size of pixels in digital cameras.

Processing power

The main limitations are processing power and speed. The need for speed of processing becomes greater as people complete more tasks using ICT. People expect the technology they are using to

Tip

There are many limitations of using ICT. You will need to keep up to date with new advances in technology and the limitations of using ICT. Up-to-date news and information can be found on the internet (e.g. on the BBC website) by watching TV programmes such as Click and by reading magazines and journals.

react immediately, for example they are impatient when waiting for applications to load. Although processing speeds are getting faster, and continue to do so, the speed will never catch up with the developments in software. More power and speed will always be wanted and needed.

Storage capacity

More and more data is being stored and the format of that data is changing over time. The most common format of data used to be text. Today, people are storing high-resolution photos, videos in HD and audio books. People are also storing an increasing number of television programmes and podcasts. Hard drive storage capacity has been consistently increasing since the devices were first introduced in the 1950s, but at any given time that capacity is not infinite. A drive's storage capacity cannot be changed – it is impossible to 'upgrade' a hard drive to include more storage capacity.

The first computer with a hard drive was the IBM 305 RAMAC. This computer was released for sale in 1956. The actual computer was bigger than a fridge with the storage being fifty 24-inch platters that, when combined, could store 5 MB of data.

Seagate Technology designed the first hard drive for a PC in 1980. The drive was twice the physical size of current hard drives and had a maximum storage capacity of 5 MB. Also in 1980, IBM announced its first 1 GB hard drive – it weighed 550 lbs and cost $40,000.

Along with increases in storage capacity, hard drives have also got (physically) smaller, faster and less expensive over the years due to improved design. There have also been other technological advances, such as high-speed computer cables and faster processors, that allow quicker data access. In August 2012, the greatest amount of storage capacity on a PC hard drive was 2 TB (terabytes), which is more than 2,000 GB.

Many people also need to back up their data, so they need a second storage medium for their data in addition to the computer's main storage. The advances in storage capacity and the reduction in price of solid state storage means that a second storage device is more affordable.

Size of technology

Technology is getting smaller. Most devices have, over the years, decreased in size. Since PCs (then known as desktop computers) became available in the 1970s, their physical size has decreased. Other devices have also become smaller in size. For example, monitors once used cathode ray tubes (CRTs), but now they have become smaller and slimmer with new technology enabling them to provide better display capabilities (see Figure 4.4).

Example

Over time the size of photos taken by digital cameras and other devices has increased and is still increasing. However, these larger photos require extra processing power to be displayed. The processing power is often not large or fast enough to display these photos as quickly as people would like.

Note

More and more data needs to be stored on portable devices, such as laptops and notebooks. This means that the storage capacity of the hard drive needs to be large. The power for this is taken from the battery and the vibration caused by the hard drive running can be significant. Advances in solid-state drive (SSD) technology have meant that solid-state memory capacity has increased and SSDs have become more widely available and cheaper. SSDs are more expensive than a 'normal' hard drive, but the new technology provides faster access speed and instant turn on, is silent with little, if any, vibration, and requires about one third of the power.

Figure 4.4 CRT and flat-screen LCD monitors

Other devices have also been introduced that are now smaller and thinner than their predecessors. Mobile phones and tablet computers have decreased in size. The new iPhone 5 is hailed as being slimmer than its previous versions. The iPhone 5 weighs just 112 grams and has a depth of 7.6 mm. These dimensions are 18 per cent thinner and 20 per cent lighter than the iPhone 4.

A netbook can have a width of 20 cm and weigh just 1.17 kg. Whilst this is great for portability, this miniaturisation can cause some problems: smaller displays can be a disadvantage for users with poor eyesight; smaller keypads are difficult to use by users who do not have tiny fingers! Poor usability can cause frustration to the user and can give incorrect, and unwanted, instructions to the device. Manufacturers might feel that to stay competitive they need to make their devices smaller, but this could be a major limitation to some users who might demand bigger devices to enable them to use them more effectively.

Bandwidth

Bandwidth is defined as the volume of data that can be transferred in one second by the communication channel.

Huge numbers of people need access to the internet. Many people wish to be connected to the internet at all times. This might be, for example, for work, social networking or to stream live events and multimedia (such as films or live news coverage). The large amounts of data being transferred by all these people means that the finite bandwidth of an internet communication channel can limit access to these broadband facilities. High bandwidth channels are required to cater for these user needs.

Many users access the internet using hand-held or portable devices, so the need for wifi access points has increased. These allow users to access the internet wherever they are using any form of device, so long as it is capable of internet access.

Example

Display components, such as screens, are generally getting smaller but users have an ever-increasing need to be able to access the internet wherever they are. Web pages cannot be fully shown on these smaller sized screens without the user having to scroll across the page.

The telecommunications industry is attempting to fulfil this need. However, upgrades to the services take time and money and, whilst the upgrade is being carried out, can cause loss of service to users. Another limitation is that buildings and other structures can degrade the bandwidth size and accessibility. Developments to overcome this could be to introduce transmission services with the capability of going through man-made and naturally formed, structures.

Security

The security of the technology that is used every day to carry out a wide variety of tasks is of paramount importance because an increasing amount of sensitive data is being transmitted and stored. There are always going to be people who attempt to hack into systems to gain access to data.

The security of any system is a limitation to the use of ICT in society. The technology used has the facility, if activated and used, to provide high levels of security, however users do not always find it easy to implement. One of the main issues is that users need to be educated about the need for security and how to increase the levels of security of the ICT systems they use.

User IDs, passwords and access levels are just some of the ways that users can secure the ICT systems they are using. However, if a user chooses the same password for everything and it is found out, then everything secured with that password can potentially be accessed. Security is not just concerned with access to data. Security can also be connected with, and have an effect on, privacy. For example, the use of CCTV cameras is increasing, and these devices are now giving better image resolution.

Users are sharing more information about themselves through the use of social networking websites. People might access this information to invade privacy or commit identity theft.

Developments and advances in technology might be able to overcome some of these limitations, For example, some devices now have built-in biometric security facilities such as fingerprint recognition. These do, however, need to be activated and used by the user.

Battery life

The battery life on any device is related to the use of the device and its power consumption. The less a device is used, and the lower the power consumption, then the longer the battery charge will last. The charge in batteries in devices that are used a lot, such as smartphones and netbooks, usually run out quickly so the batteries need to be recharged frequently.

Note

Users now require constant access to a broadband connection with ever increasing bandwidth. This can cause problems in towns and cities where building can cause transmission and reception issues. Wifi networks that provide localised coverage to 'black spot' users is one solution. WiMax is another solution for metropolitan area networks.

Figure 4.5 Using a password on a smartphone

Activities

Investigate recent developments in security relating to hand-held devices.

Connection to a mobile network can also cause battery charge to decrease more quickly (because the device power consumption is greater). The amount of power used also depends on the type of network (e.g. accessing a 3G mobile network will degrade the battery life quicker than accessing an EDGE network). This can be a problem for users accessing mobile networks. To overcome this limitation, and the general issue of battery life, manufacturers are developing batteries that have an extended life, and electronics that have lower power consumption.

Question

Discuss the limitations of the use of ICT in a hotel and how advances in technology might overcome these limitations.

Discuss the use of networks of computers at work and at home

A network can be defined as one or more computers connected together, either physically or wirelessly, in order to communicate and share data. This means that the basic function of a network, at home or at work, is to communicate data. This includes the use of, for example, email, the internet or an intranet, uploading and sharing photographs, and creating and sharing documents or presentations.

A home network could be used to allow several computers to connect to the internet. It could also be used to stream music and videos around the house and allow files, such as photographs or music, to be accessed by all the networked computers. A central data store could be established with videos, pictures and music. Printing could be centralised.

A work network could help management and staff collaboration. Work files could be shared so teams can work on them. Printing could be centralised, and management features, such as antivirus and backups, could be conducted and monitored. Networks can be used to monitor and record the users' actions as well as provide security to files.

A typical network is shown in Figure 3.14.

There are many different situations, at home and at work, where networks are used. Each situation will have advantageous and disadvantageous impacts on the users who are using the network.

Note

Manufacturers have been decreasing the size of technology to meet users' needs. However, with the reduction in size of the actual device has come a decrease in the size of the battery used to power the device. This has meant that, in most cases, the life of the battery has also been decreased. Manufacturers are now developing batteries that do not need any physical contact to a static power source to be charged.

Advantages	Disadvantages
• Backups can be centralised so there is less chance of data being lost. • The internet connection can be shared across the network. This means that filtering of websites can be carried out centrally. • There is one cost for the internet provision, this might mean it is cheaper than providing internet access to each computer individually. • Peripherals (e.g. printers and scanners) can be shared. This can lead to a reduction in cost of purchasing these peripherals. • Software applications can be purchased on a site licence. This might be cheaper than buying licences for each individual computer. • Virus scans can be carried out centrally so there is less risk of a virus attacking the network. • The network can download, automatically or manually, updates to security and antivirus software. This increases the level of security available on the network. • Users can be monitored centrally. • Access rights can be set using log-ins. • Files can be shared so that, for example, documents and reports can be worked on collaboratively by a team of users. • A user can log on to any computer anywhere on the network and access their files.	• Potential loss of security. Centrally held data can be accessed from any computer on the network. • External access to the network can be achieved via the internet or intranet. • The internet (e.g. web access, email) could be used inappropriately. • The hardware required to set up a network (e.g. servers, cables) can be expensive. • Network staff will be needed to supervise and maintain the network – extra staffing costs. • The speed of access to data stored centrally or the internet might decrease if many users try to access at the same time. • If a virus does get into the network it can spread very quickly. • If the file server crashes then, unless there is a back-up server, data might be lost or corrupted. • The cost of installing and maintaining security (e.g. firewalls and software could increase). • Hardware, such as servers, might need to be installed in a secure location. This might mean finding an appropriate location, leading to an increase in cost.

One disadvantage given in the table is that the internet could be used inappropriately. In a work situation this could mean that employees might access social websites during working hours rather than focus on their job. At home this could mean that family interaction reduces because children spend a long time on social networking websites.

Another disadvantage is that cabling costs can be high. If the house network is large, then cables running around the house might be unsightly and dangerous unless they are clipped to the walls. If the network is wireless, then the signal might be degraded if the walls are thick.

One advantage given in the table is that access rights can be set. In a work situation, this means that departments (e.g. human resources) can have access to files and software that are not needed by any other department. This will also enable compliance with the legal requirements of the Data Protection Act.

Figure 4.6 BT Homehub

Activities

A business publishes a monthly magazine – *Our Pets*. There are ten journalists, three editors and two administration staff. Currently all staff have a stand-alone computer on their desk with all the software they need installed.

There are two printers, which are connected to the administration staff's computers. The journalists and editors pass a memory stick to a member of the administration staff when they need something printing.

There is one scanner, which is connected to one of the administration staff's computers. If something needs scanning, then a memory stick is used to move the scanned data.

Identify and explain the advantages and disadvantages to this company of installing and using a network.

Questions

1 Identify and explain **one** advantage and **one** disadvantage to a university of using a network.

2 Explain **two** advantages to a home user of installing and using a network.

3 Identity and describe **two** advantages to the staff of a large organisation of using a network to share files.

4 Explain how the management of a business could use a network to ensure compliance with the Data Protection Act.

Describe how distributed databases may be stored in more than one physical location using the following approaches: partitioned between sites (vertical and horizontal), entire databases duplicated at each site, central database with remote local indexes

A distributed database is defined by BCS, The Chartered Institute for IT, as 'one where several computers on a network each hold part of the data and cooperate in making it available to the user.'

This means that data neither has to be stored in the same location as where it is used nor stored at one location. The use of distributed database management software makes it appear to the user that they are accessing a single locally stored database.

There are three main approaches to storing a distributed database in more than one physical location. These are:

- partitioned between sites (vertical and horizontal)
- the entire database is duplicated at each site
- a central database with remote local indexes.

Partitioning

This approach is where parts of the data are stored at different locations. This means that no one location holds all the data.

There are two types of partitioning: vertical and horizontal. These are shown in Figure 4.7.

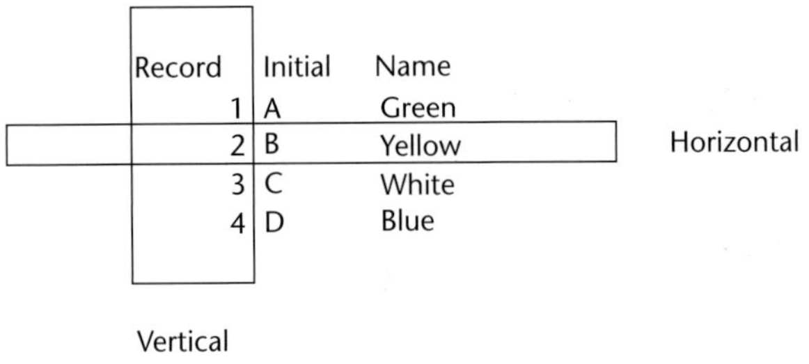

Record	Initial	Name
1	A	Green
2	B	Yellow
3	C	White
4	D	Blue

Horizontal

Vertical

Figure 4.7 Vertical and horizontal partitioning

Vertical partitioning

This is where the data is partitioned on individual fields. Each location has access to their data with the complete database held at a central site. This means that each location has access to a table that only contains the fields that it requires. Normalisation is a type of vertical partitioning.

For example, a retail organisation has different shops, each of which stock different items based on local demand. The stock is ordered centrally from the head office. The table below represents the distributed database.

Product ID	Description	Supplier ID	Supplier
1	Red pens	1	Jones
2	A4 white paper	2	Lead
3	A4 white card	1	Jones
4	Green pens	3	Smith
5	Pink staples	4	Castle
6	Blue pens	2	Lead

Each shop has access to the details about the stock they supply and the supplier ID. The database is distributed between two of the shops as shown in the next table.

Shop 1		
Product ID	Description	Supplier ID
3	A4 white card	1
4	Green pens	3
5	Pink staples	4

Shop 2		
Product ID	**Description**	**Supplier ID**
2	A4 white paper	2
4	Green pens	3
6	Blue pens	2

The central department who will do the ordering of the stock will access the next table.

Product ID	**Supplier ID**	**Supplier**
1	1	Jones
2	2	Lead
3	1	Jones
4	3	Smith
5	4	Castle
6	2	Lead

Each shop and department only accesses the data required and relevant for their needs.

Horizontal partitioning

This is where the data is partitioned based on records. The data is split into different tables and each table contains exactly the same structure. However, each table will contain different rows. This can be used where only certain users access the data that is relevant and required by their job role or function.

For example, a retail organisation has different shops, each of which stock different items based on local demand. Each shop is responsible for ordering its own stock. The next table represents the distributed database.

Product ID	**Description**	**Supplier ID**	**Supplier**
1	Red pens	1	Jones
2	A4 white paper	2	Lead
3	A4 white card	1	Jones
4	Green pens	3	Smith
5	Pink staples	4	Castle
6	Blue pens	2	Lead

Each shop has access to the details about the stock it supplies and the supplier. The database is distributed between two of the shops as shown in the next table.

Shop 1			
Product ID	**Description**	**Supplier ID**	**Supplier**
3	A4 white card	1	Jones
4	Green pens	3	Smith
5	Pink staples	4	Castle

Shop 2			
Product ID	**Description**	**Supplier ID**	**Supplier**
2	A4 white paper	2	Lead
4	Green pens	3	Smith
6	Blue pens	2	Lead

The data structure remains the same, but the records that can be accessed are different.

The entire database is duplicated at each site

This is where each location that requires the data has an entire copy of the database at its own location. For example, the entire database is:

Product ID	**Description**	**Supplier ID**	**Supplier**
1	Red pens	1	Jones
2	A4 white paper	2	Lead
3	A4 white card	1	Jones
4	Green pens	3	Smith
5	Pink staples	4	Castle
6	Blue pens	2	Lead

Shops 1 and 2 each hold a copy of the entire database, so each shop has access to the following:

Product ID	**Description**	**Supplier ID**	**Supplier**
1	Red pens	1	Jones
2	A4 white paper	2	Lead
3	A4 white card	1	Jones
4	Green pens	3	Smith
5	Pink staples	4	Castle
6	Blue pens	2	Lead

There will be some records, in the preceding table that each shop might not need. Using the example, Shop 1 will not need to access records 1, 2 and 6, whilst Shop 2 will not need to access records 1, 3 and 5.

Central database with remote local indexes

An index is a data structure that works like the index in a book. It contains references to the data that allow it to be looked up and accessed quickly.

The database is held in a central location and the indexes, either those specific to a particular location, or to all locations, are held locally. This allows each individual location to perform the processing locally and just use the central database for retrieval of the required data.

No data is held at each individual location, but an index is held. This index is used to search and locate the required data in the central database. The data is then directly accessed in the central database. The indexes will need editing to ensure they are up to date and that any searches for data held in the central database return the correct results. For example, the database is held only at the head office of the retail organisation. Each shop holds an index so that the central database can be searched and accessed. The index enables the searches to be completed more quickly.

Each shop will search the locally held index. This will provide the address, in the central database, of the data being searched for. The result of this local search (the address) will then be sent to head office (the central database) where the address is accessed quickly, returning the required record to the shop.

Shop 1 local index

Product ID	Record address
1	6
2	3
3	4
4	1
5	2
6	5

Central database

Record address	Product ID	Description	Supplier ID	Supplier
1	4	Green pens	3	Smith
2	5	Pink staples	4	Castle
3	2	A4 white paper	2	Lead
4	3	A4 white card	1	Jones
5	6	Blue pens	2	Lead
6	1	Red pens	1	Jones

If Shop 1 needs to search for details about Product ID 6, then the index will be searched for this and it will be identified that the product details are held at Record address 5. The central database is then accessed and Record address 5 is quickly found. The data is then sent back to Shop 1.

Questions

1 Describe the difference between vertical and horizontal partitioning.

2 Using examples, describe how horizontal partitioning could be used by a chain of sports clubs.

3 Describe how a local index can speed up searches for a record.

Discuss the use of different types of distributed database systems

Each different type of distributed database has its own advantages and disadvantages. The differences between the different types relate to:

- creation and maintenance
- speed – how quick is it to run queries and get the data that is required
- flexibility – changing the data structure and queries to meet the needs of the organisation
- storage space
- communication links – the method by which data is transferred (broadband, satellite etc.)
- backup
- integrity/consistency of data.

	Partitioned	Duplicated	Central database with remote local indexes
Creation and maintenance	Very complex, requires trained staff to create and maintain.	Can vary from simple to complex depending on the nature of the initial creation of the database. A flat file is simple, but a relational database can be complex. The actual duplication is, however, a simple process.	Follows normal rules of relational database design and normalisation. Creation and maintenance of the indexes might become complicated to maintain. This depends on the needs of the user and any changes they need in the database.
Speed	If the data is stored locally then the speed is high because of local access. If the data required is held in a different location (e.g. the central location), then the speed decreases.	The speed is high because of local access.	The speed is relatively high because of the local index. Only the data is transferred so no processing is required centrally. If the query/report is not available locally, then there is slow speed.

	Partitioned	Duplicated	Central database with remote local indexes
Flexibility	Any local queries that are carried out on the local database are quick. If other partitions of the database have to be used to complete the query, then the speed of the return of the data will be slower.	The complete database is stored at each location so any queries are performed locally making the speed quick.	The results of the query will be quick if the required data is held in the local index. If the query has to be performed over a range of indexes, then the result will be returned slower.
Storage space	The amount of storage required differs at each location. This will depend on the amount of data held at each location. The central location will require less storage space because the database is partitioned and so can make use of storage space at the different locations.	This is the most expensive type of database in terms of storage requirements. Every location needs a complete copy of the database. This increases the amount of storage and backup space required.	The location holding the central database will have a large storage requirement. This storage will need to allow multi-user access to data. This might require powerful processors to provide a high access and retrieval speed. Locations where the local indexes are held will have a smaller storage requirement.
Communication links	Communication links are required to perform updates to each site. If the link is down, the integrity and consistency of the data suffers.	Communication links are required to perform updates to each site. If the link is down, the integrity and consistency of the data suffers.	A large amount of data passes between the central storage and the offices so communication links are very important. If these fail then no data can be received/sent.
Backup	Backing up is the responsibility of each individual location. It might be possible to recreate the data from different sites if there is an incident but this is not an absolute certainty.	Backing up is the responsibility of individual locations. There are multiple copies of the database available if something goes wrong, for example data becoming corrupted.	The data is only held in the central location so the backup is centralised at this location.
Integrity/ consistency of data	These are a major problem because a change in one database will need to be reflected in all of the databases held at different locations. There are also more points of access for viruses.	These are a major problem because a change in one database needs to be reflected throughout all of the databases held since they should all be exactly the same.	The integrity and consistency is high. The central database means that there is only one instance of all the data. It is also easier to secure against viruses.

There is one specific issue relating to the use of a central database with remote local indexes. This is record locking. Record locking is the technique of preventing simultaneous access to data in a database to prevent inconsistent results. Data integrity needs to be maintained. It must be impossible to have one record updated by two sites at the same time. For example, in a retail organisation, two accounts staff members attempt to update the same supplier account for two different transactions. Account staff A and Account staff B each copy the supplier's account balance at the same time. Account staff A applies one transaction and saves the new balance. Account staff B applies a different transaction and saves a new balance that overwrites the information saved by Account staff A. The balance no longer includes the first transaction and is inaccurate.

Action	Balance
Starting balance	£750
Account staff A inputs £100 credit	£850
Account staff B inputs £150 debit (from original balance of £750)	£600
Balance on the supplier account should be	£700

Each type of distributed database has its own advantages and limitations. Partitioned (horizontal and vertical) distributed databases have the same advantages and limitations. These are shown in the following table.

Advantages	Limitations
<ul><li>If the data is local, then it is available quicker leading to an increase in efficiency.</li><li>The data that is being held locally can be optimised. Only the rows or columns that are available will be optimised, which improves the performance of the database.</li><li>Only relevant and required data is available, which leads to better security.</li></ul>	<ul><li>Accessing data across partitions (different sites) usually leads to inconsistent access speed.</li><li>No data replication (i.e. only a single copy of the data exists), which makes backups essential.</li><li>Potential exists for inconsistency in the data stored.</li></ul>

There is an additional limitation to vertical partitioning. Combining data across partitions is more difficult because it requires more complex joining than horizontally split data.

The advantages and limitation for the centralised database with local indexes and duplicated distributed database types are essentially the same. These are:

- A centralised database is useful for statistical analysis (e.g. sales figures) and backup.
- A distributed database might be less secure with more points of access for hackers.
- Decentralising increases complexity but reduces network traffic.
- Poor record locking and DBMS causes data reliability/integrity problems.

Explain security issues of distributed databases: interception of data, physical access to data, consistency and integrity of data and analyse methods of overcoming these issues

Distributed databases have security issues, as do databases stored at a single location. There are different security issues with distributed databases: these are due to the nature of the storage of the data. The different types of distributed databases have different security issues.

The main threats to a distributed database are:

- interception of data
- physical access to data
- consistency and integrity of data.

Interception of data

Interception of data is the gathering of data by a third party (e.g. hackers) whilst the data is being moved. All the different types of distributed databases move data between them, through communication links. This provides opportunity for the data to be intercepted. The most common way of gathering the data is through the communication links, which can be wired or wireless.

Some distributed databases have more access points. This enables data to be intercepted easier. For example, a duplicated database has the entire contents at each location and the centralised database with local indexes has the central database stored at one location with other locations having access to local indexes. These types have a central point from which all the data can be obtained.

A partitioned-only database has elements of the data at each site, so to obtain all the data, more than one security breach needs to be made.

Interception of data usually occurs during the communication of data. The partitioned and centralised databases make greater use of communication links and so could be at a greater risk of having data intercepted.

The duplicated database uses communication links when it is being updated. However, the database might be constantly updated, so there is an increased use of communication links and, therefore, an increased risk of data being intercepted.

Encrypting the data does not prevent the data from being intercepted. The use of encryption simply prevents the person from understanding the intercepted data.

Physical access to data

Preventing physical access to data is about preventing the individual from getting to the terminal.

The partitioned and replicated types of distributed database have the data stored in many locations. This means there are many locations from where to gain access to the data. Therefore there are many locations that need to implement physical security. Each location needs to implement and maintain the same high level of physical security.

Physical security methods include:
- security guards
- access control on entrances (including locks on doors).

In addition, there are some software methods that can be used to prevent physical access to data. These include:
- user access levels
- log-in procedures (e.g. usernames and passwords)
- encryption.

These methods can safeguard the data if the physical security methods are breached.

Figure 4.8 Door access control

Figure 4.9 Log-in screen

Consistency and integrity of data

Consistency of data is making sure that, where more than one copy of the same data is stored at different locations, the data is the same at each. For example, if one shop changes a supplier's details, then those details are updated with the changes at all the other locations as well.

It is difficult to maintain the consistency and integrity of data in a duplicated distributed database. This is because each location will make changes to the copy of the database it holds, but the copies of the database held at other locations will only be updated when a global general synchronisation is carried out.

In a partitioned distributed database, the consistency of data can be a major problem. This is because changes in a database held at one location will need to be reflected in all of the databases held at the different locations.

In a vertically partitioned database, this can be done through the use of the primary and foreign keys. The consistency of data will also be enforced through referential integrity, cascade updates and deletions.

In a horizontally partitioned database, the consistency of the data can be easy to maintain if each piece of data (the records) is stored at a single location. However, if the same data is duplicated, then maintaining the consistency becomes more difficult. A record-locking system could be implemented and used to maintain the consistency of the data held across the different locations.

The record locking system could also be used to maintain the consistency of data in a duplicated distributed database.

The consistency of data is easier to maintain in a centralised database with a local index. All the data is stored at one location (centrally), so any changes needed to the data can be completed at this central location. The changes, which might need to be made at the different locations, holding the local indexes, are comparatively easy to complete. These updates should be completed on a regular basis and might be completed each time a change is made to the central database.

Integrity of data is the process of ensuring that the data stored is complete and whole. Incomplete data can cause issues to users when the data needs to be retrieved and used. For example, if only a partial telephone number of a supplier is stored, then the retail organisation and shops would be unable to contact the supplier by phone. The integrity of data is usually maintained by controlling data entry.

The data entered into the distributed database system must be validated and verified.

Validation is the automatic checking of data entered into, in this case, the distributed database system. The process of validation ensures that the data entered conforms to rules and is sensible and reasonable. The validation process might be carried out using the following checks:

- **Length** – Ensures the data is of reasonable length by using preset boundaries.
- **Integrity** – Confirms the value of a piece of data by comparing it with other stored data.
- **Range** – Ensures the data is within a preset range (i.e. an upper and lower boundary is set, and the data entered must be between these boundaries).

Verification ensures that the data entered is the same as the source. However, verification can also be used to confirm the integrity of the data as it is copied between different parts of the distributed database. The data should not be changed during the copying, or replication, process. Any detected differences will mean that an error has occurred during the process.

The process of verification can take place either on data entry or when data is copied (or replicated) between the different parts of the distributed database. Verification checks on data entry include:

- **Double entry** – ensures that the data entered is accurate. The data is entered twice and compared by the system. Differences, if any, are identified and can then be corrected.
- **Screen verification** – Ensures that the data being entered is accurate. When the data has been entered, it is displayed on-screen: the user checks the data and performs an action to confirm it is correct.

Activities

Identify and describe other validation checks that could be used to maintain the integrity of data stored within a distributed database.

Activities

Identify and describe other verification checks that could be used to maintain the integrity of data stored within a distributed database.

Remember

Neither validation nor verification can ensure complete accuracy and, therefore, the integrity, of the data stored within the distributed database.

Questions

1 Explain how the interception of data can cause problems for a centralised database with a remote indexes type of distributed database.

2 Explain, using examples, how integrity of data is a problem for partitioned databases.

3 Identify and describe the methods that could be used to overcome the problems relating to the physical access to data and the use of distributed databases.

Describe the components of an expert system and explain the advantages and disadvantages for a given application

An expert system is a computer program that is made up of a set of rules that analyse information about a specific type of problem. When the analysis has been completed an expert system can also provide a recommended course of action in order to solve the problem. The expert system attempts to reproduce the decision-making process that would be completed by a human expert.

An expert system is created and developed to carry out analysis on one specific area only. The skills, knowledge and understanding of a given expert system are not transferable. For example, an expert system created to analyse rock samples could not be used to analyse leaves from trees.

Expert systems are designed to replace a human expert in the specific area they are to be used for. The expert system will attempt to ask similar questions and give the same response that you would get from a human with expertise in that area.

An expert system is made up of three main parts:

- a knowledge base
- an inference engine
- a user interface.

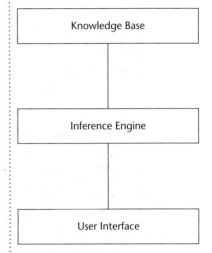

Figure 4.10 The interaction between the components of an expert system

Knowledge base

The knowledge base contains knowledge about the specific area the expert system is to be used for. When the knowledge base is being created the developers will interview experts in the specific area and input their knowledge into the knowledge base.

The knowledge base of expert systems contains both factual and heuristic knowledge. Factual knowledge is that knowledge of the specific area that is widely shared, typically found in textbooks, journals or on websites.

Heuristic knowledge is the knowledge that is acquired through experience and reasoning. It is the knowledge that underpins the 'art of good guessing'. This knowledge is acquired by experts through experience gathered over years of working in the subject. Heuristic knowledge is based on this experience and the continual acquisition of knowledge.

Examples of knowledge include:

- A cat has four legs.
- Dogs bark.
- The Moon is, on average, 238,857 miles away from the Earth.

The knowledge base also contains rules.

Inference engine

The inference engine is the component of the expert system that is designed to produce a reasoning (answer) based on rules. To produce a reasoning, the inference engine is also based on logic.

The inference engine asks the end user questions and, based on the answer, will follow lines of logic. This might lead to more questions and ultimately to an answer. The inference engine will use the knowledge from the knowledge base to carry out this process. The inference engine also works through the use of rules and will apply the knowledge and rules from the knowledge base to the questions asked by the user. The rules in the inference engine are usually based on probability.

A rule, in the inference engine, consists of an IF part and a THEN part (also called a condition and an action). The IF part lists a set of conditions. If the IF part of the rule is satisfied, the THEN part can be concluded. This might be the answer or a new set of rules.

The inference engine can run (work) in two ways: batch or conversational.

In the batch method, the expert system gathers all the necessary data it needs from the user at the beginning of the process. For the user, the inference engine works as a classic computer program: the data is provided and the results are received almost immediately. The reasoning used by the inference engine is invisible.

The conversational method is used when the developer of the inference engine knows that the user cannot be asked for all the data at the start of the process. This is usually because the problem is too complex. The inference engine software must 'invent' the way to solve the problem. This usually includes requesting any missing data from the user and, through this process, gradually approaches the answer as quickly as possible. This process gives the user the impression of having a 'conversation'.

At a basic level the inference engine can be seen as a tree structure (Figure 4.12).

Figure 4.11 Expert system interface

User interface

This is the method by which the user communicates with the expert system. The user will be asked questions through the interface. The answers to the questions will then be used by the inference engine to provide the answers.

Advantages and disadvantages of an expert system

The application and use of expert systems can provide answers to questions that are outside the user's knowledge. This makes the use of an expert system very positive and helpful. All experts have some areas where their knowledge is weak.

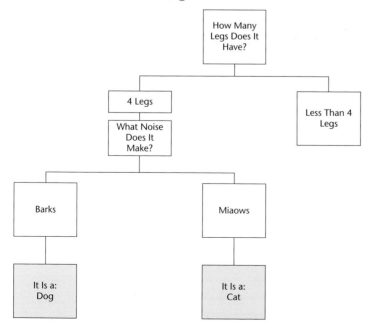

Figure 4.12 Inference engine tree

There are advantages and disadvantages to the use of expert systems in whatever field they are being used.

Advantages	Disadvantages
<ul><li>A knowledge base can hold and maintain high levels of information/ knowledge.</li><li>An expert system can provide consistent answers for repetitive decisions, processes and tasks.</li><li>An expert system will never forget to ask a question.</li><li>An expert system can be accessed 24/7 and used frequently.</li><li>If the expert system has been developed as a multi-user system, then many users can use it at one time.</li><li>The logic of any decision making can be clarified and confirmed during the development of the expert system.</li></ul>	<ul><li>An expert system can lack common sense which is needed in some decision making.</li><li>Errors might occur during the creation, or use of, the knowledge base and lead to wrong decisions.</li><li>Expert systems cannot adapt to changing environments, unless the knowledge base is changed.</li><li>An expert system cannot make creative responses as a human expert would in unusual circumstances.</li><li>It might be difficult to understand the logic and reasoning of the experts consulted during the creation of the expert system.</li></ul>

Questions

1 Describe the inference engine component of an expert system.

2 Explain **two** advantages and **one** disadvantage of using an expert system as an educational tool in a school.

Describe the features of an effective management information system (MIS) and explain the advantages and disadvantages of its use

A management information system (MIS) is a computer system designed to help managers, and other members of staff, plan and direct business and organisational operations. As such, it is a system that collects and processes business data and information to produce reports. It summarises this data in tables and graphs to make it easier to understand.

An MIS can help in decision making by presenting specific data such as sales trends or financial information (e.g. expenditure versus income analysis, reports on best sellers, overdue accounts and demographics).

Businesses with more than one department can use the same MIS. This means that all relevant and required data can be stored and accessed from one location by all the departments, reducing the risk of data loss.

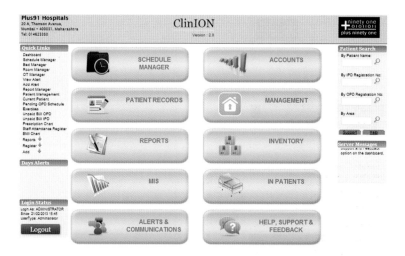

Figure 4.13 Management Information System user interface

The four main features of an MIS are:
- data collection
- report generation
- accessibility and integration
- scalability.

Data collection

Businesses and organisations use an MIS to store data and information. Typically, an MIS will store the information in one of two types of database system:

- **A relational database** – This stores the input from users, and then relates that information to other information already in the system. The database can then put the information into graphs, charts or reports so users can compare data.
- **A hierarchical database** – This stores the data in the order in which it was received, but provides no comparison tables, graphs or charts for the user.

Report generation

One of the main functions of an MIS is to use stored data to generate reports. The MIS users (e.g. the managers) will decide what type and format of report they need. Some MIS systems will include specific templates for different types of reports. The MIS system is able to compile the required report, insert data into the template and print or display the report (Figure 4.14).

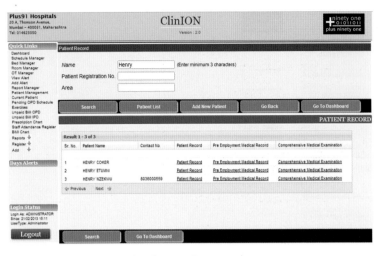

Figure 4.14 An example of an MIS report

Accessibility and integration

An MIS usually functions within a business with open access. This means that the MIS can be linked to, or integrated with, other systems within the business. This strategy enables changes to the data to be made from different sources and many locations. This function provides two important outcomes:

- The business can update the system to provide information in conjunction with needs, policies and regulations.
- The system can be maintained without needing professional technical support.

Scalability

An MIS can be expanded over time as the needs of the business change. This means that the business can add extra data capabilities, as well as system features, as required. The ability to expand the MIS system means that the business does not have to buy a new MIS as the business expands.

As with any system, an MIS has advantages and disadvantages.

Advantages	Disadvantages
• An MIS can assemble, process, store, retrieve, evaluate and disseminate information and data. • Use of an MIS can help planning by providing relevant information for decision making. • An MIS can minimise information overload. Large amounts of data can be put into a summarised and easy-to-read format.	• The storage of sensitive data requires constant monitoring to ensure security. • The quality of output is governed by quality of input (GIGO). • When analysing information and data, an MIS only considers qualitative factors and ignores non-qualitative factors (such as staff morale).

Advantages	Disadvantages
• The use of an MIS can increase data processing and storage capabilities and reduce costs.	• The effectiveness of an MIS can decrease if management and decision makers change.
• An MIS can ensure that each department is aware of problems/requirements of other departments.	• Some information cannot be captured and put into an MIS.
• An MIS makes control easier: it serves as a link between managerial planning and control.	• Computers often cannot be programmed to take account of competitor responses to marketing tactics or changes in economic conditions.
• An MIS can improve the ability of management to evaluate and improve performance.	• The value of information can erode over time.
	• Rapid changes in technology can make systems become obsolete very quickly.
	• Integration issues with existing (legacy) systems can affect the quality of output and vital business intelligence reports.
	• Allocation of budgets for MIS upgrades, modifications and other revisions must be considered to be a priority. If budgets are not allocated and used to solve issues, then the MIS might not be as useful as the business needs it to be.

Questions

1 Explain **two** advantages of the use of an MIS.

2 Identify and describe **one** feature of an MIS.

Describe how management information systems and expert systems can be used by organisations

Management information system (MIS)

An MIS can help an organisation/business to analyse information by producing reports and charts that summarise the relevant and required data. It can be used to transform the data into useful information to help managers with decision making.

Managers need only to see summaries of all the data to let them make business decisions. An MIS will collate unmanageable amounts of data, which would otherwise be effectively useless to managers, into relevant reports and graphs. By studying these reports, managers will be able to identify patterns and trends that would not have been seen in the raw data.

The MIS will produce reports and charts that are relevant to the manager who has requested the information. Different management levels within an organisation will have different information requirements.

An MIS also saves time over older manual systems because data input and information output is quicker.

An organisation might use an MIS to:

- highlight strengths and weaknesses (e.g. by analysing financial reports)
- identify sales trends (e.g. based on marketing and promotional campaigns, times of year or seasonal factors, customer types and ages etc.)
- produce financial information (e.g. forecasts, comparisons of projected and actual sales etc.)
- measure staff performance (e.g. to make necessary changes in organisational plans and procedures, to improve business processes and operations)
- give an overall picture of the company's market position
- act as a communication and planning tool
- manage customer data to help target direct marketing and promotion activities
- run simulations that answer a range of 'what if?' questions regarding alterations in strategy (e.g. to provide predictions about the effect on sales that a price change might have).

It is important to remember that an MIS will not make the decisions for the managers. The parameters for the production of any required reports and graphs will be set by the managers based on the decisions they need to take.

It might be that a specific report is required on a regular basis, for example weekly or monthly. This request can be input into the MIS and the required reports and graphs will be automatically produced. For example, a product might be part of a promotion which lasts for eight weeks. The MIS can be programmed to produce the required reports and graphs about the sales of this product each week, possibly on a specified day, for the time of the promotion. In addition to this, reports and graphs can be requested from the MIS on an 'as and when' basis.

It is not just commercial organisations that use management information systems. Most educational establishments, such as universities and colleges might also use an MIS to:

- track actual student performance against predicted performance
- identify department strengths and weaknesses
- identify trends in subjects taken by students
- analyse expenditure by academic departments.

Activities

Investigate how a charity organisation might use an MIS.

Expert systems

An expert system might be used to provide answers to questions that are outside the user's knowledge. This makes the use of an expert system very positive and helpful. Questions are asked by the expert system and, based on the answers input by the user, a solution is given.

Expert systems can be used in many areas, for example many car manufacturers will provide the garages that maintain and service their cars with a diagnostic system (Figure 4.15). Each car will have a port into which the system is plugged. Data from a car's on-board computer is downloaded into the diagnostic system, which can then analyse the data. The mechanic working on the car can also ask the diagnostic system questions relating to a specific problem with the car. Based on the answers, the diagnostic system will provide a solution to the problem and can, in some cases, provide the steps the mechanic needs to take to solve the problem.

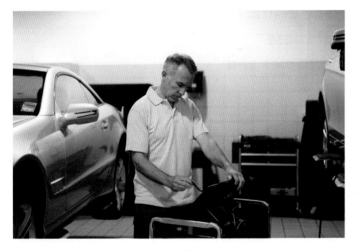

Figure 4.15 A car mechanic's diagnostic system

Expert systems can also be used to plan routes and schedules for delivery vehicles (Figure 4.16). For example the system can allocate customer orders to a route and schedule based on a customer's requirements (e.g. delivery time, vehicle access etc.), the size of the vehicle and the length of the delivery route. The expert system will ask the user to input information such as:

- collections/deliveries to be made
- vehicles and drivers available
- legislation relating to driving hours
- time constraints.

Activities

Investigate how expert systems can be used when:
- finding ore deposits from geological information
- diagnosing medical conditions.

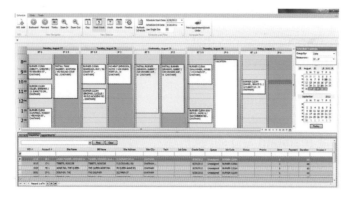

Figure 4.16 Delivery scheduling

Question

Describe how an expert system could be used when producing a
weather forecast.

Discuss the range of services offered by digital television networks and the impact of these services on individuals, television companies and broadcasters

There used to be two ways by which TV channels could be received:
digital and analogue. All the analogue channels have now been
switched off and viewers can only receive TV channels through the
digital medium.

Following the digital switchover, viewers have to use equipment
that is capable of receiving digital signals. There are many options
available. These include:

- **Freeview** – some channels are free to watch, such as BBC and ITV
  channels. The number of channels that can be received is usually
  between 15 and 40 depending on the type of digital transmitter
  sending the signal. This service is free, but the special equipment
  needed to receive the digital signal has to be bought.
- **Free Sat** – this service is available from a number of companies.
  It requires a satellite dish and a receiving box. There is a one-off
  subscription cost, but then most channels can be viewed for free.
  The average number of channels available is 115.
- **Subscription** – This service is available from a number of
  companies. The viewer can select the package they wish to
  subscribe to. The packages include many channels as standard,
  but then other options can be added, such as sport or films
  channels, subject to an extra monthly subscription. A satellite dish
  and some form of digital receiver are required.

Activities

Investigate the digital
switchover that recently took
place in the UK.

Digital television transmits digitised pictures and sound to a TV set (the receiver). A range of services are available to the viewer by pressing a button on the TV's remote control unit, for example:

● selecting different camera angles
● selecting different languages
● recording and live pause
● pay per view
● games
● voting systems
● audience participation
● selecting different ending to programmes.

Some of these services are broadcast to the user (e.g. camera angles) and others make use of telephone lines to send data back (e.g. voting systems).

Digital television can also include information services for the viewer. These can include TV guides, either day by day or weekly, being able to search for a specific genre of programme or series title, and scheduling a series for automatic viewing or recording.

Figure 4.17 TV remote control unit

Impact of services

Each service provided will have an impact on individuals watching the programme, television companies providing/making the programmes and broadcasters delivering the service/programmes to the end user.

For the end user, the impact is about interactivity and services on demand. For the company, the impact is about providing the service that will generate the most income and gaining feedback to improve the service. For the broadcaster, the impact is about providing features that will enable them to gain more subscribers and therefore increase advertising revenue.

Changing the camera angle

Digital television can offer a service that enables viewers to choose the camera angle they want to watch. This could include, for example, the different cameras that are placed around the track at a sports event, such as the Olympics or a Formula 1 motor race. You might also be able to choose to watch the performance of a particular individual, for example to select the camera on the car of your favourite F1 driver.

Figure 4.18 On-car camera view

Impact of a viewer being able to select which camera to watch

Individuals – Some events might have the option to re-watch exciting moments.

Key moments might not occur on the camera angle the viewer is watching so something might be missed.

TV companies – A greater number of cameras are required with staff to operate them which could lead to extra cost.

This service might lead to an increased number of viewers, providing extra income for the company.

All content broadcast has to be appropriate for the viewer. This might require extra staff and a time-lag facility being required to ensure no inappropriate content is broadcast.

Broadcasters – Extra bandwidth might be required to broadcast the different camera angles to ensure all viewers can access this service. If the broadcaster is commercial, then adverts need to be synchronised across all the different cameras.

Recording and live pause

Most digital TV services provide the viewer with an electronic TV guide. As well as letting the viewer know what is being broadcast and when, it can be used to record a programme or series of programmes. This can be activated in advance, for example when the viewer is away on holiday.

Figure 4.19 Electronic TV guide

Some digital equipment enables a viewer to pause a 'live' TV programme. This means that, if the viewer needs to stop watching the programme, they can pause it, but the equipment will record the programme from when the pause was activated. The viewer can then continue to watch the programme from the pause position at a convenient time.

Impact of being able to record or live pause TV programmes

Individuals – As 'live' programmes can be paused for later viewing, the viewer will not miss any part of the programme if interrupted.
One programme can be watched whilst another is recording so there is less chance of a viewer missing a favourite programme.
All episodes in a series can be recorded with a single selection.
Favourite programmes can be set to record whilst the viewer is, for example, away on holiday.
The viewer might have to pay to access this service.

TV companies – Viewers can fast-forward any programmes they have recorded so they might not view the adverts. This can lead to lost revenue for the advertisers and the TV companies.
One programme can be watched whilst another is recording so viewers might subscribe to the packages with more channels included knowing that they can record a programme if there is a scheduling clash.

Broadcasters – There is a cost to keeping the TV guide regularly maintained and up-to-date.
The cost of developing the technology might be high in terms of research, development and production costs.
If the service is not offered, then viewers might go to another broadcaster.

Pay per view

Pay per view is a service that enables viewers to watch, for example, a new film or a sports event. New films are usually those that are leaving the cinemas but have not yet been released onto DVD or Blu-Ray media. The pay-per-view service can also be scheduled, by the viewer, to start at different times. The times might be provided by the broadcaster or selected by the viewer. Viewers can book the event or film they want to watch with the cost being added to their monthly subscription amount.

Impact of pay to view

Individuals – Extra costs will be added to the monthly subscription. The pay per view cost might be cheaper than subscribing to a package if only a small number of events are watched.

TV companies – Popular events can raise extra income for the company.
Extra viewers might take out a subscription package based on their experience of using pay per view services.

Broadcasters – Security needs to be implemented for each pay per view event to avoid viewers who are not paying from accessing the event.
The cost of setting up the service will be high in terms of extra bandwidth, identifying and charging viewers and in security.

Figure 4.20 Sky Box Office

Activities

Identify and describe **one** extra impact of pay per view for each stakeholder.

Audience participation / voting systems / selecting different ending to programmes

Audience participation can take many forms. It might include voting on the results of a show (e.g. the UK entry for the Eurovision Song Contest) or having a say in a live TV debate between politicians. Participation can be carried out by the viewers by, for example, text/ voice message or by using the different coloured buttons on the digital equipment remote control unit.

Figure 4.21 A studio voting screen

Impact of audience participation, including voting

Individuals – Viewers become involved in the programme and feel they can have 'their say'.
Contact numbers are often charged at premium rates.
Votes can reach the programme after the closing time – this means the viewer might still be charged but the vote will not count.
TV companies – The costs of the calls/texts made can create extra money.
More than one ending has to be made to enable viewers to vote – this can cost extra money in terms of production costs.
A relatively small minority of viewers might participate, meaning that any decision is not indicative of the viewing public.
More viewers might be attracted, which means advertisers can be charged more for the adverts shown during the programmes.
Broadcasters – It might be expensive to set up and moderate the service.

Activities

Access a digital TV network service. Identify **two** other services that are offered and consider their impact on viewers, TV companies and broadcasters.

> **Questions**
>
> *1* Identify and describe one impact on TV companies of the recording and live pause feature.
>
> *2* Explain one impact of being able to select camera angles to the viewers of a sports programme.
>
> *3* Identify and describe one impact on broadcasters of the pay-per-view feature.

Discuss the range of services offered by mobile communication services and the impact of these services on individuals and organisations

Mobile communication services enable users to communicate whilst on the move and from any location where there is an available signal.

The most common services offered are voice calls, text messages, multimedia messages and access to the internet. However, some providers will offer different services to their customers. The range of services is expanding all the time. For example, in October 2012, the 4G system was launched. This system aims to provide mobile broadband internet access to smartphones and other mobile devices that have the facility to access the internet. The system will enable users to access applications such as mobile web access, high-definition mobile TV, video conferencing and 3D television. It is hoped that the 4G system will provide users with a higher internet data transfer rate.

Activities

Investigate other services offered by mobile communication providers.

Impacts

The range of services offered by mobile communication providers includes access to the internet. This access, together with the increased use of social networking websites has changed the way that people communicate.

The availability of fast and reliable access to the internet whilst on the move enables people to keep in touch with friends, family or, in the case of personalities, their fan base. This has had major impacts on people's lives, both positive and negative. The examples below are just some of those which have been high profile.

Example

In January 2010, a tweet on the social networking site Twitter caused a negative impact on one user. When prevented from flying out of Robin Hood Airport during snowy conditions, a traveller threatened to 'blow the airport sky high'. The tweet was seen as a security threat by police who arrested the man. The man was released on bail, but later fined in court. Stephen Fry, a user of Twitter, offered to pay the costs and fines accrued by the man. As a result of this tweet, the man, who was training to be an accountant also lost his job.

Example

Tom Daley was a diver on Team GB during the Olympics 2012. An offensive tweet was made relating to Tom's private life by another user. No action was taken against the original tweeter, but this case has opened up the debate about the use of social media sites and the concept of free speech.

Example

In the summer of 2012, a cricketer found, to his cost, the impact of texting. Pietersen sent texts to some of his friends on the South African cricket team. The texts related to the then England cricket team captain, Andrew Strauss. The texts resulted in Pietersen being dropped from the England cricket squad. It was a communication that led to his exclusion, but Pietersen also used YouTube to broadcast a very public apology.

Example

At the start of 2012, a primary school pupil from Scotland began a daily blog with photographs and comments about the school dinners being served at her school. Very soon, the education authority wanted to ban the blog because they thought it showed the school dinners in a bad light. This was, after a legal battle, not allowed.

These examples demonstrate some of the impacts that mobile communications media, and its use in relation with social media, can cause.

There are other impacts to the use of social media, not all linked directly with mobile communications.

Activities

Investigate some other high profile cases relating to the use and abuse of mobile communication media. Consider the impact these cases have had on the individuals concerned.

Advantages	Disadvantages
• Increased contact with friends and family – this can be useful if, for example, someone is travelling because they can keep in touch and, if posts fail to appear, then friends and family can raise the alarm. • Celebrities can post news to their fan base about their activities, instantly. For example, it was confirmed in September 2012, that Adele would sing the theme tune to the new James Bond film – Skyfall. At the beginning of October, Adele posted a tweet showing the cover of this single. • Charities can increase their public awareness • Pleas for help can be sent 'viral' very quickly. For example, in October 2012, a five-year-old girl went missing in Wales. Thanks to Facebook many people turned out to help look for her. • Businesses can use social media websites for marketing purposes.	• There have been cases, one including a premier league footballer, of houses being burgled because posts have been made saying where people are going to be at a specific time. This has led to insurance being invalidated. • If users put a lot of personal detail onto social media websites, then it can be easier for identity theft to occur. • A digital footprint is left – pictures, posts and tweets that have been posted are there forever. For example, there could be implications later on in life, of posting a party picture while at university. • Bad publicity, untrue comments, can be posted and go 'viral' very quickly. For example, bad/untrue comments posted on TripAdvisor have caused some hotels/guest houses to go out of business. • Employers are able to access social media home pages by being accepted as a friend. This enables employers to view what their employees are posting – some of which might be detrimental to the business.

Activities

Identify and describe **two** other advantages and **two** other disadvantages of using social media.

The future

It was after the Tom Daley case, described above, that the Director of Public Prosecution (DPP) said that 'the time has come for an informed debate about the boundaries of free speech in an age of social media.' The Tom Daley case was one of a growing number of cases and there were likely to be many more. In October 2012, approximately 340 million messages a day were sent on Twitter alone and 'banter, jokes and offensive comment are commonplace and often spontaneous', said the DPP. 'Communications intended for a few may reach millions.'

The DPP went on: 'To ensure that CPS decision making in these difficult cases is clear and consistent, I intend to issue guidelines on social media cases for prosecutors. Social media is a new and emerging phenomenon raising difficult issues of principle, which have to be confronted not only by prosecutors but also by others including the police, the courts and service providers. The fact that offensive remarks may not warrant a full criminal prosecution does not necessarily mean that no action should be taken.'

Questions

1 Identify and describe **one** negative impact to a business resulting from the use of social media.

2 Explain **one** positive impact of social media on charities.

3 Explain the future impacts that might occur as a result of using social media.

Describe the internal resources of an organisation: human, technological and premises

All organisations need resources to be able to function. The internal resources of an organisation exist within the boundaries of the organisation. There are three main types of internal resources:

- human
- technological
- premises.

Human

Human resources are the people who work within the organisation. They could be contractors or permanent (full-time and part-time). The skills and expertise of the individuals will give characteristics to the organisation.

The human resources of the organisation will each have a different job role and function. The resources will range from the highest level (e.g. the managing director) to the lowest level (e.g. the staff who work on the shop floor in a retail organisation).

All levels of staff are required to keep the organisation functioning on a day-to-day basis. For example, the human resources of a veterinary practice might include:

- the vets who own, and work in, the practice
- trainee vets working as part of their course
- veterinary nurses who look after the animals
- administration staff who deal with the paperwork, such as booking appointments, taking payments for treatments and ordering the medicines and equipment needed
- cleaning staff who keep the premises clean and sterile.

Technological

Technological resources are the equipment in an organisation, such as computer equipment and other devices needed for the

Activities

Investigate the human resources that could be found in a publishing company.

Figure 4.22 A veterinary practice

organisation to function. The technological resources are related to the equipment the organisation has to hand.

There are likely to be areas within a company that have specialist equipment and can fulfil a requirement. For example, the technological resources of a hospital might include:

- a computer network, including workstations, printers and other peripherals
- blood pressure monitoring machines
- X-ray machines, portable and static
- operating theatre equipment
- heart monitors
- defibrillators.

Activities

Investigate the technological resources that might be found in a car repair garage.

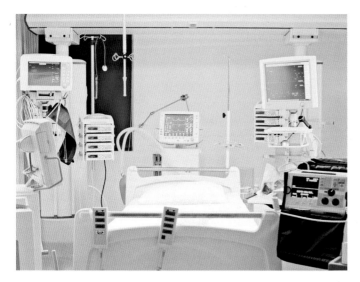

Figure 4.23 Some equipment found in hospitals

Premises

The premises can be defined as anything not covered by the human and technological resources (e.g. the buildings and the furniture). Premises are not just the office buildings, but can also, depending on the function of the organisation, include car parks, grounds and gardens, factories and warehouses.

The location of the premises is important. For example, a retail outlet might be located on a town's main shopping street or on an out-of-town retail park. Some organisations might 'cluster' with other organisations carrying out the same function. For example, a large number of financial organisations have branches and offices that are located in the City of London. (See Figure 4.24 on page 146)

Figure 4.24 The City of London

The premises resources of a haulage company might include:
- offices for administration and management staff
- car parks for staff cars and other vehicles
- garages for the repair of lorries and trailers
- a yard for the lorries and trailers to be stored in when not being used
- a warehouse to store goods that are to be transported
- a staff canteen.

Activities

Investigate the premises resources that might be found at a hotel.

Questions

1 Describe **two** technological resources that might be found in a dental practice.

2 Describe **two** human resources, apart from teaching staff, that might be found in a college.

3 Identify and describe a premises resource found at a hotel to be used only by the staff who work there.

4 Identify and describe a premises resource found at a hotel to be used only by the guests who stay there.

Chapter summary

Software training methods
Online tutorials
Computer-based training
Video conferencing

Limitations of using ICT
Processing power
Storage capacity
Size of technology
Bandwidth
Security
Battery life

Use of networks of computers
Work
Home

Distributed database systems
Vertical partitioning
Horizontal partitioning
Entire databases duplicated at each site
Central database with remote local indexes

Use of different types of distributed database systems
Creation and maintenance
Speed
Flexibility – data structure and queries
Storage space
Communication links
Backup
Integrity/consistency of data

Security issues of distributed databases
Interception of data
Physical access to data
Consistency and integrity of data

Components of an expert system
Knowledge base
Inference engine
User interface

Management information system (MIS)
Data collection
Report generation
Accessibility and integration
Scalability

Use of MIS and expert systems

Digital television networks
Features:
- changing the camera angle
- different languages
- recording and live pause
- pay per view
- games
- voting systems
- audience participation
- selecting different ending to programmes

Impact on:
- individuals
- television companies
- broadcasters

Mobile communication services
Social networking media
Impact on:
- individuals
- organisations

Internal resources of an organisation
Human
Technological
Premises

Chapter tests

Test 1

A media company produces television programmes.

1 Describe **two** human two technological resources of the company. [8]

2 The company is often involved in outside broadcasts, covering live events.

  (i) Define what is meant by bandwidth. [1]

  (ii) Explain the importance of bandwidth when transmitting live
     television. [4]

3 The company uses satellites to transfer the data to its head office.

  (i) Describe how the satellite communication system works to enable
     the outside broadcast unit to transmit its signal and for it to be
     received by head office. [4]

  (ii) Describe **one** advantage of using satellites to transmit the signal. [2]

4 The company uses social networking, such as Twitter, to promote its programmes. Explain the advantages and disadvantages of using such a service to advertise its programmes. [8]

5 Digital television has increased the range of services on offer. Discuss the impact of these services on the television companies. [11]

Test 2

A second-hand shop has expanded and now has more than ten shops in different towns throughout the country. They are introducing a new system to help them manage their stock across all the shops.

1 Describe the analysis and testing phases of the systems life cycle. [4]

2 One of the methodologies that could be used is RAD. Describe this method of software development. [4]

3 A user interface is being developed for the new system. Describe how perception, attention memory and learning should be taken into account when designing the new interface. [8]

4 The different shops are going to be linked together using a WAN. Describe **three** characteristics of a WAN. [6]

5 Describe **three** different factors that should be considered when managing the change to the new system. [6]

6 Identify a suitable method of installation for the new system and justify your choice. [7]

7 Describe hardware and software developments that are changing or might change the way that individuals shop in the future. [8]

5 | Implementing computer-based information systems

Introduction

This chapter covers the implementation of computer-based information systems. The implications of the many decisions needed here must be carefully considered. You will need to make sure that you understand the different approaches that could be taken to make an informed decision. You should also be able to apply your knowledge to a specified scenario.

This chapter covers:

- custom-written and off-the-shelf approaches
- upgrading systems
- system installation
- system maintenance.

Explain the involvement of a client when a custom-written computer-based system is produced, from the initial meeting with the client to the installation of the system

The client must be involved at every stage of the development of a custom-written information system. Initially the client will need to provide details to the development team about what the client would like the new system to do. These details form the basis on which the development will take place.

If the details are either incomplete or inaccurate, then this may lead to a system being developed which does not fully meet the needs of the client and the organisation. This will result in a system being developed that has wasted the money and the time of both the client and the development company.

Figure 5.1 shows the importance of the client being involved at all stages.

Clients must be involved at all stages of the systems life cycle. If the client is consulted at all stages, then errors, inaccuracies and omissions could be found in time to correct them. Consulting the client only at the installation stage is too late to rectify any issues.

Clients should be consulted at the end of every stage of the systems life cycle. During the consultation the developers should listen to any concerns that the client expresses, with the client being

Figure 5.1 The importance of involving the client

given the opportunity to suggest modifications that they feel are needed or to raise any concerns about inaccuracies.

The extent to which a client is involved might depend on the methodology being used during the development of the system. Some methodologies, such as the waterfall model, enable the developer to return to the previous stage in the cycle to correct any issues. Other methodologies, such as the prototyping methodology, enable the client to see a 'prototype' of the system which may enable a fuller and clearer understanding of it.

The developer, however, irrespective of the methodology being used, must ensure that the client, and the end users of the system, are consulted at each stage.

Question

Explain **two** reasons why the client should be involved at all stages of the development of a custom-written software system.

Discuss the implications of selecting, implementing and supporting the installation of custom-written and off-the-shelf solutions

Selecting a custom-written or off-the-shelf solution

The selection of either custom-written or off-the-shelf system solutions will depend on many factors. What is important is that the appropriate system solution is selected to meet fully the needs of the client.

A custom-written solution is when the software has been written to meet the specified needs of the end user – usually an organisation. It is developed by a software provider who works with the user to determine the requirements of the system design. The software provider builds the system to meet these requirements, and then implements and tests it.

An advantage of a custom-written solution is that it exactly meets the requirements of the user. The user will specify the requirements and the system will be developed to incorporate those functions. A lot of off-the-shelf software solutions have many features that are not required by the user. This is sometimes known as 'bloat ware'. These unwanted functions increase the memory footprint (the amount of hard drive space taken up by the software). With custom-written software solutions there are no extraneous functions because the software has been written to meet specific requirements.

Once the system has been developed, installed and paid for, then the user owns it and can sell it to other companies. This may cover the cost of development, however the initial cost of the development may be very high.

Specialist backup and support will be available from the system provider who developed the software. This backup may involve correcting bugs, training users or assisting in extending the functionality of the program. There will not, however, be wider support available, such as books, discussion groups etc.

One of the disadvantages of having a custom-written system is the long time it takes to analyse, design, develop, test and implement it. The end-user requirements might even change during the process.

If mistakes are found in the code, then it may take some time to find and fix them. Problems might even occur when the system is being used in a live environment after implementation.

Off-the-shelf software is a term used to define any software that can be purchased, installed and used immediately. One of the main advantages of off-the-shelf software is that it is generally cheaper than having software specially written. The cost is a one-off purchase price.

Also, because off-the-shelf software has a large number of users, it is likely to have been tested by many people and a lot of the bugs will have been removed. It must be remembered that a piece of software can never be fully tested but the more testing that is done the more likely it is that it will work.

Another advantage of implementing a system that includes off-the-shelf software is that the choice of software manufacturers is sometimes greater. For example, word-processing software is available from companies such as Microsoft, Corel and Lotus, and as open source. The software is readily available, and can be installed and used almost immediately.

Off-the-shelf software is widely used, and this means that support can be got from books, discussion groups, websites and trainers. Bug fixes and patches are often released by the manufacturer and registered users can often upgrade to the latest version at preferential rates.

There are disadvantages to using off-the-shelf software in a system solution. Among these is the fact that there are likely to be many features and functions included in the software that are not needed by the user, and which cannot be removed because ownership of the software stays with the software manufacturer. The software may also not fully meet the needs of the user and so compromises will need to be made.

The software is also more likely to have a large memory footprint.

The table below shows a comparison of the main features that should be considered when deciding whether to install a custom-written or off-the-shelf system solution.

	Off-the-shelf	Custom-written
Cost to the end user	• Either a one-off cost or a yearly rental cost, possibly thousands of pounds plus additional costs for each station it is used on.	• Need to hire the company/person to write the software which could cost many thousands of pounds. • The end user owns the system and can sell it to recoup some of the development cost.
Support	• Discussion groups, online help, books and training courses are readily available.	• Only likely to get support from the people who write the software – problems may arise if they choose not to support it or go out of business.
Purpose	• May have to be altered and edited to fit the purpose. May never meet the purpose precisely. • Will have many additional features that may or may not be used. Better to have them there and never use them rather than to want them and not to have them?	• Will fit the purpose precisely and do exactly what was asked. Possible problems might arise if the analysis was wrong. • If something it is not specified then it will not be there in the final product.
Testing	• Will have been tested by many individuals. Bug fixes will be released regularly by the company.	• Will only have been tested by a few people and there may be many bugs. Correcting them will take time.
Availability	• Immediately available.	• Will take time (possibly a few months) to complete the analysis etc.
Choice	• Choice between packages available – but none may be an exact fit.	• There is choice of who to get to write the software and the end user will have a lot of influence over the end product.

	Off-the-shelf	Custom-written
Upgrade	• Likely to use a standard file format and the company is likely to release upgraded products. • Support for new peripherals and operating systems as standard.	• New printers and drivers for peripherals may not be supported and major upgrades might not happen. If the software does not use a recognised file format it may not be possible to upgrade.
New staff	• May be already familiar with the new software.	• Unlikely to be familiar with the new software.
Memory footprint	• Likely to be larger than a bespoke solution.	• Likely to be smaller than an off-the-shelf solution.

Questions

1 What are the advantages of off-the-shelf software over custom-written software?

2 What are the disadvantages of off-the-shelf software over custom-written software?

Implementing and supporting the installation of custom-written and off-the-shelf software

The staff who will be using the system will need to be involved during the implementation and installation stages. There may be some staff who feel that the new system might lead to job losses. There might also be staff who feel that they do not have the skills required to use the new system. Staff will need to be involved in discussions that should enable them to voice their concerns and to have their worries addressed. If staff feel supported, then they are more likely to accept the changes and to feel confident when using the software.

Staff should be offered training sessions to ensure that they are confidently able to use the system. This should be appropriate to both their job role and the level of skills they already possess.

Staff need to be reassured that their jobs are not in jeopardy and the benefits of the new system should be emphasised, so they feel more loyal towards the organisation and, hopefully, use the system efficiently.

Staff should be given easy access to user guides and documentation to help them use the new system effectively. The user guides, and associated documentation, should also be readily available after installation so that staff can refer to them if any problems occur. This means that staff should become more independent and confident, which in turn will make them more efficient in their work.

Most organisations have customers (clients). The needs of the customers should also be considered during the installation of new system solution. The new system may cause some problems for the

Activities

Investigate the different types and format of software user guides that are available, indentifying the strengths and weaknesses of each.

customers. It may be that, despite testing having taken place during the development of the solution, some teething problems are still present.

This may have an impact on customers, for example, incorrect invoices being sent out or details not being transferred to the new system correctly.

The organisation, and the staff dealing with the customers, should offer some explanation to the customers and attempt to rectify any issues as quickly as possible.

The implementation and installation of the new system should be managed carefully with the needs of the staff and customers of the organisation being considered as much as possible. By considering these needs there should be no loss of confidence in the organisation for either the staff or the customers.

Explain how the expertise of staff, costs, benefits and current systems affect decisions about upgrading or installing software and hardware

The decision about whether or not to upgrade or install new software and hardware should be taken during the analysis stage of the systems life cycle. The decision should be taken after considering the expertise of staff, the costs involved and the budget given by the organisation, the benefits the system will bring and the system currently in use. A cost–benefit analysis should be completed with the results influencing the decision.

The cost–benefit analysis should consider the costs incurred. These will include the costs of any staff training which will be needed. If the software and hardware is being upgraded, then the staff are likely to have already some of the skills that will be required to use the software and hardware competently, but it is likely to be dependent on how much the versions differ. It is also possible that the planned changes may affect the administrative and operational procedures currently in place in the organisation. This may lead to extending the training required by the staff.

If new software and hardware are to be installed, then the training costs are likely to be high. If the software is custom written, then the training will have to be bespoke because it is unlikely that any commercially available training courses will be appropriate. Any training, however, will cause some disruption to the organisation. This means that when the training takes place and which staff receive it needs to be carefully planned.

If software is to be upgraded or a new package is to be installed, then the cost of licences needs to be considered. Sometimes a software upgrade might have a smaller licence cost than that of a new software package. Another cost with off-the-shelf software is for the time that will be needed to tailor and test the package in the new system environment.

Irrespective of whether the software is to be upgraded or a new package is to be installed the issue of hardware must be considered. The new software must run successfully on the old system and, in addition, the existing hardware must run the new software. Upgraded versions of software invariably add new features and as a result tend to use more memory and require faster processing speeds. To ensure that the software operates at optimum performance, the hardware may, therefore, need to be upgraded to meet these requirements. In addition, the upgrading of software may enable the organisation to use newer or additional hardware. If this is the case, then the cost of the hardware should also be taken into account when making any decisions about whether to upgrade or install new items.

In addition to the issues with software and the impact this may have on hardware, it may be that the hardware currently being used by the organisation has become obsolete or outdated. New hardware may also be required by the organisation. For example, a change in type of printer may be needed due to a change in business function of the organisation. The upgrade of new hardware may, however, require some changes to the software being used within the organisation. This is likely to be achieved by installing drivers or downloading software patches from the hardware vendor's website. It is important, however, that the software and hardware are compatible and cause no problems to the organisation. To ensure this compatibility the hardware and software must be thoroughly tested.

If the software to be upgraded was initially custom-written, then any upgrades to the software may be covered by the maintenance contract that is in place with the software development team. However, there is likely to be a limit on the number and level of revisions that can be made without incurring extra costs.

If the software to be installed is an addition to the software currently used, then the compatibility of the new software with the old must be considered. If the new software does not interact or is incompatible with current software, then it may be that the data held by the organisation will need to be transferred or reconfigured. This may add to the costs in terms of the time and personnel needed to carry out the process.

Other issues that will have to be considered, and require decisions to be taken, include the method of implementation and the available timescale.

The method of implementation must be selected carefully. (The different methods of implementation that are available are discussed later in this chapter.) The method of implementation should take into account the extent of the upgrade or installation and the impact on the organisation.

The timescale available will, in some cases, have an impact on whether an upgrade or fresh installation would be appropriate. A short timescale may not be appropriate, especially if the software has to be custom written.

The upgrading or installation of a system must, ultimately, ensure that the benefits of the new outweigh the advantages of the old. In addition, the long-term benefits need to outweigh the costs and inconvenience/disruption of the installation.

Questions

1 Explain how the expertise of staff could affect the decisions about the upgrading of hardware.

2 Identify **two** factors affecting decisions which must be made when upgrading software.

Describe a range of methods for installing a new computer-based system: parallel, phased, direct, pilot

Discuss the choice of a particular installation method or methods for a range of applications

Once a new computer-based system has been developed and tested it needs to be implemented.

In this stage of the systems life cycle, the system will be installed, new equipment will be put into operation, software will be installed and set up, data files will be created and end users will be trained.

There are four main strategies that can be taken when implementing a new system. These are:

- parallel
- phased
- direct
- pilot.

Parallel

The old and new systems are run concurrently during a parallel installation. The results from each are compared for accuracy and consistency. The old system is not discarded until there is complete confidence in the reliability and accuracy of the new system. Figure 5.2 shows the old system being used in parallel with a new

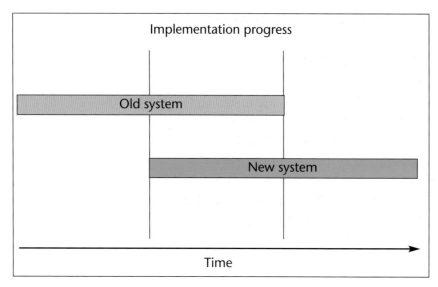

Figure 5.2 Parallel installation strategy

system for a time and then being withdrawn, leaving the new system being the only one in use.

This strategy has some disadvantages. Staff are effectively doing their work twice meaning that data is duplicated and inconsistencies can occur between the old and new systems. The inconsistencies have to be rectified, which might be very expensive in terms of staff and time costs.

However, if a problem is found with the new system, then it is possible for the organisation to function because the old system is still in place and can be used. This means that there are no detrimental effects on an organisation.

Phased

Phased installation is used with larger systems where the system to be put in place has several smaller sub-systems. Each sub-system is introduced one at a time, making sure that each one is working before the next is commissioned. The actual installation method can be direct or parallel.

The advantages are that each sub-system can be introduced with a minimum of disruption and if a sub-system fails to work, it is small enough to correct the errors.

The disadvantages are that the changeover may take a long period of time and create an extended period of unsettlement.

Direct

The direct or 'big bang' installation approach is the riskiest strategy. The new system completely replaces the old system, on a given date, with no interim parallel, phased or pilot installation. Figure 5.3 shows the old system being withdrawn and the new system beginning to be used immediately!

The disadvantages of using this strategy are great and may have potential detrimental consequences for the organisation. Any problems or bugs in the new system may lead to complete loss of data and the failure of the organisation. If this strategy is chosen, then these risks need to be minimised by careful planning by the analyst. The new system must be thoroughly and completely tested prior to installation. Staff also need to be fully trained to use the new system. It may also help if the direct installation is carried out during a slack period to ease the stress and pressure that will be placed on the staff at the switch over to the new system.

A carefully managed direct strategy that ensures a seamless transition, both in terms of the new system working correctly from the word go, and staff being adequately trained, is potentially the cheapest in terms of staff and time costs, but the analyst must consider the advantages and disadvantages of using this strategy very carefully otherwise the consequences might be very expensive.

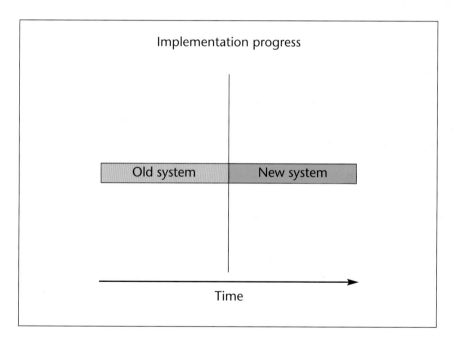

Figure 5.3 Direct installation strategy

Pilot

The pilot installation strategy requires selected departments to use the new system before other departments that continue to use the old system until the pilot has been proven to work correctly. Once confidence in the new system is high, then the new system can be implemented in another department. This continues until all the departments within the organisation are using the new system.

For example, a retail chain could implement the new system in one of its shops. When confidence in the new system is high, the rest of the shops can begin to use the new system.

The disadvantages of this strategy is that it can take a long time and is, therefore, very expensive in terms of staff and time costs.

An advantage is that the old system can still be used in parts of a company if a problem is identified with new system. These problems, or bugs, can then be rectified before installation is continued. Using this strategy limits the detrimental effects on an organisation.

A summary of the advantages and disadvantages of the different installation methods are given in the table.

Installation method	Advantages	Disadvantages
Parallel	• If a problem is found with the new system it is possible for the organisation to function because the old system is still in place and can be used. • There is little or no detrimental effect on the organisation.	• Data is duplicated. • Staff undertake tasks twice. • Inconsistencies have to be checked and errors have to be located.
Phased	• Problems or bugs are found within small sub-systems making it easier to find the error and correct it. • Limits the detrimental effect on the organisation.	• Slow to commission the complete system. • Very expensive in terms of staff and time costs.
Direct	• Potentially the cheapest in terms of staff and time costs.	• Problems or bugs could lead to complete loss of data and/or the potential failure of the organisation.
Pilot	• If a problem or bug is found with new system, it can be rectified before installation is continued. • Limits the detrimental effect on an organisation.	• Installation can take a long time. • Very expensive in terms of staff and time costs.

Questions

1 Describe the parallel method of installation.

2 Identify **two** advantages of the pilot installation method.

3 Identify a situation where the direct installation method might be used. Explain your choice.

Explain the role of reviews during the life of a computer-based information system, describing how reviews may be planned for and carried out effectively.

During the life of any system reviews need to be undertaken to ensure that the system continues to operate effectively.

Reviews should be scheduled to occur on a regular basis. Using a planned, scheduled review strategy will ensure that the system continues to provide satisfactory levels of performance to the users. Scheduled regular reviews will allow users to report any problems they have had with the system. The reviews can also ensure that the system does not become out-of-date or be perceived by the users to be 'old fashioned'.

Reviews of a system can also be scheduled to coincide with any planned changes in the operation of the organisation using the system. Planned changes may include external and/or internal changes.

External changes may include legislation changes (including tax and VAT) and data protection updates.

Internal changes relate to the organisation itself, such as a change in the mode of operation whereby new functions performed by the system will need to be included.

Other internal factors that may be considered during a review include checking that data is being processed efficiently and that there is still sufficient storage space for the number of, for example, new customers/orders. If a data entry system is part of the system being reviewed, then this should also be checked during a review to ensure that it is still working effectively and accurately.

Another role of a review is to enable developments in hardware and software to be incorporated into a system. Developments in hardware and software occur very frequently. New software might not be compatible with the system. As hardware becomes obsolete and/or needs replacing then a review of the system must take place to make any necessary changes that ensure that the new hardware works successfully with the system.

During a review of a system, users must be asked for their views on how well the system is performing. This will also enable the users to suggest improvements to the system – they are the ones using the system on a day-to-day basis so they will be able to provide relevant suggestions as to the overall system performance from a user's perspective.

Activities

Investigate different types of external and internal changes which could result in a system having to be changed.

Describe perfective, adaptive and corrective maintenance

Explain the need for perfective, adaptive and corrective maintenance during the life of a computer-based information system

Over the life of a system (post-implementation) it may be necessary to perform maintenance on it. There are many different reasons for maintenance.

The main reason for post-implementation maintenance include:

- errors/bugs that may not have been identified during the testing process but become apparent when the system is being used
- users finding that parts of the system are not working as they would like
- tasks that were not included at the design stage but now need to be incorporated into the system
- the emergence of security issues that mean the system requires an extra level of protection
- the software developer/vendor may find a way to make the system run more efficiently – this will usually result in the release of a patch/fix
- new hardware or other software may be purchased that needs to be integrated into the existing system resulting in changes needed.

Perfective

This type of maintenance usually occurs when it may be advantageous to make changes to enhance the performance of the system or to make it easier for end users to use. This type of maintenance should turn a good system into a better one. It is generally completed at the request of the end users.

These requests could include:

- the addition of shortcut keys to help carry out processes
- an improved screen design where the colours/layout of the existing system might not be appropriate
- increased levels of online help
- the rewriting of procedures to reduce the response time of the system
- the restructuring of data to reduce storage requirements.

It is important, however, to remember that perfective maintenance does not change the overall functionality of the system.

Adaptive

This type of maintenance usually occurs when the organisation using the system has a new need that the system must fulfil. The system may need to be adapted due to changes within the organisation using it, external changes such as legislation (i.e. tax/VAT rate changes) or to enable the system to operate with new hardware.

Corrective

Corrective maintenance is also known as remedial maintenance. This type of maintenance is usually completed if there are errors in the software. These errors or 'bugs' can be of two types:

- Programming errors – These occur when the programmer/s have made a mistake. This type of error should have been discovered and corrected before the system was released.

- Logic errors – These are more likely to be undiscovered during the testing stage of the systems life cycle. With this type of error the system will appear to work as it was intended but does not process the data and/or produce the output as it was designed to do.

Corrective maintenance is usually undertaken through the use of patches. The Y2K problem in 1999–2000 was solved through the use of corrective maintenance and the release of software patches.

Questions

1 Describe corrective maintenance.

2 For each maintenance method identify a situation when it could be used.

Chapter summary

Client involvement during the development of a custom-written software system

The implications of:

- – selecting
- – implementing
- – supporting

Custom-written and off-the-shelf software

Decisions about upgrading or installing software and hardware may depend on:

- – expertise of staff
- – prices
- – benefits
- – current systems

Installation methods

Parallel

Phased

Direct

Pilot

Factors to be considered when selecting implementation methods

Impact on:

- – organisation
- – staff
- – data/information

Reviews
Scheduling

Maintenance
Perfective
Adaptive
Corrective

Chapter tests

Test 1

A company wants to introduce a stock ordering system. The system can be either custom-written or an off-the-shelf package.

1 Explain the implications of selecting an off-the-shelf software solution. [6]

2 During the life of the system, reviews will need to be carried out. Describe the role of these reviews. [6]

3 Maintenance will be carried out on the system. Describe adaptive maintenance. [4]

Test 2

A boat company is updating the booking system that it currently uses.

1 Describe **two** different methods the company could use to install the new booking system. [4]

2 Identify and describe **two** different types of maintenance that might be required during the life of the booking system. [6]

3 Describe **two** factors which should be considered when managing the change in the booking system. [4]

6 Implications of ICT

Introduction

People are part of systems, so they are affected when a new ICT system is introduced. Individuals need to be managed, with any changes being carefully introduced. Change is something that can come from different areas and this chapter looks at the impact of both internal and external change.

This chapter also focuses on the ethical issues that surround ICT and different ways that data can be kept confidential and secure.

The final element of the chapter covers new developments. ICT is always changing and every day there are new hardware and software developments. You need to understand how these impact individuals, society and companies.

You will learn about:
- the impact of external change
- managing change
- ethics and ICT
- data security and confidentiality
- hardware and software developments.

Discuss the impact of external change on an organisation, on individuals within an organisation and on the systems in use

When something is done in a different way or by using new hardware or software, then change is required. Employees and companies are comfortable when they know how to do something – they do it well – but they worry about change. They even fear it because change often means upheaval. They might have to learn how to use new systems to do their jobs and there might be job losses resulting from the new systems.

There are two main types of change:
- internal change
- external change.

Internal change is change that originates from within an organisation. It is when management decides to upgrade systems or change the structure of the organisation.

External change refers to something that happens outside an organisation that has an impact on it. Reasons for external change can include:

- **Financial** – for example interest rate changes, VAT changes, lending money.
- **Research** – for example production techniques, materials that can be used.
- **Competition** – for example changes to production methods, price cuts to products, new ranges of goods.
- **Personnel**.

External change can also include the building of new roads, houses and shopping centres – all of these things can affect an organisation.

Figure 6.1 External change

Impact on an organisation

The ultimate impact of external change on an organisation is that it goes out of business. Taxes, competition and legislation can have such a bad effect that a company closes. Less extreme effects might be redundancies and organisational restructuring. All these are negative impacts.

There are also positive impacts from external change. Lower taxes might mean the goods an organisation produces are cheaper, making it more likely customers will buy them. More sales increases profit. New roads can make it easier for customers to reach the company and potentially increase sales.

An organisation is mainly concerned with two things:
- survival of the business
- growth of the business.

Figure 6.2 Survival of a business

The impact of external change is the effect it has on these two things.

Impact on individuals

If a company fails, then the impact on individuals is redundancy. If a company expands as a result of a change, then there is the possibility of new employment.

There are many impacts between these two extremes. Individuals might have to work part time if a company does not perform well. Employees might need to acquire new skills and be trained to work on new products or in a different area of the organisation. This can have an impact on their confidence (by taking them out of their comfort zone) and, in the long term, it might have an impact on productivity because an employee who has learnt new skills is not going to be working as quickly or as well as someone who already has the skills.

If a business relocates, then it might be necessary for an employee to move house, and this can impact employees' families (e.g. children's new schools and relationships with friends).

Births, deaths and marriages are other external changes that affect individuals. They might have consequences on how an employee views working overtime, flexitime or teleworking, and so affect job satisfaction.

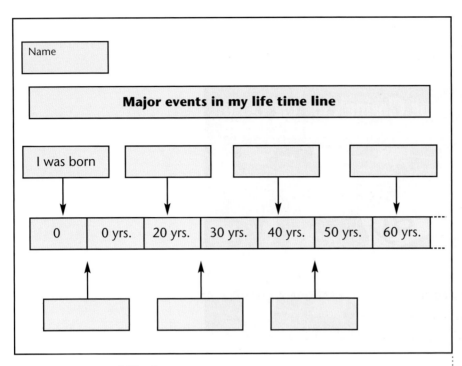

Figure 6.3 Personal life changes

Impact on systems in use

External changes such as developments in production techniques or new software mean that a system might need upgrading (e.g. in order to run new software, more RAM, a better graphics card or a faster processor might be required).

Changes to software or hardware are likely to require expenditure by a company. If their sales are poor, then this will put them further in debt and affect their overall survival.

The introduction of new software and production techniques often means that staff will need to be trained to use them. This costs money, and while staff are being trained, pressure is put on other staff who have to cover their jobs.

Also, systems might be streamlined – this might be because of less money caused by a change in the economy or an increase in competition cutting profit margins.

When systems are changed, it is either to remove something that is currently in place (hardware, software, procedure or personnel) or to add something new. This makes employees nervous:

- Is my job safe?
- Do I need to learn new skills?

Activities

Investigate the different minimum hardware recommendations for different versions of Microsoft® Windows® from Windows® 95 to Windows® 8. What would be the minimum hardware cost to upgrade a computer running Windows® 95 to be able to run Windows® 8?

1 Describe the impact on a small corner shop of a new shopping centre opening.

2 Describe **three** different external changes that could affect a local doctors' surgery.

3 Explain how external change can impact the employees.

Discuss change management and factors that must be considered (staff capability, staff views, systems, equipment and accommodation) when managing change

Change management is a complex process. There are organisations that deal specifically with change and helping firms to change. Change management has several phases (rather like the systems life cycle):

- Initially there is a source of change. This needs to be evaluated and a decision taken about whether or not a change is required.
- The nature of the change must be agreed and communicated to the workforce (if appropriate).
- The change needs to be planned with goals established. An action plan for the change needs to be drawn up and this should anticipate the effects of the change and how to minimise them.
- The change then needs to be implemented. This might require a change in culture, removing resistance and changing work practices, depending on the nature of the change.

All of this needs to be managed.

Staff capability

This is the ability of the staff to use the new system. If there are minimal changes, then they will be able to adapt their mental model and use the new system with no real issues. They might need to have the changes explained to them for a short time.

The change itself will determine how much training is required – for example there might be similarities between the old and new systems that will make the change easier, or, if the system is very different or there are lots of changes, then more extensive training will be required. This has several knock-on effects:

- The jobs of staff who are being trained will need to be covered.
- Some staff might be unable to train to use the new system and will be need to be made redundant or redeployed.
- Some staff may be worried about learning about a new system.

The workforce must be involved in the change process and where appropriate, the skills of the staff should be utilised. This means, where possible, using existing staff to do the training rather than bringing in external companies.

The timing of the training is also important. If staff are trained too soon before a changeover, they are likely to forget the skills. If the training is too close, staff might not have time to assimilate the skills.

Staff views

The employees who use a system know the most about it. They should be consulted about what needs changing and how to make the changes. This could be done by:

- meetings
- questionnaires
- interviews
- a representative on the new system committee.

Staff must feel valued and must know that their opinions are being taken on board. If they think they are being ignored, then they will be resistant to the change and, if they see something wrong, they will be disinclined to speak out.

Changes will be unsuccessful without the backing of the staff. An organisation needs to consult with employees and encourage their participation in the ways given above. Keeping everyone up-to-date and involved will improve familiarity with the new system and the reasons for the change. Resistance to the change is lessened.

Figure 6.4 Training

Systems and equipment

Nothing is worse than a new system not working. Employees need to be given equipment and systems that do their job. Some resistance to the change will be reduced if staff are confident with the new system. This means that the new system must be thoroughly tested to ensure that it does the job it is supposed to.

Hardware needs to be ordered and delivered, and any existing data needs to be transferred to the new system. The exact date and time of changeover needs to be established and all the individuals concerned need to be informed of what is happening and the role they have to play.

If the new system processes or stores data, then changing over too far in advance will mean that a second changeover of data will be required because the original data transferred will be out of date. Transferring the data too close to the new system going live adds extra pressure and the process might overrun.

Accommodation

When installing new equipment and systems, some thought must be given to where they will go. It is where the users of the system will work.

The equipment must be set up to work in its new accommodation, and this can involve additional power points, air conditioning, new rooms and new furniture.

If there are new departments (such as technical support and maintenance), they will also need accommodation and to be included in the organisational infrastructure.

Figure 6.5 Open-plan office

Having established the physical accommodation, then there is the workplace that each employee will have. This includes the style of the office (open-plan or individual offices) and where each person will work (e.g. who they are next to, how far from the water dispenser they are, and so on). While these matters might seem trivial, they are important to individual employees.

Questions

1 What is meant by change?

2 Explain why change needs to be managed in an organisation.

3 Describe how staff capability should be considered when managing change.

4 Explain the importance of accommodation when managing change.

Discuss the importance of consultation, participation and communication when managing change

Change management will work only if it has the support of those individuals who are going to be affected by the change.

The workforce is a very powerful element – in some organisations, the views of unions should be taken into consideration before any changes that affect their members can be made.

Three important elements of change management that can be used to minimise disruption and allow the organisation to gain the support of its workforce are:

- consultation
- participation
- communication.

Each is covered further in the following sections.

Consultation

Employees are afraid of things happening that they are not aware of and to which they have had no input. They are suspicious of just being informed that change is happening. The people who work every day with the system are the ones with the most knowledge about it – they understand it, they know its problems and successes. It therefore makes sense for an organisation planning to change a system to involve the people who know most about it – this involvement is known as consultation.

The greater the number of relevant people who are consulted, the more information will be available for developing the change plans. There are different ways of consulting employees:

- interviews
- meetings
- representative on committee
- suggestion box.

Individuals who have contributed will be aware of the need for change and will have a better idea about what will happen. They will have a greater commitment to making the change work if some of their own suggestions have been included – they will feel they have some 'ownership' of the new system. The key is that the employees know that they have been consulted and are being listened to.

However, the more people the organisation consults with, the greater the number of different ideas that will be put forward. Some of these ideas might conflict, which means some suggestions might not be taken on board – this might cause resentment among those whose ideas were rejected.

Figure 6.6 A meeting

Activities

Imagine that your school is looking at increasing the length of the school day. Who are the relevant parties that need consulting? How might the school go about consulting these relevant parties and what methods might they use?

Participation

It is vital to get the employees to participate. It is easy to consult employees, but if employees do not actively engage with it, then there is a problem. Participation is the involvement of all relevant individuals – it is not just their involvement in a single part of the cycle, but a continuous participation.

The more people that are involved, the better the problems will be defined and the more likely it is that the final solution will meet the requirements. The participative approach to systems analysis places the user at the centre of the process. The key is that not only should the users be consulted (as occurs with all systems analysis), but that they should be heavily involved in the rest of the cycle. For example, a designer of user interfaces will show them to the users for their opinion. The participative approach is a joint effort in which the users play a part in the design process from the beginning ensuring that the chance of rejection at the end of the cycle will be much less. However, there are problems:

- Some staff might have a very strong idea of the roles of management and employees, and will claim that new ideas are management's responsibility and that employees should not be involved.
- There is likely to be extra work with meetings, proposals etc. This takes the employees away from their main job, which will still need to be covered.
- The employees involved in the process might see themselves as being better than other employees because they were involved – they might develop a superiority complex.

Communication

Communication is the process of informing the employees of the change. There is nothing worse than a surprise or a workplace that is full of rumour. Change that occurs without communication is doomed to failure from the start.

The communication must be continuous and relevant – there should be no secrets or surprises. Communication with employees allows them to get involved, to monitor the project themselves and to know what the future holds. An organisation must not spring a new system on its employees – they need: to be led towards it; to understand why it is necessary; to be a part of its development; to take ownership of it; and to be protective towards it. Only then can it be introduced and, hopefully, be accepted.

Activities

Go through the systems life cycle and identify all the different parts where participation could take place.

There are three parts to communication:

- **What** – What do you tell employees? How much information do you give them about the reasons, the timescale, the idea? The managers will not wake up one morning and decide that they need to change. There will be a catalyst (this may be external change) and they will have some ideas of the direction of the change.

- **When** – At what point do you inform the employees that change is going to happen? If it is left too late, then rumours will have started and there might already be some resentment from employees that they have not been told. Too early in the change process and employee concerns and worries could last a long time and have a negative effect on work and productivity.

- **How** – This is the method used to tell the employees about the change. This might be:
  - email
  - a notice on a board
  - verbally in a meeting.

Figure 6.7 Communication

Questions

1 Describe the importance of participation when managing change.

2 Describe what is meant by 'ownership' of a system.

3 Describe what is meant by 'resistance to change'.

4 Describe **three** different methods of communication that could be used to inform shift workers in a factory that they are relocating. For each method identified, give its advantages and disadvantages related to the scenario.

Discuss ethics relating to ICT with reference to codes of conduct, for example, BCS, The Chartered Institute for IT's Code of Conduct and the Association for Computing Machinery (ACM) Code of Ethics and Professional Conduct

Ethics and ICT has been an issue for some time, but it is growing in importance as ICT affects all walks of life. Ethical issues can be difficult to grasp especially in its relationship to ICT. This definition by James Moor seems to fit best: 'The analysis of the nature and social impact of computer technology and the corresponding formulation and justification of policies for the ethical use of such technology.'

What do we mean by ethical use? A definition of 'ethics' is 'a code or set of principles by which people live.'

The internet is a good place to start when considering ethics and ICT. The internet is accessible by billions of people and anyone can post anything. The ethical considerations of the internet include:

- accessibility to age-restricted information – for example children being able to access pornography
- views that are inconsistent with historical evidence – for example information on historical events that individuals claim did or did not exist, such as the holocaust or landing on the moon
- access to opinion without related facts – for example religious, racist and sexist opinions given without challenge.

There is a difference between ethical and legal. Sometimes the two cross over. Gary Glitter, a 1970s pop star, took his computer to PC World for repair. The technician, who was repairing the PC found offensive material on it and called the police who investigated. Gary Glitter was later jailed. (For more information visit http://news.bbc.co.uk/1/hi/uk/517604.stm.)

The ethical and legal aspects seem quite clear. However, why was the technician at PC World looking through the files? Was there any need to do so in order to complete the repair? If you take your computer to be repaired, while there might not be illegal material on it, there might be sensitive material (e.g. copyright books, letters, emails) that you do not want others to see. Do you expect or anticipate the technician to go through your files? Was it ethical for the technician to report what they had found? Of course it was. Was it ethical for the technician to have been looking through the files on the computer? No it was not. Ethics and ICT is a grey area.

Activities

Investigate http://zapatopi.net/treeoctopus/

Here are some other ethical issues involving ICT:

- **Software licences** – The need to make sure that all software that requires a licence has one on every single computer.
- **Abuse of resources** – Using company bandwidth for downloading personal emails. Is it acceptable to surf the internet using company resources during a lunch break? What are the consequences of listening to internet radio at work?
- **File sharing** – A huge area of ethical and legal implications, including ownership and copyright issues.
- **Copyright** – Using images and text from non-credited sources or without payment.
- **Preferred suppliers** – Buying from an equipment supplier who might charge a little more than another, but who gives you a really nice hamper at Christmas and treats you to nights out.

Codes of conduct

Codes of conduct have arisen as a way of establishing what an employee can and cannot do in the workplace. It sets out the expectations of both the employee and the employer with respect to different issues.

A code of conduct is required so that the employees know the boundaries of the system. With fixed boundaries, they know what they can and cannot do. From the employer's point of view it is a method of shifting responsibility – if the employee has signed a code of conduct stating that they will not load any software onto the company's computers, but does so and the company is charged with software theft, they can pass the blame onto the employee.

Example statements based on the BCS, The Chartered Institute for IT, code of conduct include:

- You shall conduct your professional activities without discrimination against clients or colleagues.
- You shall act with integrity in your relationships with all members of your professional body and with members of other professions with whom you work in a professional capacity.
- You shall seek to upgrade your professional knowledge and skill, and shall maintain awareness of technological developments, procedures and standards that are relevant to your field, and encourage your subordinates to do likewise.
- You shall not claim any level of competence that you do not have. You shall only offer to do work or provide a service that is within your professional competence.
- You shall accept professional responsibility for your work and for the work of colleagues who are defined in a given context as working under your supervision.

Activities

Read your school's code of conduct for ICT use (if it has one). Does it cover all types of ICT use and behaviour? Is it comprehensive? What else do you think it should cover?

Activities

Investigate the BCS and the ACM codes of conduct. How are they different? Are there some things that are particular to one country? Are they reasonable?

ICT and ethics are continually changing. A code of conduct, because it is not a specific part of a contract of employment, can be updated to take into consideration the shifting environment and technical nature of ICT.

This can be a disadvantage. With the goalposts and the boundaries ever changing there is no stability. What might have been acceptable one week might now not be allowed. Other disadvantages may include a perceived lack of trust in the workforce – having to spell out exactly what is and what is not allowed might be like being back at school! Following an ethical policy can put a company at a competitive disadvantage – other, less professional, companies might not follow the code and this might mean they can sell their goods cheaper.

There is, however, a niche market for ethical companies. In ICT, being 'green' and carbon neutral is important. A company that is ethical is fair and treats its employees and customers with respect. This can gain customers and the loyalty of staff (who might increase their efficiency).

Questions

1 Explain why a company should make its employees sign a code of conduct.

2 Describe how a code of conduct promotes ethical behaviour.

3 Describe the difference between ethical and legal.

4 Describe **four** ethical issues an internet hosting company should be aware of.

Discuss the need to keep data confidential and explain how this can be achieved

There are two reasons to keep data confidential:
- to meet the requirements of the Data Protection Act (1998)
- to protect against competitors.

One of the requirements of The Data Protection Act (1998) is that personal data held by an organisation is kept secure. This means that details such as name, address, date of birth and so on should only be accessible by those that need it. Anyone else should not have access to the data and it should be protected in some way.

Competition is based around keeping company information secure. This includes information on new products and financial records. A company does not want its competitors to know what is happening because it might lose its market advantage.

Activities

Investigate the rumours surrounding iPhone and iPad launches. Many websites predicted what the products would be. How accurate were they?

Data confidentiality

There are two main ways that data is kept confidential:

- by preventing access to the data
- by preventing it from being read or understood if it is accessed.

Preventing access to the data is done through physical security, logical security and personnel measures.

If the data is accessible, then it can be encrypted to prevent it from being understood. Data is encrypted to make it unreadable by anyone that does not have the key to interpret it. This is discussed further in the next section.

Physical security

This is the use of physical methods to prevent access to the data. It includes things such as locked doors and security guards. Some physical measures do not prevent access but alert security guards to the fact that access has occurred. These include measures such as camera and alarms.

Logical security

This is the use of software measures, including:

- using up-to-date antivirus software
- installing software patches
- installing a firewall
- locking the computer so a password is required for access (this might be part of a screensaver) – a variety of settings can be used to increase the security of the password, such as:
  - not allowing the use of old passwords
  - specifying a minimum password length
  - not allowing a dictionary word
  - specifying that the password must contain upper and lower case characters , numbers and symbols
- locking an account if three incorrect passwords are entered in succession.

Personnel measures

This includes:

- educating users to be aware of who is around them when entering passwords so unauthorised people cannot see what is being typed
- not writing passwords down
- not choosing obvious (i.e. easy-to-guess) passwords.

Activities

Use the internet to research the most common passwords that people use. Why do you think they are used?

Questions

1 Explain why companies need to keep data confidential.

2 Describe **two** different logical security measures a company can use to keep data confidential.

3 Explain why an alarm will not keep data confidential.

Discuss how encryption, authorisation, authentication, virus checking, virus protection and physical security can be used to protect data

Encryption

Encryption is the process of taking plaintext and using an algorithm to convert it into ciphertext (encrypted data). A key is used to decrypt the text and turn it back into plaintext.

Figure 6.8 Encryption

Encryption does not prevent the data being intercepted or acquired, but it stops it from being understood. This protects the data because the contents cannot be read and used by anyone who does not have the key.

One of the simplest methods of doing this is the Caesar Cipher. This is part of a family of ciphers that are known as substitution ciphers or shift ciphers. They are called this because each occurrence of a letter in the plain text is replaced with a different letter in the encrypted text. In simple ciphers, the plaintext letter is always replaced with the same letter in the encrypted text.

In the Caesar Cipher you replace the plaintext letter with a different letter a certain number of positions ahead in the alphabet. For example:

Plaintext: A B C D E F G H I J K L M N O P Q R S T U V W X Y Z

A shift of five letters ahead would mean that A is replaced by the letter five characters to the right: in this case F. B would be replaced by G, and so on.

Encrypted text: F G H I J K L M N O P Q R S T U V W X Y Z A B C D E

It is called the Caesar Cipher because it is rumoured that it was used by Julius Caesar to send messages to his army.

The security of encrypted data depends on how complex the cipher and the key are. Something like the Caesar Cipher is relatively easy to crack. Others are much harder.

Authorisation

This is permission. It can relate to an individual or a computer. For example, individuals can be authorised to access certain files on a computer. This authorisation can be verbal or written. If someone who is not authorised tries to access the files they are breaking the law as defined in the Computer Misuse Act (1990). Authorisation given to an individual can be implemented through the use of access rights allocated to their username.

Computer authorisation is the process that allows only a certain machine to access a particular resource. Authorisation might be further limited by time restrictions.

Authentication

Authentication is making sure that the person (or computer) requesting access is who (or what) they say they are prior to allowing access. Authentication is therefore combined with identification. This can be achieved by using a key, code word or PIN known only to both parties. Once a person (or computer) has been authenticated, the system allows access only to the authorised level of that person (or computer). (Note that having only the password or the PIN does not prove that you are the rightful owner, you may have found it out or been given it to use.)

Putting the above another way, a system needs to identify and authenticate a user before authorising access. This security measure is often a username–password combination, but a physical attribute, such as voice or a fingerprint (a biometric), might be used for authentication. (Note that biometrics are a very poor method of identification and should be used only for authentication.)

Activities

Use a Caesar Cipher with a right shift of 7 to decipher the message:

`vbiaxkl tkx yng`

Create your own messages using a different shift and don't tell anyone what it is. Try to get them to crack it.

Activities

Investigate different methods of encryption. Each person in the class pick a method and give a presentation about it to the class.

Figure 6.9 Cashpoint

At a cashpoint, a card and associated PIN are used as authentication to authorise access to the facilities of the cash machine. (Note that it is the card–PIN combination that authenticates at a cashpoint – obtaining the PIN is no use without the card – but it is the card alone that authenticates with online transactions.)

Virus checking and virus protection

A computer virus is a piece of software that is designed to infiltrate a computer and perform unwanted processing such as file replication or deletion, or transferring of data.

There are two different aspects to viruses: protection (i.e. preventing the virus getting onto the machine in the first place) and virus checking (i.e. scanning the computer to find any viruses that are present and getting rid of them).

Activities

Investigate 'man in the middle' (MITM) attacks and how SSL certificates are used to prevent them.

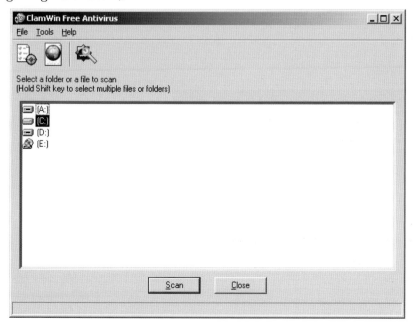

Figure 6.10 Antivirus software

Creators of viruses and antivirus software manufacturers are constantly trying to create software that will defeat each other. When a new virus is detected, the antivirus software firms very quickly release an antivirus software update to eliminate it.

Viruses can infect computers in many different ways, but there needs to be an entry point. This could be:

- an email attachment
- by running code downloaded from a website
- via a USB memory stick
- via CD/DVD.

An antivirus scanner scans these entry points in an attempt to find and stop the virus entering the computer.

Physical security

Physical security prevents access to data by devices such as locks and guards. For example, physical systems can lock down a computer so it cannot be stolen.

Figure 6.11 Physical security on a laptop

Activities

Look at the latest virus threats at http://home. mcafee.com/virusinfo/threat-activity?ctst=1. What is a Trojan? Why do you think people create viruses?

Questions

1 Describe how encryption can protect data.

2 Explain, using examples, the difference between authentication and authorisation.

3 Describe the difference between virus checking and virus protection.

4 Explain how educating users can help to protect data.

Discuss hardware and software developments that are changing, or might change, the way we live. Examples might include advances in treating injuries or disease, leisure activities, the environment, the home, education and freedom of speech and movement. This list of examples is not exhaustive as questions will reflect the current use or abuse of ICT in society.

In meeting this requirement, you are expected to read widely and keep up with breaking news. You will need to be able to express your own opinions. You need to understand and write about the consequences and impacts of the introduction of new developments.

How do you keep up to date?

There are many ICT magazines and websites that give up-to-date news, for example (links may change):

- The Register: http://www.theregister.co.uk/
- BBC Click: http://news.bbc.co.uk/1/hi/programmes/click_online/
- TeachICT: http://www.teach-ict.com/newshome.htm
- Gadget Show: http://fwd.channel5.com/gadget-show

This section of the specification is about showing your understanding. It is not about the ability to regurgitate information, but to show that you understand the content and are aware of the implications of the introduction of the technology.

Future developments of ICT

There are always changes in ICT: to the hardware, the software and how the technology is used. There are key areas identified by the specification:

- treating injuries or disease
- leisure activities
- environment
- home
- education
- freedom of speech and movement.

These have been provided to give you topics to research. They are not the only topics that you might be asked about. The exact nature of the answer is up to you: what areas of those topics you are familiar with and wish to discuss. Some ideas have been given below for each topic listed above. You would need to develop positive and negative impacts and consequences of these to get high marks on the final question on the paper.

Treating injuries or disease

This could include the use of ICT in research, remote surgery through robotics, expert systems for diagnosis, the use of ICT in creating medical components, biometrics and androids.

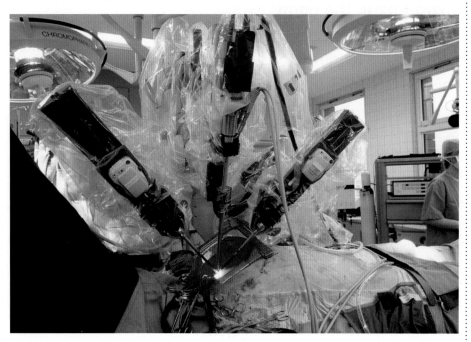

Figure 6.12 Remote surgery

Activities

Discuss future developments in hardware and software that will affect how patients are treated. Copy and complete the table.

Point	Positive/Negative	Impact	Consequences
Remote surgery – surgeons from anywhere in the world can control a robotic device to perform the surgery.	Positive		
Step-by-step mobile applications for assessing and treating accidents that a lay person could use.	Negative		

One positive and negative point has been given. Complete the table giving the impacts and the consequences of the point, clearly stating why you think the point is a positive or a negative development.

Leisure

Developments in the leisure area might include the use of virtual reality to go on 'holiday'. They could include: advances in games machines; in cinematography (for example, as used in Avatar); in theme park rides (design and control); in mobile technology; or in sound and music devices.

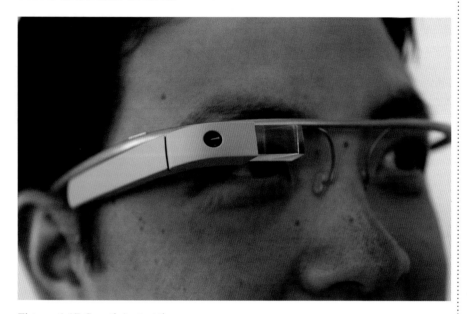

Figure 6.13 Google's goggles

Environment

Developments affecting the environment might include the use of technology: to reduce vehicle emissions; to reduce emissions released in energy generation; to reduce energy consumption (in manufacturing, business and domestically, and by vehicles – e.g. to manage deliveries to plot the best route to minimise fuel consumption); to monitor the weather and the ability to use this to forecast future weather (including the use of satellites) etc.

Activities

Complete the advantages and disadvantages of the following possible future environmental developments.

Development	Advantage	Disadvantage
Models and predictions on climate and rainfall to make suggestions for crops to plant.		
Use of technology to change the weather (e.g. to make rain or remove rain as required).		

Home

Many areas in the home might be affected by ICT developments. Devices (such as fridges, cookers, lawn mowers and vacuum cleaners) and the infrastructure of a house (e.g. electricity, water, heating and security systems) might be further updated by technology. The future use of biometrics to authenticate users and computer control are two other areas for possible discussion.

Activities

Complete the advantages and disadvantages of the following possible future development in the home.

Development	Advantage	Disadvantage
Personalised TV goggles (each person wears goggles that gives them their own TV channel).		
Holographic telephones (3D video phones).		

Education

ICT in education currently involves the use of online tutoring and testing, and, in the classroom, the use of mobile devices, teleconferencing and associated software. It can involve online marking and submissions, software to see if you have plagiarised (copied) from the web, and the provision of materials (books, 3D modelling and sound/video and different methods of utilising it, for example electronic readers).

Freedom of speech and movement

Freedom of movement includes the tracking of individuals using CCTV or implanted chips. It could be the use of data and technology (such as iPhones) to monitor the location of convicted criminals. It is possible to track individuals and bring together information on their movement by gathering data on their purchases, passports and photo records.

There are privacy issues centred on how personal data is collected and is used – 'If I am not doing anything wrong, why is data being collected about me?' or 'If I am not doing anything wrong, why should I care what data about me is being collected?'

Activities

Here is an essay. Read it and decide how many marks out of 11 you would give. Justify your marks and make suggestions for improvements.

Discuss hardware and software developments that allow an individual's movements to be tracked.

Phones can have their locators switched on and this can be tracked and the position of the phone sent to the internet where it can be seen. This means that the phone needs to have enough power to broadcast its position and there needs to be enough signal strength to send its position to the internet. There is also the frequency of the update to consider: if the position is only updated every half an hour, someone travelling could be over 30 miles away from the last known point.

If you are on the other end, you need a device that can connect to the internet and have an internet connection. You can become obsessed looking at the screen waiting for the next track to come in. The track will tell you where the phone is. It does not tell you who has the phone – it may have been stolen – or if the person is in trouble. A parent would want more than just a track.

Future developments can include a button that can be pressed and send an emergency signal – this can go to parents and, based on the location, the nearest police car. There could also be a facility on the phone to allow the camera to be used and the microphone to broadcast images and sound. If you are walking home at night, then your parents can see what you are seeing and keep you company.

Chapter summary

Impact of external change on

An organisation
- individuals
- systems in use

Change management

Staff capability
Staff views
Systems
Equipment
Accommodation
Important to consider when managing change:
- consultation
- participation
- communication

Ethics and ICT

Principle of work
Code of conduct
- ACM
- BCS

Keeping data confidential

To comply with the Data Protection Act (1998)
Competition
Achieved by:
- preventing access to the data
- encrypting the data

Protecting data

Encryption
Authorisation
Authentication
Virus checking
Virus protection
Physical security

> **Future developments of ICT**
> Treating injuries or disease
> Leisure activities
> Environment
> Home
> Education
> Freedom of speech and movement

Chapter tests

Test 1

A company runs an online dating website and is expanding, and introducing new systems.

1 Describe how staff capability should be taken into account when managing the change. [4]

2 Explain the importance of participation when managing the change to the new system. [4]

3 Describe **two** ICT ethical issues that the employees might be confronted with when working for the company. [4]

4 Describe **three** statements that the company could have in its code of conduct. [6]

5 Explain why the company needs a code of conduct. [4]

6 Explain why the company needs to keep its data secure. [4]

7 Describe **two** logical security methods the company could employ to keep its data secure. [4]

8 Discuss future hardware and software developments that may change the way people date. [11]

Test 2

A local successful bed and breakfast business has bought the property next door and is opening a restaurant.

1 Describe **two** external changes which could occur that would have an impact on the new restaurant. [4]

2 Describe how staff views on accommodation should be taken into account when managing the change. [8]

3 Describe **three** different methods of communication the business could use with its staff when managing change. [6]

4 The business has written a code of conduct for ICT use. Describe two reasons why a code of conduct is required. [4]

5 Explain, using examples, how encryption can be used to keep the business data secure. [4]

6 Explain the difference between physical and logical security. [4]

7 Discuss future hardware and software developments that may change the way people dine out. [11]

7 | Introduction to the project

The project is based on the systems life cycle. You need to, in conjunction with a third-party user, choose a well-defined client-driven problem that enables you to demonstrate your skills to:

- analyse a problem
- design a solution to the problem
- develop the software solution
- test the solution against the requirements specification
- document the solution
- evaluate the solution.

What makes a suitable project is a key question to consider before starting the project. If you make the wrong choice of project, you could waste weeks of work by having to start again. In the very worst case scenarios, it might not be possible to do anything about it and as a result your grades will suffer.

The project is worth 20% of your final grade (40% of the A2 grade) and it is vital to get the choice correct from the very beginning. The project should take approximately 80 hours to complete – this is the recommendation from the examination board and you should try to stick to this amount of time.

Some points to consider in the selection of appropriate projects are given below and should be looked at and read before beginning the project.

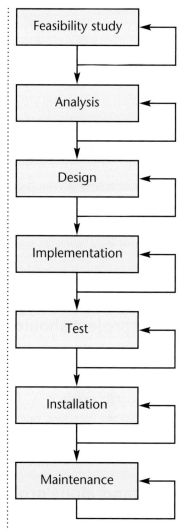

Figure 7.1 Systems life cycle with recursion

1 The project should fit the specification

This is a general statement but important. The project should be able to meet all the requirements of the specification and be of sufficient complexity to allow the top marks to be reached. If you read the marking scheme for the specification, it is possible to achieve all the required elements with a relatively simple project. It is because of this that the problem itself must have a certain degree of complexity – it must be of A-level standard.

2 How complex must the solution be?

This is a difficult question. The specification does not give specific information on complexity. The project must be logically correct – the flow from 'analysis' to 'design', to 'creation', to 'documentation' and to 'evaluation' must be correct. Each section is based on the previous and it must reference and follow it – you cannot add something in 'creation' that has not been designed and appeared in the analysis.

The complexity of the project is based, to a degree on the analysis, however the solution developed must be a level of complexity greater than a simple linear-type solution. This means that a simple singular problem with one output is not sufficient to gain full marks.

- In a database, a single table, form, query and report is a linear solution.
- In a spreadsheet, data entry, formulae and functions based on a single output is a linear solution.
- In websites, a purely content-driven information website, even if hierarchical in nature, is a linear solution.

To get into the higher band, your project will need to be:

- a database which uses the data from the tables to create multiple different queries and reports
- a spreadsheet which can use functions and formulae to provide different outputs on different sheets
- a website that takes data from the user and can store and use it in some way, such as sending documents, log-on areas etc.

The complexity should be there from the beginning and included in the analysis. It should not be 'bolted on' when you get to development.

3 The project should enable the student to achieve all areas of the marking criteria

In the evaluation section, there are marks available for 'a range of possible extensions'. If your project is a complete unit with no extensions, you will not be able to achieve marks in this area. Therefore, you must make sure that when you are stating the problem you do not solve all of it, but leave room for extension at a later date.

4 A stand-alone problem or a redevelopment of an existing solution?

Projects do not need not be stand-alone; the enhancement or modification of an existing system provided that all these elements are covered is acceptable. They are more likely to be a real-world situation. Unfortunately projects of the type 'a shop has a paper-based system that it wants to computerise' are unlikely to exist nowadays. It is still perfectly acceptable, if you can find one, to computerise a manual system. It may be, however, that the system has a computer system and you are updating a part of it.

5 A suitable problem with end-user interaction

The project work ideally requires user interaction, that is there should be a 'real' problem to solve and people to help you. It is recognised that it is not always possible for you to solve a real problem, but you should try and get 'real' people to help you. 'Real' people refers to people who actually work in the area where your problem lies. The people need to be prepared to help you with questionnaires, interviews and testing of the final solution.

You need to involve a client and/or third-party user, who may be different people. The people will need to provide information for the analysis, use the solution and contribute towards its evaluation.

A teacher could act as the third party, but this arrangement is far from ideal and if you can find a person who is involved with the organisation that has the problem you will produce a better solution. Ideally, you should try and look for projects beyond school life and into business and organisations in your community.

It is a good idea to inform the individual of the level of involvement that you will require from them. They should be willing and able to assist:

- in the analysis of the problem (where their requirements are obtained) – this will include an interview
- at the design stage to comment on the designs that you produce
- at the software development, testing and installation stages (where they may be involved in prototyping)
- at the evaluation stage (where they are involved in checking that the system is completed as specified).

Leading on from these, they should be willing to critically comment on the system.

6 The project should demonstrate the complete systems life cycle

You need to show the successful completion of a whole task from its initial definition involving a third-party user, to its acceptance and evaluation by that third party and other possible users. This starts with the definition of the problem, through to designing, creating, testing, documenting and evaluating the solution that has been created.

7 Work within the limits of the available hardware, software and personal skills

You may have an excellent problem and brilliant design, but unfortunately find that you do not have either the hardware or the software to implement it. It is a balancing act to make sure that the solution does what you want within the resources available.

The solution may be implemented using one or more of:

- a standard generic applications software package
- prewritten modules
- toolkits/authoring/publishing software, interface/client software (including HTML/Java).

You need to ensure that you have the skills to use the packages to create the solution. You do not want to have to learn how to use new software as you will not have the time.

8 An organisation or a person?

The size of the organisation is always a question that arises. You can create a project that gets full marks even if there is only one person. The size of the organisation is not important – it can be a multinational company or just one person. What is important is that you differentiate between the end user and the person in charge. Even if there is only one person in the organisation, they may have to 'put on different hats' to help you with different parts of the project – some parts require an end-user response, some require a 'management' contribution. Even if this is the same person, there will be no problems as long as you make this distinction.

9 Evidence to submit

You need to submit a report on what you have done. This report is the evidence that is sent to the moderator, so if any evidence is not included in the report, it cannot be marked.

The project report should contain:

- a title
- a contents list
- page numbers.

The report should be spellchecked and appropriately formatted. There are three marks available for the presentation of the final report. You must have created the report yourself. If you use a report template supplied to you by a third party you will not be able to gain these marks and effectively your project will be marked out of 77.

You should not submit magnetic or optical media as supporting evidence, but you can make references to web pages available over the internet or to photographs where appropriate. Ideally, all evidence will be submitted on paper and it will follow the sequence laid out in the following chapters. You want the moderator to be able to sit down and read the report sequentially (rather than to have to flip backwards and forwards through it) confirming the marks.

10 Final points to consider

Interest

You will be working on this project for a considerable period of time. It must be something that will hold your interest for that length of time. If you become bored with it after three months and still have another five months to go, it may affect the quality of the work you produce.

Teacher supervision

At all times, the teacher must be convinced that the work you are producing is your own work and nobody else's. This can be a problem if you do the majority of work at home. It is essential that throughout the project each component is monitored by the teacher.

Teacher expertise

Although your teachers will have many skills, they will not be an expert in every piece of software written and every problem. You must be aware that if you require assistance and support, but have chosen software in which your teachers are not experts, then you will need to find it from elsewhere. This may affect how well your teachers are able to supervise the project, so choose carefully and weigh up the advantages/disadvantages of using specialist software.

Reference to real data

You must be careful not to enter real data into your system. For example, if you are entering names and addresses, one way around this is to pick a name from an address book, a different address and a different telephone number. This way the data entered will not relate directly to a 'living identifiable human being' and contravene any of the principles of the Data Protection Act.

Programming and customisation

A common question is 'how much programming must I do in the project?' The answer, unfortunately, varies. It will depend on the project. It may be none or it may be a fair amount. You are more likely to customise an existing software package.

The course is ICT, it is not computing, so the examiner is not expecting a custom-written solution in a programming language. They will be expecting you to take an existing package (spreadsheet, word processor, database etc.) and tailor it to your solution. This may involve creating menus, toolbars, macros and *some* programming.

Types of problem

There are many different types of problem that you could choose, but in general, they can be divided into four categories:

Database

This involves accessing a database, and sorting and searching data. You will be required to print reports and maybe mail merge a document.

Examples of database-type projects include:

- a video shop – for storing data on customers, on videos, and on hiring and reservation of videos
- a hotel – for booking rooms in a hotel and calculating the bill
- an employment agency – for matching job vacancies to people.

Data analysis/mathematics

This involves collecting data and then analysing it by producing graphs or tables of data. It may involve calculations of some kind.

- Data collection and analysis – collecting data via questionnaires and analysing it.
- Booking a holiday – holiday data entry and calculation.
- Budgets – working out a budget for an organisation.

Measuring/control

This involves monitoring or measuring using some form of control equipment. It may be a mock up of a real situation.

- Traffic control – setting up a sample of a traffic light sequence, questionnaires to see what to implement, analysing data and informing people of the new lights.
- Burglar alarm system – setting up a mock system, user instructions etc.

Internet/web-based

This involves the use of the internet in some way:

- e-commerce – selling goods over the internet
- setting up access to a database over the internet
- chatrooms and discussion boards.

These are only a few examples and are not complete. You would need to develop the project and complete all the sections to score marks.

You are better off choosing a topic where you will be able to complete all sections of the documentation with a database or spreadsheet that is fairly simple than having a very complicated database or spreadsheet and not being able to completely document it.

Log of events

You are required to keep a log of events for your project. This is a diary of when you worked on the project and what you did. This log is important because without it the number of marks you can get in the final section is limited.

It is an ongoing account of the project. It can be handwritten or typed on the computer. It should be logically correct – this means that the dates on letters in the project and the project plan should correspond with the log of events.

Two main questions asked about the log are:

- How long does each entry need to be? – It does not need to be an essay for each day, a few sentences about what you did that day.
- Do I need to write an entry every day? – No you do not. You only need to fill in the log if you do some work on your project.

  An outline for the log might be as shown in Figure 7.2.

Make sure you get into the habit of filling in the log after working on the project.

Date	Activity
4/9/09	Completed background to the problem
7/9/09	Wrote questions for interview
8/9/09	Planned date for interview

Figure 7.2 An example project log

8 Definition, investigation and analysis

Introduction

There are a total of 23 marks available for this section: 2 for the definition of the problem, 12 for the investigation and 9 for the analysis.

As this is the opening section of the project, first impressions are important. This is the part of the project the examiner will read first, so it is important to get it right. If it is vague, waffly, indistinct or incorrect it will set up an unfavourable impression in the mind of the examiner that may be difficult to change later in the project. Imagine opening up a project to find it untidy, with spelling mistakes, and different font types and font sizes all over the page. What would your initial impression be? Perhaps it is not fair that impressions contribute to the mark, but they do. It is in your best interests to follow the guidelines to gain the highest mark you can.

The amount of work involved in this first section is disproportionate to the number of marks available. However, much of the work done here will be re-used in the design and evaluation sections. From your point of view, this section is very important – it will let you clarify, in your mind, what the problem is and what you will be developing as the solution. You will not be able to produce a good project unless you are clear about what the problem is and what your solution is going to be prior to attempting the design.

Overview

The section can be broken down into six stages.

1 **Problem definition and organisation:** A new computer system must have a purpose. There will be a problem, or perhaps several problems, that the system you create will be required to solve. You must first define the problem, so that you can select a system that will solve it. You must also outline the organisation that has the problem.

2 **The gathering and analysis of data about the existing system:** This involves you in detailed fact finding and identification of why the problems with the existing system have arisen.

3 **The gathering and analysis of data about the new system:** This involves you in detailed fact finding and identification of what the new system is to do.

4 **Establishing objectives for the new system:** Once you have defined the existing problem, and gathered data about the existing and new situation, the next step is for you to decide what the new system will be designed to achieve.

5 **Analysing alternative systems:** There will always be several different ways of designing a system to meet the stated objectives. You need to think of, analyse and evaluate several different options. The alternative systems need not necessarily be computer systems.

6 **Hardware and software selection:** Having selected the system that best meets the system objectives, you need to compile a reasoned list of the hardware and software required.

There should be a continuous process of re-examining and re-assessment of each stage of the system selection process, until the preferred system is eventually selected. In other words, you should be continually asking:

- Have I properly defined the problem?
- Have I correctly gathered and analysed all the relevant data about the current system?
- Have I collected information on what the client/end user wants for the new system?
- Have I created a detailed requirement specification for the new system?
- Have I satisfactorily defined the objectives for the new system?
- Have I identified and properly evaluated all the available system alternatives?

You should not be asking these questions in isolation, but in conjunction with the end user – the project should be a partnership. It is the end user – the client – who makes the decisions based on recommendations from you.

Everything you do must be documented. This includes interviews, questionnaires, subsequent analysis of the data collection and conclusions reached. If you make mistakes and the re-examining process brings these to light, it is very tempting to change the project to make it seem that you got it right in the first place. Don't do this, document the process and show what has changed. You will not lose marks for getting it wrong, as long as you show why and what you have done to correct it.

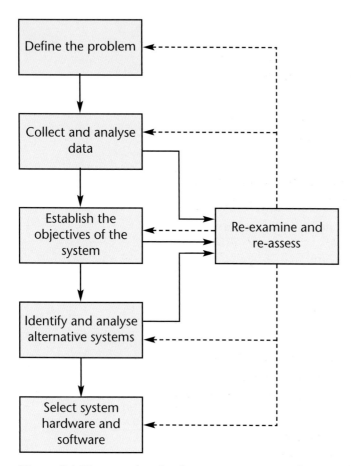

Figure 8.1 Diagram showing how re-examination fits into the life cycle

Definition – The nature of the problem to be investigated (2 marks)

There are many different problems and many situations and circumstances from which you can select your project. The examiner will not be familiar with all of them. This introductory section is your opportunity to make the examiner familiar with the particular scenario on which your own project is based.

You should begin with an introduction to the organisation. The level of detail required is not great, as long as you give enough information for the examiner to understand the outline of the scenario into which your project will fit.

Having obtained the answers you require you need to write it up in an easily understood way.

Marking

1 mark   A brief description of the organisation or group that has the problem and an introduction to the client and/or the end user(s) and their place within the organisation or group.

1 mark   An outline of the problem that needs to be solved.

Example

Sample questions that you might choose to ask in order to complete the section might include:

- What is the name of the organisation?
- What does it do?
- Where is it located?
- How many people does it employ?
- How many shops/offices are there?
- What are the names and positions held of people who are going to be involved with the project?
- What is the problem that they have?

Investigation (12 marks)

This section is about collecting information on the existing system (that is the system that is in place at the moment). There are two main types of project:

- Those that put a new system into place – this may be a complete new system or adding new functionality to an existing system.
- Those that use ICT to replicate a manual system.

Both types of project need to have information on the existing system in order to be successful in their use – that is 'how does the existing system function?'

You need to plan the mechanics of the collection of information, decide on the questions to ask, carry out the collection and record the findings.

Investigation into the existing system to find more information about the problem

In the previous section you gave a very basic outline of the company and the problem. It is necessary to do some more research and find out some detailed information about the system as it currently stands and the problem.

You will do this by investigating the existing system, so you will need to find out the facts ('fact finding') and then record them ('fact recording').

Fact finding and recording

Methods of fact finding include using questionnaires and interviewing to find personal knowledge of the situation, observing the current system, and reading existing documentation and manuals. You may need to use more than one method in order to find out what you want. The main method will be an interview.

Interview

There are four components to the collection of information by an interview:

- planning the interview
- planning the questions
- conducting and recording the interview
- post-interview analysis.

Planning the interview

You need to plan the interview before conducting it. This involves thinking about who you are interviewing, and where and when the interview will take place.

You need to set up an interview – you cannot just turn up and interview people. There should be a set of letters or emails between you and the person you are interviewing setting the time, the date and the venue. As mentioned above, it is good practice to include a copy of the questions you are going to ask so the interviewees can make sure they have all the relevant information to hand.

OCR Systems
Birmingham
B7 4DR

22nd June 2012

Dear Mr Jenkins,

Further to our telephone discussion last week I am writing to you to arrange an interview to look in detail at the system that you currently have in place. If you could get back to me with times when you are available next week I can see when I am free and arrange to meet up.

Yours sincerely,

A Student

Figure 8.2 An example letter to arrange an interview

Planning the questions

Before conducting an interview, you need to plan a set of prepared questions, and have one or two follow-up questions for each that you may or may not ask depending on the interviewee's initial answers.

It is good practice to let the interviewee see the questions before the interview.

The questions you ask need to give you more information about what happens now, such as the inputs, the processes, the outputs and the storage in the current system. You may also ask questions about the personnel.

When planning the questions, think about the 'flow' through the system. For example, for a stock control system:

- How is the stock level updated?
- When is the stock level updated?
- How do you know when stock needs to be reordered?
- How do you know that stock has been reordered?
- How is the order to suppliers generated?
- What happens when an order from a supplier arrives?
- How many stock items do you have?
- How many different suppliers do you have?

This is not an exhaustive list of questions. Several of these questions might have follow-up questions.

To get high marks for this section you need to have included some reasoning – why you have asked this question? There also needs to be some follow-up questions. You do not need to include these for every question, just for some. For example:

- Do you have any security on the system?
  - Ask whether different areas are read-only or read/write.
  - Ask what type of security – guards, locked room, passwords?
    - If passwords – does everyone have the same or do you use usernames and passwords?

Conducting and recording the interview

You need a record of the interview as evidence that it has taken place. This can be in the form of a typed transcript. It should match the details you gave in the planning stage but some of the questions might be different. There should be a clear differentiation between question and answer. There needs to be a record that both the interviewee and the interviewer agree with the contents of the interview – this usually involves both people signing the transcript.

Name of Interviewee:	Mr Jenkins		Position in Company:	Manager
Date of Interview:	28/6/2009		Location of Interview:	Manager's Office
Purpose of Interview:	To gain a clearer understanding of the current system for stock ordering			
1 What is your role within the company?				
I am in charge of looking after the customers				

Figure 8.3 Record of interview with informative headings

Post-interview analysis

After the interview you need to analyse the responses and extract the important points.

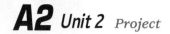

Following the analysis you may be aware that you have not got all the information you need. If this is the case you will need to conduct additional interviews repeating the four steps above.

The post-interview analysis should not rewrite the interview but needs to draw conclusions about the problems that need solving. This may include a repetition of the initial problem to be solved or it may be a sub-set of that problem. It needs to be presented to the client and agreed by them.

So far, the focus has been on what happens now and what are the problems with the existing system. There is an implicit assumption that the new system that you are going to create will resolve the problems. This assumption needs to be made explicit. In the next section you are going to develop requirements for the new system. In order to do this, you need to know what the client wants the new system to do. This means collecting information about the new system.

This collection may be by interview, questionnaire or other appropriate method. The method used to collect the information must be justified. The focus must be the new system – what the client wants the new system to do. The information collected needs to be recorded so that it can be used in the next section.

Marking

2 marks   For the existing system, a thorough planning of the mechanics of the interview situation.

3 marks   Reasoned set of questions to elicit important information (possible responses have been considered and follow-up questions have been planned).

1 mark   Record of key responses of interview(s).

3 marks   Evidence of analysis of the current system or of likely problem areas, arriving at reasoned conclusions that will show evidence of being agreed by client.

2 marks   Information collected about the requirements of the new system.

1 mark   Clear presentation of the information collected about the new system.

Analysis (9 marks)

You should now know what the problem is and what they want the new system to achieve. It is now time to begin to develop the solution. There are three parts to the solution:

- the requirements specification, that is the requirements of the solution
- possible approaches to solving the problem
- the justified approach you are going to use to solve the problem and what software and hardware are involved.

Requirements specification

The end result of the investigation is an understanding of what the finished system must be able to do. These will form the requirements.

The requirements must describe the external behaviour of the system. You need to write it in terms understandable to the end user. The requirements should not contain too much information but describe what the system should do.

The requirements specification lists features of the system without saying how they are to be implemented.

If you are given any limitations or constraints, then you must include them as part of the requirements. For example, if you are told that it must be a menu-driven system, then one of the requirements is that it must be a menu-driven system.

It is essential that the requirements are detailed and get to the very core of the system. There may be several user requests that are ill-defined and difficult to clarify (e.g. the interface needs to be 'user friendly' or 'easy to navigate', or the design needs to include 'warm colours' or 'documentation' etc.). It is not useful to list these as part of the requirements specification without adding more detail. For example, you might replace 'easy to navigate' with 'no option is more than three mouse clicks away', or you might redefine 'user friendly' as 'appropriate error messages', 'readable user guides', 'screen tips on icons', 'accessible online help' etc.

A requirement to store data is too vague. This should be rewritten to:

A requirement to store the following data on customers:

> Forename
> Surname
> Address
> Telephone Number
> Email

You must revisit the data collection section to check that is possible for the examiner to link each of the requirements listed to the conclusions you have drawn from the data collection, and to backtrack to the data itself. It may be necessary to redo this section several times, each time revisiting the system to find more evidence. This is acceptable as long as it is documented. Do not fall to the temptation of making it seem as though you got it right the first time. You will get more credit if you show your mistakes and how you have corrected them.

How many requirements should there be? This is a totally open question. Some projects might have four or five detailed requirements, other projects may have 10–15 less-detailed requirements.

Example

For example, when describing an e-commerce site, the following requirements may apply (not complete):

- Allow the user to log on using a password.
- Allow the user the opportunity to change their password.
- Be able to add and remove items from the shopping basket.
- Be able to change user details.

It is vital that all the requirements are achievable because they will be used in the evaluation section of the project.

Once you have listed the requirements, you need to get them agreed (e.g. with a signed statement) by the organisation.

Here is an outline requirement specification agreement with some examples. The text in italics should be replaced with appropriate text.

Requirement Specification Agreement

• To be able to find all members with overdue books.

• To print a list of overdue members.

• To order books using email.

I *name*, of *organisation*, have discussed the requirements and I am in agreement that a system that delivers these will fulfil our requirements.

Signed:

Name (printed)

Position

Figure 8.4 Example agreement of requirements specification

Approach to be used

Several alternative designs should be considered and compared. You should look at each from the point of view of:

• its feasibility (i.e. how it will operate and how it will succeed in achieving the system's objectives)

• its expected costs and benefits.

Any alternative system you look at must be compared with the requirements specification.

You **must** compare at least three solutions. One can be the current solution and at least two others, or they can be three completely new ones.

The alternative approaches that you look at must be possible solutions. For example, if you are looking at a solution that requires data handling, it is not appropriate to look at the use of a word processor. You may be able to match it against the cost, training and other requirements but it is not a valid solution in the first place. Make sure that all the alternative solutions that you are looking at could be used to solve the problem and deliver the requirements.

There may be constraints put upon the solution by the organisation (e.g. the solution must be developed in a specific package). If this is the case, the alternative approached will be primarily based on differences in data structures (e.g. relational versus flat file, file sizes etc.), and you need to take these into account.

Even if there is a limitation, this does not stop you from discussing alternative solutions. The discussion can still take place, it is only the conclusion that is affected.

System justification

You should not recommend a new system unless you can justify it. Criteria for basing your justification are an evaluation of:

- the costs and benefits of the proposed system
- other performance criteria
- whether the system meets the requirements specification.

The costs of the proposed system

In making a recommendation for a particular approach, you need to make a full study of the economics of the proposed system(s). This is unlikely to be possible for you, but some attempt at financial justification should be made.

The costs of a new system may include:

- equipment costs (capital costs, leasing costs etc.)
- installation costs
- development costs
- personnel costs
- operating costs.

The benefits of a proposed system

You must also evaluate the benefits of a proposed new system. As with financial costs, this may be difficult for you to do, but some effort should be made. Benefits of a proposed approach can include:

- savings, because the old system will no longer be operated
- extra savings or revenue benefits, because of the improvements or enhancements that the new system should bring
- possibly, some one-off revenue benefits from the sale of equipment that the existing system uses, but which will no longer be required. Second-hand computer equipment does not have a high value but it does have some. It is also possible that the new system will use less office space (filing), and so there will be benefits from selling or renting the spare accommodation.

Some benefits might be intangible or impossible to give a monetary value to. These might include:

- greater customer satisfaction, arising from a more prompt service (e.g. because of a computerised sales and delivery service)
- improved staff morale from working with a better system.

Once you have a general analysis of the potential approaches to the problem, you can evaluate them against the requirements specification in the form of a grid.

Alternative approaches listed across the top

Requirements can be listed down the side

	Database	Spreadsheet	Paper system
To perform complex searches	Yes, both static and dynamic, can be given a forms interface	Yes, both static and dynamic, can be given a forms interface	Yes but very time consuming and difficult to guarantee results
To integrate with the Web	Yes – with ActiveX	Yes – with ActiveX	No automatic integration

Figure 8.5 Grid for alternative approaches

The approaches to be used are not names of specific packages but applications. The move from application to specific software is made in the next section.

You need to select a final solution giving reasons for the choice. Having assembled the evidence, you need to discuss your chosen solution with the client – this needs to be recorded. The end of this discussion should be an agreement to move forward with the selected approach.

Hardware and software choice

Once the solution has been agreed, you can specify the hardware and software required. This should be a justified selection, and not simply a list. The hardware and software specified should be all the items required for a full installation of the solution, even if you are not personally implementing all of the end product (e.g. a network installation of 20 PCs in an office where there are currently no computers will require 20 PCs, cabling, a server etc. and you are unlikely to implement this fully, however you do need to specify the complete requirement).

The software list must include the operating system, and if the internet is to be used, then you must state the additional software required (such as an email package, protocol etc.). You need to state the network software required if a network is being used as part of the end product.

The hardware list must also be fairly detailed. Make sure that you have covered the input, processing and output requirements.

For input, you may need items such as a keyboard and a mouse, a scanner and an optical mark reader. If the system receives data via a network or the internet, then you will need a network card/router and appropriate software. Do not forget to specify what sort of disk is needed for input (e.g. DVD, CD) and what type of monitor.

Output requirements may cover many of the same items as input (e.g. disk type, internet connection, network connection, printer type).

Processing requirements can include what is inside the machine (e.g. RAM, hard disk drive, processor).

You must justify all the hardware and software you specify. Here is a sample layout.

Example

Software/hardware	Justification
Microsoft Windows 7	Operating system required to run Microsoft Access 2010 with minimal problems
Microsoft Access 2010	Software selected to develop the system and required by the end user
Microsoft Internet Explorer 9	Internet browser required to run web elements of product
TCP/IP	Internet protocol required to connect to the internet
17-inch monitor	Required to see the data that is being entered into the system
Keyboard	For manually entering data
Mouse	To move the cursor around the screen in the WIMP interface that has been developed and for the client to select items from the drop-down list in the customer form
Router	To connect the computer to the internet so that web access can take place
1 GB RAM	Required for running Microsoft Windows 7, Microsoft Access 2010 and Microsoft Internet Explorer 9 at the same time
500 MHz processor	Required for running Microsoft Windows 7, Microsoft Access 2010 and Microsoft Internet Explorer 9 at the same time
Black and white laser printer	For black and white printing of invoices
4.5 GB HDD	Required for storing of software and additional storage space for records
CD writer	For loading software and creating backups

Table 8.1 Table of software and hardware justification

Note that a specification has not been given that cannot be justified. The operating system is the minimum required to run Microsoft Access. The hardware is the minimum required. You may choose to go above the minimum but justification must be given.

Marking

3 marks A requirements specification containing a number of clearly defined objectives that the solution should meet. These must be arrived at through consultation with the client.

3 marks A comparison of a number of different methods of solution, one of which may be the present solution and at least two others to allow a reasoned decision to be made in consultation with the client.

3 marks A reasoned list of hardware and software requirements for the new system, providing clear justification for each choice in relation to the problem to be solved.

9 Design

Introduction

There are a total of 15 marks available for the design: 13 marks for the nature of the solution and 2 marks for the project plan.

Meeting the requirements of the Design section is difficult, particularly since you do not have a very detailed knowledge and understanding of systems analysis. Design is the link between the analysis and software development. It is important to match your stated requirements of the previous section (on definition, investigation and analysis) with the design created in this section, and with the results of the next section (on software development). In other words, what you say you are going to create in the requirements section is covered by the design in this section and created in the next. It is very tempting to get carried away with the design and create masterpieces of screen design, but if the reality of software development does not match the design you will lose marks. Keep the design functional and as simple as possible.

Overview

The section can be broken down into two stages. The first is the most important.

1. **The nature of the solution:** This is where you create the designs of the input, output and processing, and files required to implement the requirements. You will also design a test plan to be used in the next section.

2. **Project plan:** This will require a breakdown of the tasks and a time plan.

You will draw many diagrams as you undertake this section and it is very easy to get page numbers mixed up and out of order. You can draw diagrams by hand and there is no reason why you cannot add blank pages to the project and, once printed, draw in your designs. This will keep the correct page number order that is vital to the marking of the project.

Nature of the solution

This is where you create all the designs that will be used to develop the solution. The overall aim is that you should be able to pass all the design diagrams to a third party and they should be able to create the required solution. The test plan should be able to be passed to a third party, who, once the solution has been developed, can test it to see if it works.

You should actively involve the end user in the design process.

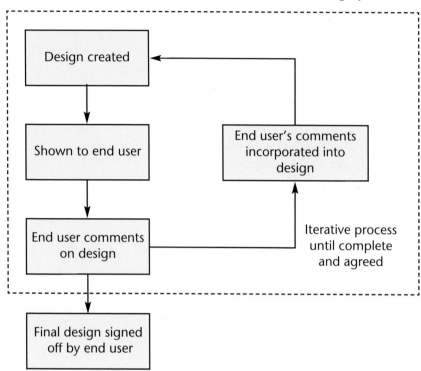

Figure 9.1 The design process

Design specification

The design specification is a document that shows how each of the elements in the requirements specification can be created and included in the end product. The design specification shows how the data gets into the system, what happens to it, where it is stored and in what format, the processing, the output and the user interface, as well as back-up procedures and any connections to other programs.

You will be required to draw up input documents, data entry screens, output documents and the user interface. There are three ways you can design the screens and documents:

- on paper (hand drawn)
- in the package in which you intend to create the final product (e.g. Microsoft Access, Microsoft Excel, Microsoft Word, Corel Paradox)
- in a package that will not be used to create the final product (e.g. by using Adobe Photoshop to mock up the screens).

Which method should you use?

The choice is yours. You will not be marked down whichever one you choose. However, the second option is the one to be wary of – designing in the package in which you will create the final product – because it is very easy to create the product and then print out a created, working form and claim that it is a design. The examiner must be sure that you have not done this. The easiest way to prevent any doubts is to choose one of the other options.

What to include in a design?

Any design needs to be annotated – you should not submit any design that has not been annotated. All final versions of designs **must** be signed off by the end user.

The following elements may or may not appear in your design. It may not be appropriate for your particular project to have all of the elements – choose the ones that fit your project.

The design specification comprises the following elements:

- input
- processing
- output
- user interface
- files and data structures
- error messages
- house style.

Exactly what goes into your design will depend on the solution you are creating – a website, spreadsheet, game, database; all will have different elements to each other.

Input

The input section can be broken down into two sections:

- **Input documents:** These are the documents that will be filled in as part of the manual system. They are paper-based documents: the data capture forms. The data collected on the forms will be entered into the computer system. There needs to be some correlation between the data capture forms and the forms on the computer where the user will enter the data. Look at all the data entry points going into the system, as identified in the data flow diagram, and if they are paper based, then there needs to be a data capture form.

- **Input interface:** This is the computer screen that will be used to enter the paper-based documents identified above. You will have one computer input form for every data capture form.

    If the form automatically looks up data (e.g. you enter a postcode and the system automatically returns the street name, town and county), then this must be detailed. If any data is calculated (e.g. you enter a hotel room number and a number of nights and the system calculates the price), then this must be documented.

    Where appropriate you need to specify any screen tips or associated help.

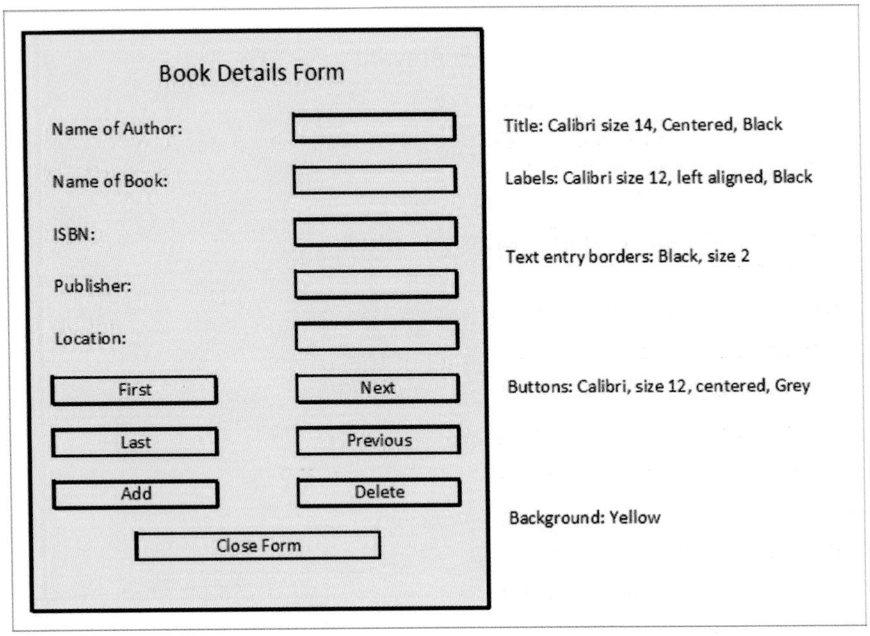

Figure 9.2 Sample design of a form

You must have considered how the data is to be collected and prepared for data entry: how the paper-based data that is received is to be sorted or changed to be suitable for data entry.

- Are there any coding procedures that need to take place?
- Does it need to be sorted by customer number?
- Does it need to be matched with any other documentation (e.g. matching a dispatch note from the company to the order placed by the end user)?

Forms can be included in web-based, database and spreadsheet projects.

It is not anticipated that you will get the designs correct first time. Do not throw away any initial designs – the moderator will want to see the progression of the design. There may be user comments written on early versions of the forms: these will indicate that the end user is involved in the process.

Processing

The processing section must detail what happens at each stage. It can be written in text form, pseudocode or any other appropriate method. You must list:

- the action that begins the processing
- each action that occurs during the processing, indicating what data and files are being used
- what happens to the data, that is, where it is saved to (variable, file, table etc.).

The processing is a logical list of what happens. Where necessary it must include queries (if in a database), formulae (if in a spreadsheet) etc.

Example

Processing example

This is an example is of the processing requirements of the hire component of a library system.

```
Enter code number of book to hire.
Look up code number of book to hire in book table and
return book details to form.
        If book does not exist, give error message.
Look up customer number in customer form and return
details to form.
Look up customer number in outstanding fines.
        If there is a fine give the customer a chance to pay.
                If they pay, flag fine as paid and continue.
                If they do not pay, end transaction.
        If customer does not exist, give error message.
Automatically enter the date (today).
Automatically enter the date+3 as the date of return.
Add a record to the hire table that includes customer
number, book number, date of hire and date due back.
Flag the book record in the book file as being hired.
```

This can be completed as a diagram if necessary.

Where appropriate, you should specify the security procedures (e.g. what security is in place, how it is applied and on what areas it works). Each 'object name' is a table, a form, a query, a report etc. The 'access rights' are full, read only, write, edit and delete. The 'user' is the name of a user or a group who have the specified rights to the object.

Example

Object name	Access rights	User
Members Form	Read Only	Mrs Jones, Mrs Adams, Mrs Lee
Members Form	Read, Edit	Daily Managers
Members Form	Full	Administrator

Table 9.1 Security form

You must also include a backup and a restore procedure for the files used.

Output

The output section is similar to the input section. There are three types: the output that appears on the screen, output documents (printed output) and other output such as email, files etc. You need to design and annotate each type (as you did with the input).

User interface

The user interface is what the user will see and it must remain consistent throughout the project. This section requires a specification of the general rules that you will apply to the user interface (e.g. the colours used, what buttons appear on all screens, menus and general layout of the screen). Remember to include items such as menus that do not appear under the input or output sections.

You must design and annotate the user interface in a similar way as for other designs.

Files and data structures

The design specification needs to contain details on all files and data structures that you will be using.

The file specification needs to include:

- the name of the file
- a description of the file's contents and the use of the file
- the location of the file (if known)
- the name of fields contained within the file
  - a description of the contents of fields
  - the data type of field
  - the length of the field
  - an example of contents
  - validation on the field.

The following format can be used.

Example

Format of file details

File name: TbookHire

Location: C:\Program Files\A level project\book.mdb

Purpose: To hold details about a book hire in a library

Field name	Description of contents	Data type	Length	Sample values/ range/set	Type of validation expected
HireID	Primary key	Autonumber	3	45	Auto-generated
MemberID	Who has taken out the video	Number	3	121	Looked up
BookID	What the book is that has been taken out	Number	4	1065	Looked up
Date Out	When the book was taken out	Date	8	15/08/09	Calculated as today

Table 9.2 Format of file table

For data structures, you must specify:

- what the structure is (e.g. record structure, array)
- where it is used (list the names of the procedures, forms etc. where it is used)
- what it is used for (detail what it contains and why).

For a spreadsheet-based project, the data structure is likely to be combined with some of the processing. It will include the functions and formulae used and descriptions of variables (including type).

Example

Name of Item:	☐	*Drop-down list from items worksheet*
Price of Item:	☐	*Looked up using VLOOKUP from items worksheet and Name of Item to return price – formatted currency*
Number Purchased:	☐	*Entered by user – integer value only between 1 and 100*
Total Price:	☐	*Multiplication of Number Purchased by Price of Item – formatted currency*
VAT:	☐	*Multiply Total Price by VAT variable in Variables worksheet – formatted currency*
Total to Pay:	☐	*Add Total Price and VAT – formatted currency*

Figure 9.3 Part of the structure design for a spreadsheet

If appropriate, you must include security features (e.g. what access rights exist on the various files/cells/worksheets).

Error messages

You need to design a basic format for an error message box.
A standard error message box should tell the user what has happened to cause the error and what they need to do to correct it.

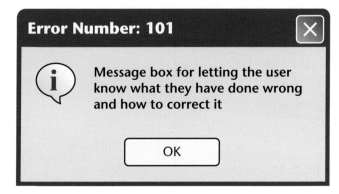

Figure 9.4 Custom error message

The message box should give a unique error number to help trace the error. You need to create a list of the error numbers and what they refer to. The following format is appropriate:

Example

Message ID	Error
101	Incorrect date entered into Hire form
102	No name entered in Customer form
103	No book entered into Add Book form

Table 9.3 Format for error message listing

House style

You need to include the house style – how each element is to be formatted. This can be completed on the design itself or as a separate document. It needs to include all the information required to implement the design exactly as intended.

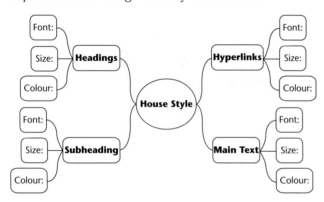

Figure 9.5 House style

System diagrams

You may have already completed several system diagrams that relate to the existing system. In the design phase, you need to draw the diagrams for the new system. The diagrams you may choose to include are:

- data flow diagrams
- entity relationship diagrams
- data structure diagrams.

Not all projects will include all items. The main projects will be:

- data handling (databases)
- calculations (spreadsheets)
- informative (web-based/Flash).

The following table gives examples of the different areas that could be included under each section.

Example

Example	Data handling	Calculation	Informative
Input forms	Forms	Forms or worksheet	Web form, buttons
File structure	Tables	Functions, formulae, variables	Navigation diagram, file locations
Output forms	Forms/Reports	Forms or worksheet	Web pages, display

Table 9.4 Representation of data in a system

All projects are likely to have:
- backup
- security
- error messages
- a test plan.

It is entirely possible for a project to include more than one element (e.g. a web-based project that stores customer information collected from a form in a database or a web project that uses a spreadsheet to return quotation information).

Marking

4 marks Design of data handling, including capture, preparation and storage, to include map and diagrammatic representation of links where relevant.

4 marks Design of inputs, queries/processing and outputs, including error capture reports as appropriate, based clearly on the analysis of the client requirements

Iteration of designs/end-user involvement

The project is about development, from initial problem through requirements to design. It is not about putting a set of final designs in place. The process of getting to the final design needs to be shown.

Iteration is the process of creating a design, showing it to the end user/client, taking their changes on board and redesigning. But, I hear you say, what if I am so good that the first design that I do is perfect and needs no changes? Then give the user some choices – look at two alternative layouts and ask which one they want. These can be rough sketches and then, once they have decided, create a final neat version.

The involvement of the end user needs to be more than a letter to them and a letter back saying 'everything is fine'. There needs to be specific involvement.

The easiest way to do this is to get them to hand write on a set of designs (not all of them) with their suggestions for changes.

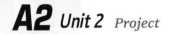

Marking

1 mark Clear evidence of iteration and development of designs in the form of annotated drafts; where relevant this should include feedback from the client and evidence of how these have had an effect on the solution.

Test plan

A test plan is a formal document that lists the tests that will be carried out on the completed system. It should check:

- the requirements
- pathways
- validation routines.

There is no minimum or maximum number of tests that can be carried out. The rule of thumb is whether the solution has been tested against the requirement and the tests will prove that it works.

Example

This test plan layout is an example that could be used.

Test number	Description of test	Type of test	Data used	Expected result

Table 9.5 Example of a test plan layout

Column headings

- **Test number:** a unique identifier for each test.
- **Description of test:** an everyday language description of what you are testing.
- **Type of test:** is the test 'normal', 'extreme' or 'incorrect'?
- **Data used:** the data that will be entered to run the test. It must be specific and, if appropriate, where it will be entered will be indicated. All data used must be given.
- **Expected result:** what you expect to happen when you run the test. For normal tests it should be a positive result; incorrect data should result in an error message.

Test number	Description of test	Type of test	Data used	Expected result
1	To test if correct price of delivery is calculated.	Normal	In E4 enter 3.6	In E7 £7.99
2	To test if the maximum weight allowed for delivery of 10 kg can be exceeded.	Incorrect	In E4 enter 12	Message: The Maximum Weight We Can Accept For Delivery is 10.0.

Table 9.6 Example test plan with sample entries

At this stage, you will not include the results of testing (because you have not yet implemented the system).

Testing against requirements

Take each of your requirements from analysis and write a test that will demonstrate that it has been implemented. It may require more than one test to show this. For example:

Requirement:

> To store details on customers: Forename, Surname, Email Address

Test:

Test number	Description of test	Type of test	Data used	Expected result
1	To test that the system can store details on customers	Normal	Forename: Eleanor Surname: Oliver Email Address: EJO@EJO.net	In data table under field: Forename: Eleanor Surname: Oliver Email Address: EJO@EJO.net

Table 9.7 Requirement tests

The test plan also needs to show normal, extreme and incorrect data.

- **Normal data** is the data that is in everyday usage. It is also known as correct data.
- **Extreme data** is data at the edge of tolerances. This is data at the ends of the ranges specified. For example, if a number is entered with a validation set of between 1 to 20, then extreme data would be 1 or 20.
- **Incorrect data** is data that is wrong. It is also known as erroneous data. This is data that, when entered into the system, should produce an error message and not be accepted by the system.

User testing of the system

There needs to be evidence of the planning of user testing. The user testing must be detailed and needs to cover the following questions (as appropriate):

- Are the buttons in the correct place?
- Are the colours correct?
- Is data entry easy to do?
- Do the help instructions (screen tips and labels) work?
- Are forms presented in the correct order?
- Are the output requirements correct?
- Is the correct data being stored?
- Do drop-down boxes/list boxes/option buttons work correctly?
- Are error messages useful?
- Does the security work?
- Are the user guides easy to follow and use?
- Is the main menu easy to use?

This list is not exhaustive and other questions may be appropriate for different systems.

Marking

4 marks A test plan that will identify a number of tests that will be carried out on completion of the work. All requirements should be tested. The specific test to be carried out should be included in the plan together with the result expected. Some elements of testing should involve the end user(s).

Project plan

The task model is a list of the order in which you will undertake the various tasks. You can complete this using a Gantt chart, timelines, tables or calendars. It should make some reference to the timescale for each task.

The task model needs to show the tasks in order, when you will begin and when they will end. The chart should also show predecessors. Predecessors are events that must be done before another particular task. For example, if creating a form in a database that is based on a table, you must have first created the table.

The task model needs to be detailed. (Do not, however, go into too much detail – you can specify when to create a procedure, but do not go into detail about the procedure.)

The date started and date ended do not have to be totally accurate – at your age and level of skills it is not expected that you will be able to correctly judge time plans.

Task number	Task	Date started	Date ended	Predecessor
1	Create table of library members	12/6/09	13/6/09	
2	Create table of book genres	13/6/09	13/6/09	
3	Create table of books	12/6/09	13/6/09	2
4	Create form of members	13/6/09	14/6/09	1
5	Create form of books	13/6/09	14/6/09	3
6	Create form of genres	13/6/09	14/6/09	2
7	Create main menu	13/6/09	14/6/09	
8	Link forms to main menu	13/6/09	14/6/09	5,6,7

Table 9.8 Sample tasks and how they are related for a time plan

Gantt charts are a graphical method of displaying tasks and dependencies between tasks.

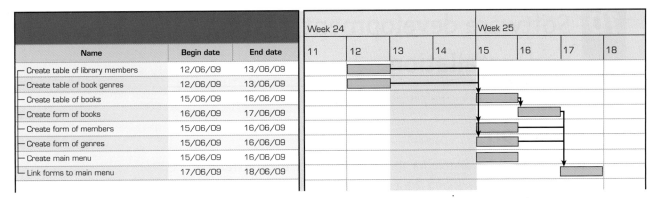

Name	Begin date	End date
⌐ Create table of library members	12/06/09	13/06/09
├ Create table of book genres	12/06/09	13/06/09
├ Create table of books	15/06/09	16/06/09
├ Create form of books	16/06/09	17/06/09
├ Create form of members	15/06/09	16/06/09
├ Create form of genres	15/06/09	16/06/09
├ Create main menu	15/06/09	16/06/09
└ Link forms to main menu	17/06/09	18/06/09

Figure 9.6 Sample Gantt chart showing the tasks in Table 9.5

Open source Gantt chart software can be downloaded from http://ganttproject.biz/webstart.php

The project plan covers **only** the development section. This is the creation and the running of the test plan. It does not cover the entire project.

Marking

2 marks Clear description, diagrammatic or otherwise, of the different tasks necessary to complete the solution and a clear timetable.

10 Software development, testing and installation

Introduction

There are 21 marks available for this section: 14 for the software development and testing, and 7 for the installation.

Overview

This section can be broken down into three main stages, of which the first is the most important:

- **Software development:** This is where you print out the project. You produce evidence of what you have actually created – including printouts of any programming, table definitions, HTML coding etc.
- **Testing:** You must test everything that can be tested against the requirements and using normal, extreme and incorrect data.
- **Installation:** This requires the cooperation of the end user. They have to see the system and comment on it. The second half of this section is about the production of an installation plan.

Software development

This is the section where you document the finished product. The only things that can be marked are what you produce evidence for – if you have not printed it out, it did not happen and it does not exist.

The technical evidence is a very important part of the project. It should contain every screen (input, output and user interface), reports and any code written. The technical evidence is the only evidence you can produce of the creation of the project. You should not include any screenshots unless they are annotated or cross-referenced. A screenshot is only useful if it is referenced and it can be understood how it fits into the project as a whole.

It is not necessary to print out the design of a form unless it is unusual. Where possible you should group together a form and any related code. Annotation of individual items is not necessary as the design of the form details this, and any code will support the names of the objects.

It must be possible for a third party to copy the software development from your printouts, so you need to make sure that everything is included.

The following is a list of what you need to provide. Of course, it will depend on your exact project whether you have them all.

Example

Database	Spreadsheet	Web page
Tables	Worksheet(s)	The web page itself
Forms	Formula view	Associated data structures
Queries	Macros	(database, spreadsheet,
Reports	User forms	text file)
Macros		Macro code

Table 10.1 Evidence of software development

The printouts that you provide should show how the project meets the client's requirements. It should also show how you have met the stages in the project plan.

One method of producing the evidence might be to reproduce the tasks from the project plan and, this time, take a screenshot as evidence.

Example

Task	Evidence
Create Table of library members This is the design of the table created to hold details on the library members.	 Figure 10.1 Example of database fields used in Library Members table
Create Table of book genres This is the design of the table created to hold details on the book genres.	 Figure 10.2 Example of database fields used in Book Genre table

Table 10.2 Using the tasks to order software development evidence

Annotation

Note the additional notes in Table 10.2. It is always useful to give as much additional information as you can – the annotation should refer to the screenshot.

Your printouts of procedures, modules and macros also need to be annotated. Ideally you should annotate the code as you write/edit it, but if this is not possible then you should write on the printout.

Annotation should tell the reader what is going on, therefore you need to strike a balance between annotating everything and only those items that need annotating for clarity. Remember to annotate all variables.

It is not necessary to print and annotate every piece of code. For example if code is generated when placing a button on a worksheet to take the user to another worksheet, and this is recorded, it does not need to be printed. Wizard or recorded macro-generated code does not need to be printed and annotated. If, however, you write your own code, then this must be annotated and printed.

It is good practice to begin each piece of your own code with a header section. The header should contain:

- a line that identifies where it is (makes it easy to find)
- the title of the procedure
- the final date of editing
- the version number (incremented after each edit), and
- the name of the editor (i.e. your name).

Example

```
'***************************************************
'FINES FORM
'26/06/12
'Version 1.3a
'Writer: G Millbery
'***************************************************
```

Figure 10.3 Sample annotated header from a procedure

Marking

8 marks

- 6–8 marks: the candidate has solved a problem that has needed a level of complexity greater than a simple linear type solution.
- 3–5 marks: the candidate has attempted to solve a problem that has needed a level of complexity greater than a simple linear type solution and has been successful in some aspects.
- 0–2 marks: the candidate has produced a solution that is a linear style of solution in the use of software.

If your project is a simple linear solution, you cannot get any more than two marks. A linear project is one that has a single aim and a straight path from data entry to output of results.

If you have created a complex solution, but some of the tests fail and you cannot make the solution work, then you will not be able to achieve more than five marks.

A complex solution that works can gain the full eight marks.

The evidence for the solution working comes from the test results and the screenshots of software development.

Development of one aspect of the system that processes data

You need to make sure you are testing a solution at the same time that you develop it. For example, you need to enter data into a formula as you develop it, and make sure it works before moving on. This is a combination of development and testing, and for this section you need to document one aspect that involves the processing of data.

Processing of data for this section is:

- searching – using a parameter search to locate specific information
- updating data – automatically marking an invoice as paid
- deleting data – automatically archiving and deleting data
- retrieving data – a function that looks up data to retrieve.

The processing needs to be automated. It cannot be pressing a delete button or ticking a box on the screen.

Example

For example, in a project involving delivery of items, the delivery price needs to be calculated:

Weight of final Products	1.30 kg		Delivery Prices Data Table		
			0	£	2.99
			1	£	4.99
			3	£	7.99
Price for delivery	£ 4.99		5	£	10.99
			10	£	25.00

Figure 10.4 Example of testing spreadsheet formulae

It is important to test that the function for the delivery price works before integrating it into the solution. The testing that occurs during development is informal and does not need a test plan.

There might be instances where the development does not work.

Example

A form has been created to search for orders by customer. The customer name is selected from a drop-down list, but the query is not returning any values.

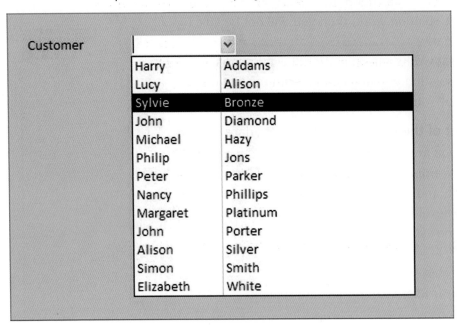

Figure 10.5 Example of drop-down list

A message box has been set up to identify the value being passed to the query.

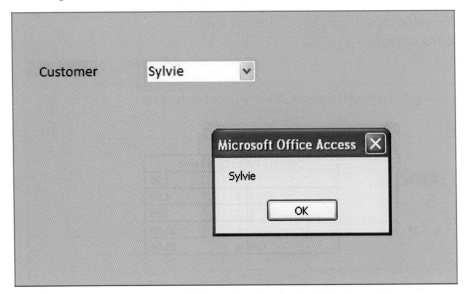

Figure 10.6 Message box showing value passed to a query

As can be seen, the value being returned is the forename and not the expected CustomerID.

In this instance, the testing has revealed a problem which can then be rectified. It is essential that where you need to rectify a mistake, you give evidence of this. It is very easy to find an error and correct it without writing down what you have done. If you do this, you will lose marks.

In this example, the primary key had been missed out when the combo box was created. The solution was to include the CustomerID in the row source as the first field.

Property Sheet	
Selection type: Combo Box	
Combo0	
Format Data Event Other All	
Control Source	
Row Source	SELECT TMember.MemberID, TMember.Forename, TMember.Surname FROM TMember ORDER BY TMember.Surname;
Row Source Type	Table/Query

Figure 10.7 Correcting the error

When a customer is selected, the message box now shows the CustomerID. When this is passed to the query it works.

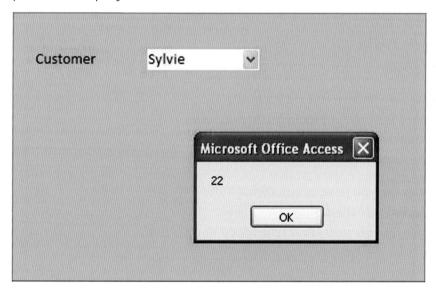

Figure 10.8 The correct message box

After each major section that involves queries, formulae, functions etc., test the solution and document the process.

It is possible that a problem encountered cannot be solved easily, and the design or even the requirements need to be revisited. Marks will not be lost if this is the case, so long as the procedure is documented and the end user is involved in the discussions.

Marking

2 marks Evidence of the development of one aspect of the system that processes data.

Evidence of the HCI

The HCI (human–computer interface) is the form or web page that the user sees. It is how the information is presented to the user and the means by which they interact with the system.

This section is where you demonstrate how you have customised the user interface. For example, in a database, how you applied the house style and contextualised it to the client rather than leaving it as created by a wizard.

You need to show what you have customised and why. The 'why' needs to link back to the requirements.

Customisation can include:

- changing colours/backgrounds
- applying appropriate font size, type and style
- removing record selectors and scroll bars
- adding customised buttons
- including a company logo in the interface.

Marking

2 marks Hard-copy evidence of an effective HCI with annotations explaining its effective solutions for problems that had been highlighted in the requirements specification.

Test results/Testing

Having created a test plan in design, you need to run through the tests listed in it and provide evidence of the results. This is best done by giving the results under the test plan cross referenced to the 'Test number'.

Example

Test number 1:

			Delivery Prices Data Table		
Weight of final Products	3.60 kg		0	£	2.99
			1	£	4.99
			3	£	7.99
Price for delivery	£ 7.99		5	£	10.99
			10	£	25.00

Figure 10.9 Sample test result 1

3.6 has been entered into cell E4 and the result £7.99 is displayed in E8. This answer matches the expected result.

Test number 2:

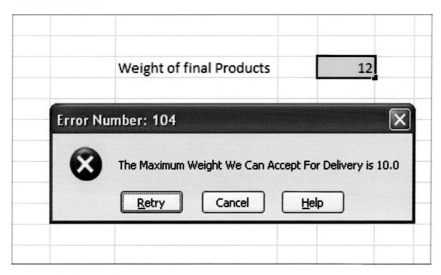

Figure 10.10 Sample test result 2

12 has been entered into cell E4. The correct error message has appeared. The test has passed.

If a test fails, then you need to correct the error and run the test again. Remember to provide evidence of the correction and the re-test.

User testing of the system

The user testing specified in design also needs to be run on the completed system.

It is possible to create a questionnaire for the end user to fill in. If there is more than one end user, then all (or as many as is practical) should test the system and the results should be summarised in a graph or table. Not all responses need to be 'pass' and 'fail'; some can have an explanatory comment.

Example

User test	Pass	Fail	Comment
Is the main menu easy to use?	✔		All required options are coved.
Do the labels on the button make sense?	✔		They are easy to understand.
Are all the error messages easy to understand?		✔	Error Message '531'.

Table 10.3 Sample questionnaire for user testing

The user must write a letter to you detailing the fact that they have tested the system. The letter needs to contain:
- their name, position and address
- a reference to the project
- a reference to you (your name)
- a date on which the system was tested
- some comments.

Example

This is a sample letter from the user. The italics are to be replaced with relevant details.

Their address
The date

Your name
Your address (or the address of the school)

Dear *Your name*

With reference to the system you are developing for us, I am writing to confirm that on **XXX** *date, I and* **XXX** *(if others)* tested the system.

We/I have filled out and returned a questionnaire on the test and would like to make the following comments.

Enter comments here.

Yours sincerely,

Signature

Position within organisation

Figure 10.11 Sample letter from user

If the end user has any problems or comments, you must address them and, if necessary, re-test the system.

Marking

2 marks Evidence that each of the tests specified in the test plan has been carried out, that they are linked to the hard copy evidence, that the results have been analysed and that any necessary action has been identified.

These marks are awarded for running the tests from the test plan. If tests fail, the system must be corrected and a re-test carried out.

Installation

There are seven marks available for the installation section.
The specification recognises that it is not always possible to install the system. However, as long as the user is involved, it is still possible to gain full marks without actually putting the system completely into place.

The end result of this section should be a written installation plan that could be followed by a third party.
The implementation section has three stages:

- user training
- files, hardware and software
- method of changeover.

User training

It is likely that staff will need to be trained to use the new system. You need to give details of the training that will be required and, if necessary, when and how this training will take place.

The dates for training need to be agreed with the client and take place at a time appropriate to the method of changeover.
The types of training to be agreed include:

- one-to-one training
- using a start-up guide/user manual
- a group presentation
- post-installation training.

You will need to consider the data that will be used for training purposes and how this will be created/entered. The training, hardware and software sections will merge into each other.
A calendar/diary of events is useful to show what will happen and when. This needs to be agreed with the end user.

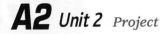

Example

The installation plan should contain dates, which you need to agree with the end user.

Date	Phase of implementation
1/2/12	Acceptance meeting
2/2/12–5/2/12	Data changeover
6/2/12	Budget meeting for equipment
6/2/12	Delivery of user manuals
7/2/12	Group training
8/2/12–10/2/12	Individual training
9/2/12	Acquisition of equipment
13/2/12	Installation of equipment
15/2/12	Data changeover update
16/2/12	Direct changeover
18/2/12	Training session

Table 10.4 Sample format for calendar

Marking

3 marks Details of the training that will need to be available for the staff who must use the new system.

Files, hardware and software

The system that you have created will require either:
- new data to be entered, or
- existing data to be transferred.

You need to indicate the volume of data that is to be transferred/entered and to make an estimate of how long it will take.

If data is entered into the new system too early, then by the time it is ready to be used, the existing system will have generated more data. This will need to be entered and a cycle is entered into. If the data entry is started too late then it may not all be completed in time. You need to consider:
- the volume of data involved
- the number of people to be involved in data entry/data transferal
- the time taken for data entry/data conversion.
- how the process is to take place.

An organisation may not have in place the hardware and software required for the new system, so it may be necessary to upgrade or purchase them.

The hardware and software required needs to be listed along with the dates by when it is to be delivered and installed.

The hardware and software listed need to match the hardware and software from the analysis section.

Marking

2 marks Details of the means by which the new files are going to be created, including some indication of the scale of the problem, and also the possible need for hardware installation and the installation of the software on the hardware.

Methods of changeover

There are four methods available for changeover:

- direct
- phased
- parallel
- pilot.

Direct changeover

Direct changeover is likely to be the most appropriate. It is where the use of the old system stops and the new one begins. There is a cut-off point when the old system stops working.

The advantage is that it is fast, efficient, requires the minimum duplication of work, only one system needs supporting and no interfaces between old and new systems are needed.

The disadvantages are that if the new system fails to work, there will be disruption. The new system has to be completely implemented during a period of time when the system is not required and there may be some disruption to customers while staff get used to the new system.

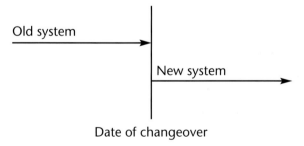

Figure 10.12 Direct changeover

Phased changeover

Phased changeover is used with larger systems where the system to be put in place has several smaller sub-systems. Each sub-system is introduced one at a time, making sure that each one is working before you begin with the next. The actual implementation method can be direct or parallel.

The advantages are that each sub-system can be introduced with a minimum of disruption and if a system fails to work, the system is small enough to correct the errors.

The disadvantages are that the changeover may take a long period of time and create an extended period of unsettlement.

Parallel changeover

In a parallel changeover, the old system and the new are run side by side for a determined period of time.

The advantage is that if there is something wrong with the new system, the old system is still in operation and can continue to work. The disruption to the customers is minimised and the results from the old system (which are trusted and known to be correct) can be compared with the results from the new. This will establish trust and confidence in the new system.

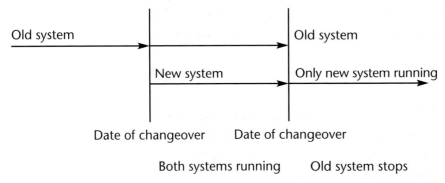

Figure 10.13 Parallel changeover

Pilot changeover

Pilot changeover is used in large organisations and involves the new system being tested in a small portion of the organisation for a determined period of time.

The advantages are that bugs can be worked out with the minimum of disruption, and training and testing can be completed in a small section of the organisation.

The disadvantage is that several changeovers need to take place.

You must detail the different methods of changeover, with advantages and disadvantages in such a way that the client can make a decision. The advantages and disadvantages must be contextualised to the scenario – they cannot be generic 'bookwork' responses and you need to apply them to the client's business.

Marking

2 marks Details of appropriate, different, methods of changeover explained so that the client can make a reasoned decision.

11 Documentation

Introduction

There are 10 marks available for this section. Documentation is often an area that is not done particularly well. Guides are often difficult to follow and presented badly, and could not be used by the end user. Documentation should stand alone and be presented in a binder/ section separate to the numbered page sections of the project.

Overview

The user guide is for the end user of your system. As such it should tell the end user how to use the system you have created. It should not detail how to use any application software you might have used to create your system. You must include all routes through the system and how to troubleshoot errors.

Manual

There are ten marks available for the user guide and all marks should be easily accessible. You should include a collection of screenshots and associated text, but you must never include a screenshot unless it is annotated in some way. You must also make sure that the user guide is a sequential document. This means that it follows the standard routes through the system that the user will use.

The guide must be easily used, that is, it should be an everyday reference guide that will help users of all levels. To separate different aspects of the guide, it can extend to a manual containing more than one document.

In order to achieve marks for the highest band, you must include some documentation that exists only on the computer, such as an on-screen help/electronic guide. On-screen help can also be included within the interface. It can include items such as tool-tips, descriptive elements on a form informing the user what to fill in, and text on buttons giving information about the function of the button. It is possible that all the documentation exists only on the computer, and if this is the case there are two points to note:

- How does the system cope with novice users? – A novice user is unlikely to have the skills to begin by reading on-screen documentation.
- You still need to print out the documentation for the examiner. Here are some basic rules for the production of user guides:
- Always annotate your printouts.

- Test the guide yourself to make sure that it works.
- Make sure that someone other than you has tested the guide.
- The guide should be a separate document and not be included as part of the project documentation.
- The guide layout should be easy to follow and logical. For example, you may start with the main menu and cover all the options on a screen-by-screen basis or you may choose to cover first input, then processing, then output. The choice is yours but it must be easy to use.
- Make sure that you have spellchecked the document – there are marks for written communication.

The various elements that you may choose to include as documentation are:

- a 'Getting started' guide
- a user guide
- a troubleshooting guide
- on-screen help.

'Getting started' guide

A 'Getting started' guide contains information for the novice user on how to start using the system. It will be only a few pages long. The guide should not begin with how to switch on the computer (unless there is some special reason why this needed), but should start with how to run your system and show its opening screen.

The 'Getting started' guide should contain the purpose of the software: what is it to be used for and where is it to be used. You should include all the initial information required to use the system, such as whether or not a username and password are needed, and if they are, where the user can get them etc.

It should be written for the novice user. This means that you should use as few technical terms as possible and include a glossary of terms used (e.g. defining 'mouse click').

User guide

A user guide is the most important of all of the guides. It should contain all the information needed to run the system on a day-to-day basis within one standalone document. When writing the user guide, you need to remember at all times that the audience of the document will range from novice to expert users.

You need to include in the user guide text on the following:

Entering data

This will include the data needed to be entered into the system and where to enter it. You must illustrate this with annotated screenshots which show examples of the actual data to be used wherever possible.

If there is more than one data entry point, each needs to be covered in separate sections.

Processing

All options must be covered. Processing includes anything that happens to the data: sorting, searching, updating, deleting etc. If there are several options that cover a similar item, such as four different methods of searching, they can be grouped together.

You need to cover every button/option. For example, you may have a main menu with lots of buttons, or there may be options on a data form to go to the first, last, next and previous records. All of these must be documented. However, if you have several forms with the same buttons on them, you only need to cover the buttons on one form, not all of them.

Output

There are likely to be three main methods of output: screen, disk and hard copy (paper). Each of the different outputs must be included in the documentation, covering what each is and how to produce it.

Backup and recovery of data

You can document data backup and restoration with a simple set of instructions and screenshots.

Security

Different systems will require different security options. You need to document how the end user can get through the security or, if appropriate, change security levels.

Reference material

The guide must contain an index, a glossary of terms and a table of contents – remember to add page numbers.

Professional user guides are written in many different styles. You can get some idea of how to write one by looking at user guides produced for applications by major software providers and independent companies. You will not be expected to produce a guide that is up to the same standard (although no one is going to stop you!), so long as you remember that it needs to be usable and helpful.

Different projects will have different types of end user. Some systems might have more than one type of end user. For example, a website with a back-end database is unlikely to have a guide in the form of a manual for the user of the site itself, but it will have a hard-copy guide for the use of the database part of the system.

When you collect images for a user guide, make sure they:

- are what the user will see
- have been cropped so there is no background
- have real data in them so the user can see what they are supposed to do.

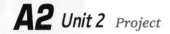

Once you have collected the images, they must be positioned on the page so they can be easily annotated with text and arrows.

Example

Here is a simple example of how you might lay out a user guide.

This screen is for viewing and changing details about companies. You need to search through the companies by pressing the Find, Next, Previous and Last buttons, until you come to the name and address of the company you want.

When you begin, some of the buttons will appear faded, for example the Previous button in the screenshot below. This is because the screenshot shows the first record and there is nothing before it. If you moved to the next record, the faded button would become active (i.e. the text turns black and you can click it).

You can edit the details and press the Update button to save your changes.

If you want to exit from the screen, press the Close button.

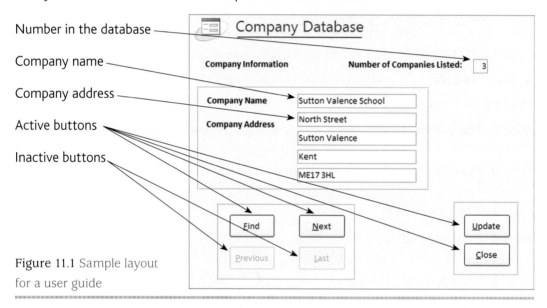

Figure 11.1 Sample layout for a user guide

Troubleshooting guide

A troubleshooting guide is a guide to likely problems with their solutions. You need to list all the different problems the user might encounter, what caused them and how to get out of them.

You must include any error messages the system generates. (If you have used the recommended format for error messages, with each message represented by a unique number, the errors can be sorted and presented by number.)

The troubleshooting guide is a collection of screenshots of the errors with explanatory text about each.

In general terms, you should include anything that generates an error message within your test plan.

The format for representing each error in the troubleshooting guide is:

- What screenshot evidence will the end-user see to tell them they have an error?
- What does this mean? What has the user done to generate the error?
- What do they need to do to correct the error?

Example

An example layout of a troubleshooting error is given below.

When entering the weight of the package to be delivered, you might see this error message:

Figure 11.2 Example of an error message

This error has appeared because you have typed a value that is greater than 10 into cell E4 (highlighted yellow).

To correct the error, click Retry and type a value between 0 and 10.

On-screen help

You will need to print out evidence of this type of help because you are not allowed to submit disks. The on-screen help will depend on the package you are using. It could be web-based online help using HTML, or a collection of screen tips or a series of text files accessed by clicking a button.

On-screen help must be accessible and relevant. It is usually a collection of concise documents, the content of which will depend on individual requirements. You should again include table of contents, a glossary and index to help the user.

One of the most effective ways of providing on-screen help is to make it context sensitive. This means providing specific help for the screen that the user is currently on. The easiest way of providing context-sensitive help is to create a Help button on the screen on which you want the help. The button links to an external file (this may be a PDF or a text file) and when clicked the relevant help text appears.

Example

				Delivery Prices Data Table		
Weight of final Products	8.00 kg			0	£	2.99
				1	£	4.99
				3	£	7.99
Price for delivery	£10.99			5	£	10.99
				10	£	25.00
			Help On Delivery Prices			

Figure 11.3 A context-sensitive help button

The Help button is linked to code which will open and run the help file.

(General)	▼	Delivery_Help_Click

```
Sub Delivery_Help_Click()
    'Code for opening Help.doc
    Shell ("c:\progra~1\micros~2\office12\windowd.exe c:\help.doc")
End Sub
```

Figure 11.4 Help code

When the Help button is clicked, the help text given in the file will be displayed.

Delivery Prices Help

The yellow box is the only box you can fill in on this screen.
Enter a value between 0 and 10. Do not add the units (e.g. kg)
to the value you enter – the system does this automatically.
The Price for Delivery is automatically calculated.

Figure 11.5 Online help displayed

Marking

8–10 marks   Candidates will produce detailed and accurate
documentation. The manual will be presented in a
well-structured and coherent format. Subject-specific
terminology will be used accurately and appropriately.
The documentation will include a complete and detailed
user guide covering all operations that the user would be
required to perform. The on-screen guide should be well

presented and easy to follow. There will be few if any errors in spelling, grammar and punctuation.

4–7 marks Candidates will provide clear documentation. The documentation will be well presented. There is clear on-screen help to support the end user. The supporting documentation and on-screen help is well presented and covers most aspects of the operations that the user would be required to perform. Some subject-specific terminology will be used. There may be occasional errors of spelling, grammar and punctuation.

0–3 marks Candidates will provide a superficial documentation with weak supplementary user documentation covering few aspects of the operations that the user will be required to perform. The information will be poorly expressed and limited technical terms will be used. Errors of spelling, grammar and punctuation may be intrusive.

12 Evaluation

Introduction

There are a total of 8 marks available for the evaluation.

This is the final section of the project. By reading the first section (the analysis) and this final section, a moderator can get a good idea of the quality of your project: that is, what you have done and how successful you have been.

Overview

The evaluation of your project needs to be done by you and by the end user.

Your evaluation needs to tie in with the objectives given in the Analysis section, so without a good analysis (i.e. with poor objectives), you will not score many marks in the evaluation.

The evaluation by the end user requires any individuals you identified early in the project (in the analysis) to look at the system and given a written response.

The evaluation is an assessment of what the finished product you have created can and cannot do in relation to what it was required to do. It is not about how well you think you have done or how much fun you have had doing it.

Honesty is the best policy with any evaluation. If something has not worked, then say so. Explain why and what you have done about it. If you try to cover it up, the likelihood is that evidence will be in the rest of your project to prove that it has not worked and you will be caught out. If you have lied here, how can the examiner be sure you have not lied elsewhere?

The section can be broken down into three main stages:

- an assessment of the final project against the requirements from analysis
- identification of possible future extensions to the system
- evaluation of the finished development against the project plan.

Comment on the success in meeting the original objectives

It is not possible to achieve marks in this section unless you have completed the requirements specification earlier in the project. You need to take each objective listed in the requirements specification, comment on the degree of success you have had in meeting it and provide evidence of how the completed solution meets the requirement.

What are the 'degrees of success'? There are four possibilities:

- An objective has been met completely.
- An objective has not been met in its entirety, but most of it has.
- Most of an objective has not been met, but a small part has.
- An objective has not been met at all.

Initially, you can note the success attained by referencing the requirements in the form of a table. This will give the examiner an immediate overview of how successful you have been in implementing the requirements specification. However, you will need to list the objectives and your evaluation of success more fully at some stage to prevent the examiner from having to flick backwards and forwards through the project. A simple tick or cross in the table is not enough, there needs to be some commentary about the success of meeting each criterion.

Example

Requirement	Completely met	Mostly met	Mostly not met	Not met	Page number for evidence
Edit members' information	The system allows information for existing members to be edited.				65
List of overdue books sorted by date		The system gives a report of all books that are overdue but they are not sorted by date but by members.			66

Table 12.1 Format for visual reference for meeting objectives

The table is only an initial guide: on its own it will not get you many marks. To get marks, you must decide into which of the four success statements each objective falls. You must back up the objective with evidence, which may be from testing, a statement from the end user, or a printout of parts of the development.

You must comment on every objective and produce evidence to back up your assessment. You will lose marks if you miss out any requirements. You must provide evidence: the statement alone is insufficient to achieve the marks.

Where you have not completed the objectives, you must provide a reasoned comment saying why, what you have done to try and meet it, and what you could do in the future to meet it. The more honest you can be, the better!

You can still achieve full marks for this section even if you have not managed to fulfil all the objectives. It is, however, important that you give full and frank comments on the success of the project.

The evidence you need to produce can be page references to test run printouts or to specific areas of coding. If the objective you are producing evidence for is to do with the ease of use for different ability users, it might be appropriate to get a written statement from them.

If you have completed the full test plan in the development and testing section you will have gone through the design specification and provided screenshots to show that each one has been implemented and works. The page references you give in the evaluation will direct the moderator to this section to see the evidence of success.

Sometimes the evidence might not be in the system itself: you might have to go out and get it. This may require additional data collection, interviews or signed statements.

Shortfalls

Shortfalls in the system are areas where you have not met the requirements specification and the system fails to achieve its objectives.

There may not be any shortfalls in your system, and if this is the case, then you can skip this section.

If there are shortfalls, then they need to be identified with methods of correcting them so that they are eliminated.

There is no requirement to carry out the correction.

Example

Overdue books sorted by date

At present, the system sorts by Member and not by Date. To change the system to sort by Date, the date the book is due back needs to be identified as a sort field in the query the report is based on.

To ensure that this sort is made before the Members, the Date field needs to come before the Member field.

Marking

4 marks   Evaluation of each of the requirements from the requirements specification including showing how the completed solution meets the requirements. Areas from the requirements specification that have not been met are discussed.

Range of possible extensions

There are two marks available for this section. You are required to describe possible extensions to the system and how they should be carried out.

You must not only describe the possible extensions but give some idea of how to carry them out. This does not need to be a complete design, but a very general and rough description of what might be done to implement the extension.

This section requires you to use your imagination. You need to think about what you would do to improve the new system. Some ideas might be become evident as you develop your existing system, but don't be tempted to add them in as additions to your original specification. For other ideas, you will need to think further afield.

Example

Database	Spreadsheet	Web
• Connect to external applications – spreadsheets, word-processing. • Access to the system via the internet. • Payment options – credit card etc. • Move to a partitioned system.	• Replace the worksheet entry with forms entry. • Connect to external applications – databases, word-processing. • Allow web-based applications to access the spreadsheet.	• Connect to a database/ spreadsheet to store data. • Personalise the visit by storing customer information and profiles. • Add interactive elements – Web 2.0 etc. • Automatic display changes for different browsers/ resolution of screen.

Table 12.2 Example of extensions

If you were coming to the project from scratch and the project that you were asked to investigate and analyse was the one you have just created, what would your suggestions be for improving it – taking it to the next level. These form the extensions.

Do not forget that there needs to be a brief description of the possible extension and how it could be achieved.

Marking

2 marks   Details of extensions to the project and how these might be completed.

Comparing development against plan

In the design section you created a project plan for development – listing the tasks, the predecessors and a timescale for each task.

As you have limited experience in creating projects of this size it is likely that you missed out some tasks, got the predecessor wrong or under/overestimated the amount of time that each task would take.

This section of the project is a review of your project plan. How accurate was it? What was missing? If you have no project plan in the design section, then you cannot get any marks for this section.

As part of the review, where there are differences, give reasons for those differences. For example, why did the creation of the customer table take you an hour instead of the ten minutes you allocated?

Honesty is the best policy. You will not be marked down if the intended plan and the actual plan are different.

Marking

2 marks   Evaluation of the finished development against the project plan from design.

13 Presentation of report

Introduction

There are a total of 3 marks available for the report.

This is not a separate section. The marks are awarded for the presentation of your coursework.

The elements of the report that need to be present to gain full marks are detailed below.

Report elements

Detailed and accurate means of navigation

There should be a title page to the project. This needs to be followed by a contents page. The contents page should map the sections and headings of the project so that it is easy for the moderator to work sequentially. Pages in the project documentation need page numbers. A contents page references these page numbers in order for it to be useful.

You are expected at this level to use an automated table of contents. This requires the use of styled section headings within the body of the text.

The project documentation should be fit for purpose – it is the report into a systems life cycle project for an A-level ICT qualification. The presentation needs to be consistent, with appropriate use of font sizes and font styles.

Layout determined by the reader rather than the author

You, as the author, are not the intended audience of your report. The intended audience is the reader: in this instance, your teacher and the moderator. You must be aware of their needs when putting together the project. A systems life cycle project has a natural progression: analysis, design, development, testing, evaluation. This needs to be reflected in the project documentation. The user manual must be presented as a standalone document to gain high marks.

There should be very little need for the reader to flick backwards and forwards through the project: everything they need should be in the correct order.

Few spelling and grammatical errors

Most software provides spellcheckers and grammar checkers so there is no excuse for any spelling mistakes or grammatical errors in the project documentation. There should be appropriate use of technical terms and subject-specific terminology.

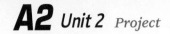

Log of events

You cannot get more than one mark if you do not keep a dated log of events. The log should have been kept since the beginning of the project. See Chapter 7, pages 196–7, for more detail on the log of events.

Use of templates

There are two types of template: task templates and document templates.

Task templates are templates that have been created to meet a specific task or purpose. For example, a test plan layout is a task template. There is a formalised structure to these documents and their use is commonplace within industry. The use of task templates is acceptable, encouraged and will not lose any marks.

Document templates are templates which set out the entire structure of a document. These include project documentation templates and user documentation templates. The use of these, while not forbidden, does have an impact on the marks. If you make use of a document template for the project report then you will not be able to achieve any marks for this section.

Marking

3 marks   The candidate has provided a detailed and accurate means of navigation of the report and has tailored the language used, both technical and non-technical, to the audience for which the parts of the report were aimed. Subject-specific terminology will be used correctly. A professional approach to the presentation will be expected and a clearly understandable, dated log of events will be kept. The information will be presented in an ordered and well-structured manner. There are few if any errors of grammar or spelling.

2 marks   The candidate will produce a navigable report. The contents will be determined by the requirements of the candidate rather than the reader. A log of events will have been kept. The information is presented in an ordered fashion that maintains some coherence. There may be some occasional errors of grammar or spelling.

0–1 mark The candidate has produced some material that explains part of the solution attempted. It will be difficult to navigate and will assume much knowledge of the solution that the reader will probably not possess. The information may be expressed without a structure. Errors of grammar or spelling may be intrusive.

Index

A

accommodation 171
adaptive maintenance 162
alternative solutions 206–7
analysis 2, 3–4, 8, 191
   project 198–200, 204–10
annotation 213, 225–6
antivirus software 181–2
attention 46
asymmetric digital subscriber
      line (ADSL) 84–5
audience participation 140
authentication 180–1
authorisation 180

B

backup 152, 239
bandwidth 64–5, 111–12
batch operating systems 39
batch processing systems
      35–6, 37
battery life 112–13
broadband connection 84–9
bulletin boards 78–9
buttons 42–3, 241–2

C

cable, types of 66
cable broadband 86
Caesar Cipher 179–80
camera angle 137–8
cellular phones 89–91
central database with remote
      local indexes 119–20,
      120–2
change management 169–74
client involvement 15, 150–1,
      219–20
client–server networks 61–2
codes of conduct 176–7

colour 39–40, 45
communication 173–4
   technologies 55–105
computer-based training (CBT)
      107–8
consistency of data 125
consultation 170, 172
controls 42–3
copper cable 66
corrective maintenance 162–3
cost-benefit analysis 155–6
critical path analysis (CPA)
      24–6
custom-written software 150–7

D

data flow diagrams (DFDs)
      28–31
data protection 177–82
data structures 216–17
data transfer 96
databases 131
   distributed 115–26
design 2, 4–5, 8, 35–54, 191
   project 211–23
design specification 5, 20–1,
      212–18
digital TV networks 136–41
direct installation 158–9, 160, 235
distributed databases 115–26
distributed processing
      systems 39
document analysis 11–12, 13
documentation 2, 7, 237–43
duplicated distributed databases
      118, 120–1, 122

E

email 77–8
encryption 178, 179–80

equipment 170
error messages 48, 217–18,
      240–1
ethics 175–7
evaluation 2, 8, 244–8
expert systems 127–30, 135–6
extensions, possible 247
external change 165–9
extranet 60

F

fax 76–7
feasibility report 1, 3, 8, 23, 191
files 216, 234–5
firewalls 72
flowcharts 32–3
font size and style 42
forms 43, 44, 213–14
future developments of ICT
      183–7

G

Gantt charts 26–7, 222–3
gateways 71
geosynchronous satellites
      91–2
'getting started' guide 238
global connectivity 98–100
global positioning systems
      (GPS) 94–5
graphical user interface
      (GUI) 16

H

hardware 156, 208–9
   installation 234–5
Help button 241–2
home networks 113–14
horizontal partitioning 117–18
house style 218
hubs 69–70

human–computer interface (HCI)   39–53, 127, 129, 216, 230
human resources   144

I

implementation   2, 5, 8, 150–64, 191
inference engine   127, 128–9
information on the screen   41
input   213–14, 238–9
installation   2, 6, 8, 155–7, 191
methods   6, 157–60, 235–6
project   224, 233–6
instant messaging   80–1
integrity of data   125–6
interactive operating systems   38
interactive processing systems   36, 37
interception of data   123–4
internet   58–60, 141, 175
interviews   10–11, 13, 201–4
intranet   60
investigation   2, 3–4, 8–13
project   198–200, 201–4
iteration of designs   219–20

J

justification   207–10

K

knowledge base   127

L

language complexity   42
layout   41
learning   48
leased line   87
limitations of ICT   109–13
live pause   138–9
local area network (LAN)   55–6
log of events   196–7, 250
logical security   178
low Earth orbit satellites   92

M

maintenance   2, 8, 161–3, 191
management information system (MIS)   130–4
meetings   10–11, 13
memory   46–8
mental models   48–51
menus   43, 44, 46
mobile phones   44, 89–93
Model Human Processor (MHP)   51–3
multi-tasking operating systems   38
multi-user operating systems   38

N

network interface card (NIC)   68
networks   55-74
of computers   113–15
see also social networking

O

observations   12, 13
off-the-shelf software   151–7
on-screen help   48, 237, 241–2
online tutorials   106–7
operating systems (OS)   35, 37–9
optical communications   67, 74–5
organisations   194
impact of external change   166–7
internal resources   144–6
output   215, 239

P

parallel installation   157–8, 160, 236
participation   173

partitioned distributed databases   116–18, 120–1, 122
pay per view   139
peer-to-peer networks   62–3
perception   45
perfective maintenance   162
phased installation   158, 160, 235–6
physical access to data   124
physical security   178, 182
pilot installation   159–60, 236
premises   145–6
problem definition   1–3, 8
project   198, 200, 200–1
processing   214–15, 227–30, 239
processing power   109–10
processing systems   35–7
programmer   23
project   191–250
analysis   198–200, 204–10
design   211–23
documentation   237–43
evaluation   244–8
installation   224, 233–6
investigation   198–200, 201–4
problem definition   198, 200, 200–1
report   194, 249–50
software development   224–30
testing   221–2, 224, 230–3
topic selection   191–6
project manager   21–2
project plan   5, 211, 222–3
evaluation against   247–8
project planning tools   24–7
project team   21–4
protocols   100
prototyping   14–16, 151

Q

questionnaires   9, 13